GW00586506

A-Z
of
Child
DEVELOPMENT

- While the younger girls were too young to be concerned about the size of their chest, they expressed concern about the size of their hips, the width of their legs, arms, thighs and shoulders and the shape of their noses.
- Many of those who dieted had mothers who were also dieting, and had probably learned the strategy from them.
- In a few instances, dieting is so extreme that it impairs growth and delays puberty.

Other studies have shown that boys, too, are vulnerable to this sort of pressure, though for males the emphasis tends to be on physical skills and strength rather than good looks. Their role models are usually muscle-bound sportsmen or macho, super-strong adventure heroes. Any body shape remotely approaching fatness is definitely out.

If you want to discourage your child from forming a connection between physical attractiveness and feelings of personal worth, then:

● *Encourage him to consider a wide range of personal features, not just good looks, when judging whether someone is nice or not.* Tell him to think about the person's kindness, his thoughtfulness, his friendliness, etc.
● *Try to select children's stories which don't emphasise a relationship between beauty and success, or between ugliness and failure.* Every now and again, read your child a story about an ordinary child who has an interesting adventure.

See also **Self-Confidence**.

Autism   Autistic children have difficulties forming relationships with other people. They seem to be cut off, living in a world of their own. Although the condition was first identified in the eighteenth century, it was not until 1943 that American psychiatrist Leo Kanner called it 'early infantile autism' (from the Greek word *autos* meaning 'self'). Kanner used this term because of the autistic child's withdrawn behaviour and disinterest in others.

Statistics from the National Autistic Society confirm that approximately four or five children per 10,000 have classic

23

autism, and approximately 15–20 per 10,000 have autistic-like features. Autism – the cause of which is unknown – affects four times as many boys as it does girls.

Experts on autism emphasise that the condition affects the child's whole system of communication. A typical autistic baby doesn't show awareness of his mother's presence, screams constantly unless rocked rhythmically all the time, and doesn't look at the world around him; at the toddler stage, he appears not to understand the meaning of speech, and is late learning to talk. Secondary problems usually develop, such as resistance to change (routine becomes very important), absence of imaginative play, socially difficult behaviour (destructive, aggressive actions), and learning difficulties. Many parents of autistic children think their child is potentially intelligent, if only he could communicate with them.

Some autistic children make no progress at all, and remain withdrawn all their lives. The majority show some improvement, however, especially between the ages of six and twelve years, but only 15 per cent are able to lead an independent life in adulthood. In recent years, new treatments aimed at helping autistic children have been developed (e.g., holding therapy which involves an adult carer hugging the child tightly during a distressed outburst, or daily life therapy, pioneered in Tokyo, which relies heavily on group dynamics, modelling and physical activity). The effectiveness of these has still to be evaluated properly.

See also **Language Difficulties**.

B

Bedtime It's not unusual for a child to resist going to bed at the end of the day: she would rather stay up and continue having fun! There can, of course, be genuine reasons underlying her reluctance to retire for the evening – e.g., insecurity, fear of the dark, ill-health, hunger, thirst. But once you have ruled out these possibilities, you can be reasonably confident that problems in getting your child to bed stem from her simple desire to bend the rules.

Take a firm approach in these circumstances, especially with a child around two or three years of age. First, talk to her about the importance of bedtime, about her need for sleep, and about the strain her misbehaviour is putting you under. Remind her that everyone in the family has set times for going to bed. Second, adopt a matter-of-fact tone when you tell her that bedtime has arrived, and make sure she goes through her bedtime routine of getting undressed, washed and so on at a reasonable pace. Third, don't give in when she asks to stay up a little bit longer. If she ignores you and refuses to stay in bed, insist that she remains in her bedroom. Don't let her come downstairs to be with you, no matter how hard she tries to persuade you. Should she leave her bedroom despite your warnings, take her right back. You will see the positive effect of this strategy after a few weeks, as long as you apply it consistently.

A child aged four or five may regularly resist bedtime because she feels she is old enough to stay up later, or because her older brother or sister has a later bedtime. Rather than blindly insisting that she adheres to the time you have set, ask her what time she thinks she should go to bed. Then reach a compromise. Even if you concede only an extra 15 minutes, this will make her feel she has been involved in the decision-making process and, as a result, she'll be more inclined to keep the agreement.

In the event that neither of these approaches works and you and your child are locked in bedtime battles every night, try an alternative method. Suppose, for example, you want her to go to bed at seven o'clock, but she struggles against this for hours and doesn't actually fall asleep until 10. Since you know that she's going to stay up late anyway, tell her that for the next three nights she doesn't have to go bed until 10.30 (i.e., half an hour after the time she is usually asleep). She will almost certainly cooperate with you now because you have removed the source of conflict between you and her. Praise her for going to bed at the agreed time without a struggle. After three nights, bring her bedtime forward by 15 minutes, and repeat this process every three nights, each time making bedtime 15 minutes earlier. Within three or four weeks, you may find your child goes to bed at seven o'clock without any of her previous misbehaviour.

See also **Fears; Nightmares; Routine; Sleep**.

Bed-Wetting Although bowel and bladder control at night is usually achieved around the age of three years, a number of children have difficulty with this stage of development (i.e., at age seven, one child in five still wets her bed occasionally, at age 10 about one in 14 does so, and by age 14–15 one child in 33 remains enuretic).

A child becomes dry at night after she becomes dry during the day. Having achieved daytime bladder control, she knows what is required of her at night. The most common sign of readiness for night training is when her nappy is regularly dry in the morning when she wakes up. Girls frequently reach this stage earlier than boys.

Common-sense rules apply to night training. Your child should use the toilet before going to sleep, and should be able to reach the toilet easily if she wakes up. Or have a potty close to her bed, if this is more convenient. Leave a light on in the toilet all night, if necessary. There is no scientific evidence that a child who wets at night is a very deep sleeper. Research confirms that a child can pass urine at any stage in sleep, not always at the deepest moment, and most commonly when moving from a phase of deep sleep into lighter sleep.

Don't worry if she takes months, rather than weeks, to become dry at night. She needs lots of encouragement, and lots of praise when her bed is dry in the morning. And be prepared to wash mounds of sheets while night training is proceeding.

Some parents lift their sleeping child when they themselves are going to bed and take her to the toilet. There is no proof that this actually stops bed-wetting. In fact, it can be counter-productive because it involves the parents taking the responsibility of toilet-training away from the child and on to themselves. Nor is there any proof that depriving a child of drinks in the evening will help her become dry at night. Of course, she should not be plied with large glasses of juice just before bedtime. But even total deprivation will not stop her bladder filling while she is asleep – and it could be a source of conflict between you and her.

Psychologists have identified two types of bed-wetting, which occur in children beyond the age of five years; *primary enuresis* applies to a child who has never achieved bladder control at night, and *secondary enuresis* applies to a child who has been dry at nights consistently and then unexpectedly begins to wet her bed.

Primary enuresis can be caused by many factors, including:

– *heredity*. Investigations have found that parents who themselves were slow to achieve bladder control at night often have children who follow a similar pattern.
– *maturation*. With some children, bed-wetting may be caused by a delay in the development of that part of the brain needed for bladder control.
– *poor training*. Not all parents adopt a consistent method when training their child to be dry, and sometimes the situation develops into a battle; inconsistent strategies only confuse the child, or make her anxious.
– *urinary problems*. Bed-wetting can be associated with physical abnormalities or urinary tract infection, which is why medical advice should always be sought in the first instance.

The cause of secondary enuresis is virtually always stress. Although a child who starts to wet at night after she has been dry consistently for a long period may be suffering from an infection or other physical illness, it is more likely that the wetting is due to an emotional difficulty (e.g., the birth of another child in the family, starting playgroup or nursery, starting school, worries about friends, and parental arguments).

Seek professional advice if bed-wetting – whether primary or secondary enuresis – continues much beyond the age of five. The type of treatment given to your child will depend on her individual circumstances; it is always necessary for her to be helped with any psychological or physical difficulties which might be underlying the condition. But even when these stresses have been removed, your child will probably need additional treatment for the wetting itself.

A 'star chart' can be effective. This is a simple technique, designed to harness your child's interest in becoming dry, and involves the drawing of a small box-chart with a space in it for each night of the week. It usually covers a four-week period. Before the chart is put into operation, tell your child that every time she has a dry night (the word 'wet' should not be used) a gold star will be stuck on to the chart. Give her encouragement and praise every time she has a dry night. Display the chart prominently by her bedside; your enthusiasm for it, coupled with her desire to please you – and to get lots of stars – may be sufficient motivation to help her achieve full bladder control. The chart should be continued until a period of three completely dry weeks has been reached.

Your GP may suggest a buzzer device which operates on the principle that when the child begins to wet herself while asleep, the urine activates an alarm which wakes her up and stops her passing any more. These are very popular devices, with a reasonably high success rate, although there are a number of factors which must be taken into account when considering their use. First, physical causes of enuresis should always have been excluded. Second, the device will require a great deal of supervision by you, and has to be used consistently every night. In addition, there's the possibility that the child may sleep right through the alarm, while everyone else in the house is woken by it! Finally, because the alarm is activated by liquid, heavy sweating can cause it to go off in error.

Some paediatricians favour the use of drugs to treat children who are enuretic. But this method has been highly criticised by other doctors because there are inherent dangers, such as unpleasant and toxic side-effects from the drugs, accidental poisoning, and even deliberate overdosing by an unhappy child. Such risks seem unnecessary when the problem can usually be resolved by psychological methods.

See also **Potty-Training; Unhappiness.**

Birth Order   Were you the youngest child in your family, convinced you were always last in line for everything? Were you the oldest in your family, fed up with being given responsibility for your younger brothers and sisters? Or were you a middle child, who had to follow in the footsteps of a clever brother or sister? There is little doubt that a child's birth order – his position in the family – affects his personality

Jealousy of younger brothers and sisters is common in first-born children. Having been the only child in the family for some time, a first-born may feel threatened when the next child arrives. It's hardly surprising that some first-born children react with anxiety rather than pleasure at the prospect of a new baby. These feelings of jealousy and insecurity can last well into adulthood. Ask any of your friends who are first-born children if they recall having felt any resentment towards their younger brothers or sisters. Chances are they did – and you'll probably find this rivalry between them still exists today.

Research has also shown that the oldest child tends to achieve more at school than his younger brothers or sisters. And this higher level of attainment often extends beyond school as well; oldest children usually have better jobs than the others in the family.

One explanation for the oldest child's greater success in life is that parents are more conscientious about 'doing the right thing' when raising their first child than they are when dealing with their second and third. They are also able to give him attention whenever he wants. This gives the first-born a head-start over his brothers and sisters. Yet this explanation fails to take into account that we make most of our mistakes with our first-born child, and are more confident when dealing with the next. A more likely theory of the first-born child's high attainments is his fear of being surpassed by his brothers and sisters – which makes him try harder to be successful.

Middle-born children frequently complain they are worse

off than any other in the family; while the oldest is allowed the most freedom, and the youngest may be 'spoilt', the middle child lies somewhere in between. The rivalry between children that drives the oldest to be a high achiever has a different effect on middle children. They tend to be less conventional than their brothers and sisters; the typical middle-born child prefers non-academic pastimes such as music and art, and likes clothes which lead, rather than follow, fashion. As adults, they often have a relaxed and carefree manner.

Perhaps these characteristics develop because a middle child – having to walk in the shadow of a successful older brother or sister – decides not to compete. Parents and teachers may be greatly tempted to motivate a younger child by reminding him of how well his older sister did when she was in that class. Instead of acting as an incentive, however, this strategy may encourage the middle child to reject traditional goals.

Sometimes the youngest in the family finds that he is the centre of attention. Older brothers and sisters, especially those aged five or six years upwards, often dote on a baby and make a big fuss of him. And parents often spoil their youngest child because he is the 'baby of the family'. At other times, though, this same child may find himself pushed to the back of the queue when sweets are being given out, or when all the children want to tell their news to mum and dad at the end of the day.

Youngest children tend to be the most self-confident of all, capable of handling worries on their own, without relying on advice from others. This level of independence probably arises from necessity. After all, by the time he arrives in the family, his parents have other children to attend to as well. Practical circumstances dictate that the youngest has to become independent or else get used to waiting a long time for help.

And youngest children also tend to be more 'street-wise' than others in the family, an attribute that develops from daily experience of fighting hard to secure their fair share of family resources. Constant competition with older brothers and sisters hones the youngest child's ability to survive, and strengthens his ability to cope with the stresses of everyday life.

The effect of family position on an individual child

depends on many factors, such as the age gap or gaps, and whether they are both or all of the same sex. But the most important factor determining how much your children are affected by their birth order is you, their parents. The way you interact with them is the strongest influence on their personality development.

For instance, you can reduce potential rivalry between an older child and his younger brother or sister by preparing him for the birth of the new baby. And when the new arrival is brought home, involve the older child in his basic care as much as possible. Similarly, a middle-born child shouldn't automatically be saddled with the achievements of the older child. Avoid the trap of using the oldest child's school performance as the standard by which your other children are judged.

And a youngest child's need to achieve independence will be less intense if you make sure he doesn't have to fight for everything that's going. Although it's tempting to share out toys, sweets and clothes on the basis of the oldest child first, then the next oldest, with the youngest last of all, let your youngest come first in the queue every now and again. Let him be the one to have a new track-suit occasionally, instead of having to wear hand-me-downs all the time.

Each of your children should be respected for his own strengths and weaknesses, not judged solely in relation to how well he compares with everyone else in the family.

See also **Age Gap; First-Born Jealousy; Jealousy; Only Child; Sibling Rivalry; Twins**.

Boasting Everybody compares their characteristics, their achievements and their possessions with those of other people. But there are some children (and some adults!) who make these judgements in a very public way, and openly show off about some object they have or about some goal they have attained. Young children are particularly prone to this.

The act of boasting, of course, makes your child feel very important. But his friends are unlikely to be pleased with what he says, and a child who constantly docs this will eventually become unpopular. This is why you should discreetly discourage him from engaging in this type of behaviour, perhaps by pointing out to him that other children feel miserable when he boasts because it reminds them of the things they don't have, or that it may make others jealous. You should also set a good example yourself (a boasting parent is likely to have a boasting child) – which will discourage him from developing this sort of behaviour.

However, a child may regularly boast about himself as a result of a deep-rooted feeling of insecurity. Outwardly he may appear very confident and successful, but inwardly he may be feeling miserable and inadequate. Boasting in these circumstances is the child's unconscious way of hiding from an unpleasant reality. Always look closely at a child who boasts regularly, in order to identify any underlying factors in his life that may be troubling him. Removal of these influences will decrease his need to rely on boasting as a way of boosting his self-esteem.

See also **Lying; Self-Confidence**.

Body Language Children communicate their ideas and feelings in two ways – verbally, using words, and non-verbally, using body movements. Body language (also termed *non-verbal communication*) reveals as much as spoken language, but what makes body language particularly fascinating is that we don't have as much control over it as we do over our spoken language. Body language leaks out, without us realising.

Sometimes a child's body language conveys the same message as her spoken language, while at other times body language and spoken language appear to be in conflict. When this happens, always believe the body language rather than the spoken language. Remember the time you asked your daughter to tidy her room because she had said she wouldn't mind, but then she sulked silently for the rest of the morning? Or the time your son claimed not to be upset by another child's aggressive behaviour towards him, and yet burst out crying a few moments later. Incidents like this – where a child's body language reveals feelings that contradict what she says – happen all the time.

Young babies have no choice over whether or not to use body language as a means of communication – they can't speak. Parents quickly learn to interpret their baby's non-verbal communication in quite subtle ways, such as the difference between a cry that signifies hunger and one that signifies tiredness, or the difference between wriggling that represents playfulness and wriggling that represents discomfort. This sort of non-verbal communication goes on between parents and their babies in a very natural way.

Body language follows the same principles no matter what age the child is, although the younger she is, the less sophisticated her body language. A young baby's non-verbal communication will include:

- *facial expressions*. A baby's smile tells you she is happy, her pursed lips tell you she is unhappy, and her pouting lip tells you she is so annoyed that she's probably going to start crying at any moment.
- *leg movements*. If her legs are gently kicking in the air, then you can be sure she's happy and playful. On the other hand, if her legs are drawn tightly up towards her tummy, the chances are that she is in pain.
- *arm and hand movements*. A baby whose hands are tightly bunched and held close to her face is probably in some discomfort, while a baby whose hands are open and relaxed is almost certainly feeling contented. Similarly gentle hand and arm movements suggest playfulness while swinging, forceful arm movements suggest anger.
- *noises*. At this stage of development, a baby also uses sounds to let people know what she is feeling and thinking, such as quiet gurgling when she's contented, loud screaming when she's irritable, and babbling when she's trying to catch an adult's attention.
- *breathing*. When a baby's breathing is slow and deep, she's either in a state of sound sleep or else she is about to enter a state of sound sleep, whereas her shallow breathing usually means she is upset.

Your ability to interpret your baby's body language is one of the factors that influence the extent to which you are able to form a two-way emotional bond with her.

Women suffering from post-natal depression often complain that they don't know what it is that their baby wants from them, that they are unable to care for their baby adequately because they don't understand what she needs. This inability to interpret non-verbal communication causes distress for both the mother and the baby. Of course, it's not possible to say whether it's the mother's depression that reduces her ability to communicate non-verbally with her baby, or her reduced ability to communicate non-verbally that increases her depression. Either way, this breakdown in communication causes psychological problems.

Bonding between mothers and babies with visual difficulties can be badly affected because of their relatively poor non-verbal communication. Compared with a baby with normal sight, a baby who is blind tends to smile less frequently and less intensely, makes no eye contact, has a narrower range of facial expressions, and appears more sombre and morose. This restricted level of body language means that mother and baby can have difficulty trying to form an emotional attachment.

Older children have a much wider repertoire of body language than babies because they have a more mature level of understanding, because they are mobile, and because they are able to use eye contact more effectively. These new dimensions greatly expand a child's non-verbal communication skills:

– *mobility*. A child who is angry can express this in a number of ways using body language. For instance, she can simply walk out of the room, or throw her toys all over the place, or even lie flat on her back and scream. Most of us have experienced this type of non-verbal communication from an irate child, and we don't have any problem interpreting the deeper meaning underlying it!

– *social distance*. The gap we leave between ourselves and another person during conversation (social distance) is normally between 18 and 24 inches; longer than that probably means there is bad feeling (e.g., when your child angrily shouts at you from the other side of the room), while a shorter distance can mean either temper (e.g., when you and she are having a disagreement), or closeness (e.g., when she is sitting on your knee while you read her a story).

– *eye contact*. When a child is tense and nervous, or when she is feeling guilty about having done something she knows is wrong, then the chances are that she will not be able to make eye contact with you – she will look at the ground, when talking to you. On the other hand, when she tells you something she is pleased about, she will probably look straight into your eyes as she talks to you.

See also **Bonding; Visual Difficulties**.

Bonding The emotional attachment between parent and baby – known as *bonding* – does occasionally occur at birth. But for most parents, bonding takes longer.

A newborn baby is already pre-programmed to interact with her parents; she is born with a number of characteristics that enable bonding to take place. For instance, a newborn baby's

– hearing is already tuned to a specific frequency so that she hears human voices in preference to any other sounds in the environment;
– vision has the sharpest focus at a point somewhere between 7 and 9 inches away from her face, which is the distance she's usually held from her parent during feeding;
– voice has a broad range of tones, in order to let her parents know when she is hungry or in distress.

Psychologists place great importance on the bond between a child and her parents, because it is this emotional relationship that has the greatest influence on her subsequent psychological development. The quality of this affectionate bond determines many of the child's emotional characteristics in later life.

But you shouldn't worry if it takes time for you and your baby to mesh together. Whereas young animals can become emotionally attached to a caring adult figure (even to humans in some cases) only during a specific short period at the start of life, a human baby does not have to form an emotional connection with her parents during a fixed time span. Bonding is a gradual process. In fact, a child has to be able to differentiate her mother from every other adult before a unique connection can develop between them – and research has shown that many babies do not acquire this skill till around the age of six or seven months. So a genuinely reciprocal mother-infant attachment isn't usually formed until then, and it can take longer.

But children who have not formed a secure relationship with at least one adult before the age of four often have difficulty with relationships in later life. In extreme cases, failure to form an emotional connection can lead to a psychological disturbance.

Psychologists once thought that breast-feeding forges a closer bond between mother and baby than bottle-feeding does. But this is a complete myth. The specific method of feeding in itself has little to do with bonding. What matters is the emotional interaction between the mother and her baby, and this interaction can take place through a bottle or a breast. What matters is the caring way she holds her infant when feeding, and the soothing words she speaks. These factors are more important to bonding than whether the milk comes out of a real nipple or a latex nipple. A mother who is tense and anxious when breast-feeding is not putting her baby at risk psychologically by changing to bottle-feeding.

Bonding is not simply a matter of the parents changing their baby's nappy, washing her and feeding her. Neither is it simply a matter of the parents spending a lot of time with her. Studies of infants living in kibbutz – a communal farm, in which a baby lives with her parents at night and is looked after by a nurse in the nursery during the day, along with all the other kibbutz children – confirm that although a baby typically spends most of her waking hours in the nurse's care, emotional attachments are still formed more often with the parents than with the nurse.

The following factors will help establish an emotional connection between you and your baby:

- *your ability to soothe her when she is upset.* Bonds are strongest in families where the mother feels she can calm her unhappy baby.
- *the amount you lovingly cuddle your baby when she is irritable and unsettled.* Physical contact by itself will not enhance the mother-child relationship, but your loving physical contact will draw you and your baby together.
- *your sensitivity to your baby's communication.* At first, you may be unable to make sense of her actions. For instance, crying could mean she is in pain, or it could mean she is bored. The more you understand her signals, the stronger the emotional attachment between you.

36

Of course, your child can form bonds with more than one person, not just with you; she is as likely to form an emotional attachment with her father as she is with her mother. Nowadays, fathers play a much more active role in their child's life, and so the chances of bonding between a father and his baby are high.

See also **Body Language; Fathers; Kibbutz; Mothers**.

Bullying Every child fears a bully. Bullying is one of the worst forms of anti-social behaviour because it involves exploiting someone else's personal weakness by frightening him into acquiescence. Some children are naturally adventurous, and enjoy rough-and-tumble play – but this isn't bullying, because these children's behaviour lacks a malicious or sinister dimension. Bullying involves a deliberate act of coercion.

A child bullies for many different reasons:

– *identification with parents*. Children 'identify' with their parents, and copy their behaviour. A child of parents who show concern for the feelings of others is more likely to be caring towards other children than he is to be uncaring. And a child of parents who believe the best way to deal with others is to threaten them with violence, is more likely to express aggression in his relationships than he is to express sensitivity and kindness. Identification means that bullying parents usually have bullying children.

– *release of frustrations*. Like adults, children experience anger and frustration which they should be allowed to release verbally rather than physically. However, some parents discourage their child from voicing negative feelings, preferring all unpleasant emotions to be concealed. A child in this situation can only express his anger outside the family, and this may manifest itself as bullying; the victim becomes the means through which the bully releases his tension.

– *extremes in family discipline*. Parents who are either too restrictive in the way they discipline their child (i.e., they have very firm and narrow guidelines for acceptable behaviour, and punish any infringement immediately) or too permissive (i.e., they avoid rules, and let their child do as he pleases) tend to have children who are aggressive and bullying. A more balanced discipline is preferable.

- *feelings of inadequacy*. A child may compensate for poor performance at school by trying to prove himself in other ways. And aggression towards his fellow-pupils may be the one field in which he can come out on top. Unconsciously, this type of child bullies others in the hope of achieving some sort of recognition.
- *unhappiness*. Any source of severe and long-term unhappiness (e.g., pressure at home, jealousy of brothers and sisters, or even ill-health of a relative) can put a child under considerable stress. When stress of this sort is prolonged, the child may hit out against others.

Always treat complaints of bullying seriously. Remember that it takes a great deal of courage for your child to admit to you that he is being bullied. He will be terrified in case you approach the bully's parents or teacher, because they may reveal to the bully that your child has lodged a complaint against him – in fact, it's fear of retaliation that makes most victims remain silent about bullying for a very long time. So reassure your child that you won't take any action without consulting him first. Try to persuade him to let you discuss the situation with the other child's teacher or parent; often, this course of action successfully puts an end to the bullying very quickly.

However, you should also teach your child how to cope with bullying, along the following lines:

- *Persuade him to walk away discreetly whenever the bully appears to be moving in his direction*. There is a pragmatic realism in the saying, 'He who walks away lives to fight another day.' Although, too often, this type of avoidance strategy is mistakenly construed by the victim as an act of cowardice, safety is the first priority, and a child who keeps a low profile is less likely to be bullied.
- *Encourage him to show as little reaction as possible to the bully's threats*. It is generally true that teasing and bullying will stop eventually if the victim displays indifference to the actions against him. Of course, ignoring verbal and physical threats is difficult, but it can be done successfully. One way to help your child achieve this is

by allowing him to practise it through role play with you at home – this will let him develop skills for coping with the real event when it happens.

- *Increase his self-confidence.* Long-term bullying has the unpleasant side-effect of reducing the victim's self-confidence. A child's realisation that he cannot defend himself from attacks makes him feel inadequate. You can try to compensate for this by reminding him of his achievements, whether these are in sport, in particular aspects of the curriculum, in music, or whatever. Your positive remarks will increase his self-confidence and may indirectly increase his ability to cope with the bully.

- *Don't tell your child to fight back.* Tempting as it may be to encourage him to retaliate, this advice can have a number of drawbacks. First, he may not have the necessary physical skills. With your encouragement, he may go headlong into battle with the bully and actually end up worse off than before. Second, telling your child to fight back simply means that there will now be two violent children instead of one. Third, if he thinks you believe in aggression – however justified the circumstances may be – he may think this is a suitable way of dealing with any problem involving others.

See also **Discipline; Victim.**

C

Cerebral Palsy   A general term which describes a range of serious coordination difficulties:

- *spasticity*, in which the leg and arm muscles are very tight and contract very strongly when the child attempts to make any stretching movement; spastic muscles often become shorter as the child grows older, resulting in limb deformities;
- *athetosis*, in which the muscles move involuntarily and uncontrollably; the child can attempt to make a purposeful movement, but it often becomes distorted;
- *tremor*, in which the arms and legs shake; continuous tremors are rare – tremor usually only occurs when the child tries to use his limbs;
- *ataxia*, in which balance is poor; the child walks with an unsteady gait, holding his legs and arms apart to help balance himself; an ataxic child often falls over.

Estimates suggest that approximately one child in 400 has cerebral palsy. All forms of cerebral palsy are caused by specific damage to part of the brain. This can occur in the womb (for example, when a mother becomes infected by German measles early on in the pregnancy), during the birth process itself (for example, if a baby is denied oxygen for a short time during labour), or after birth (for example, as a result of meningitis). The specific form of cerebral palsy depends on which part of the brain is affected and how widespread the damage is. Cerebral palsy is a non-progressive (non-worsening) condition.

The brain damage that affects the child's motor coordination frequently affects other body mechanisms as well. A child with cerebral palsy may have difficulties with swallowing; nearly half of all children with cerebral palsy have some form of speech difficulty. Hearing and visual defects may occur and in some instances of spasticity the child may experience convulsions.

Unless the condition is extreme, diagnosis of cerebral

palsy rarely takes place at birth. Indeed, several days or weeks may pass before the baby's mother and father begin to sense that he does not move his limbs in the ways that he should. Although there is no cure for the condition, the earlier it is diagnosed the better, since proper management of the child in the pre-school years can make a significant difference to the way he copes with his motor-coordination difficulties.

Once a child is identified as having cerebral palsy, a number of specialist therapies – physiotherapy, occupational therapy and speech therapy – will be made available to him if they are needed. In every instance, the therapist will be actively involved with the child, and will give parents advice on the sorts of activities suitable for him at home. An occupational therapist may also arrange for the child to be supplied with specific aids, to enable him to sit at a table, to walk, to eat independently, and so on.

Although surveys indicate that at least 50 per cent of children with cerebral palsy have learning difficulties to some extent, and although there is a higher incidence of severe learning difficulties amongst such children than there is amongst the normal child population, this certainly does not mean that every child with cerebral palsy will inevitably be a slow learner. Each must be treated individually, since his rate of development depends on the degree of brain damage.

A child with cerebral palsy should be encouraged to lead as normal, and as independent, a life as possible, and this should begin in the pre-school years. Encourage him to cope with his coordination problems so that he can interact with other children of his own age. While some are so severely affected in their motor coordination, their intellectual development and their speech that they require specialised schooling, many with this condition can cope with ordinary school. In recent years, conductive education has become more widely available in Britain. This treatment – developed in Hungary, with the aim of promoting the all-round development of a child with cerebral palsy – combines physiotherapy, occupational therapy and speech therapy in a multi-faceted approach.

Conductive education prepares a child with cerebral palsy for school by developing his thought processes, language, communication, mobility and hand control. In doing so, it

41

can enable a child to participate more fully in the education offered at an ordinary school. Advocates of this system claim that children are not taught how to use a wheelchair – they are taught to walk. They are not taught how to manage their incontinence – they are taught to be continent. They are not taught alternative means of communication because of their speech difficulties – they are taught to speak.

See also **Clumsiness; Coordination; Hand-Eye Coordination**.

Clothes Getting dressed in the morning is a skill that virtually every child masters eventually. But before she learns how to put clothes on, she'll learn how to take them off – it's a lot easier to take off a pair of socks or to slip out of a jumper than it is to put on a vest or a pair of trousers. The best age to start teaching your child how to dress herself is around 18–24 months, when she has developed some coordination skills.

At first, you will have to show her how to get dressed, item by item. Pick an easy-to-put-on garment (e.g., a pair of elasticated trousers that can be pulled into position without much effort), put it on for her, then let her try herself. Keep repeating this process until she copes without your help. Point out clues that will help her: for instance, that labels go at the back of clothes, that the front neckline of a T-shirt is often slightly lower than the back, that the pockets of a pair of trousers are usually at the front. Give her lots of time – first thing in the morning, when everyone is in a rush, is not the best time.

Around the age of three or four, your child may be able to put on a few articles of clothing at a time, without your help. You can make dressing easier for her by laying out the clothes in a fixed order, on the floor beside her bed. This way she will know which one to start with. You might even put a small sticker on the front of each garment to help her identify the way it should be worn. Pick clothes that don't involve complicated manoeuvres during dressing – tops with loose necks are better than the sort with buttons or zips; and choose footwear without buckles or lace fastenings.

Your child will be more interested in mastering dressing

skills if she actually likes her clothes. Select items that are brightly coloured, with attractive patterns. Young children particularly love clothes that feature their favourite television cartoon character as part of the pattern. Let her be involved in choosing which clothes she'll wear the following day; a pre-school child can be very fussy about what she wears, so the more you involve her in decisions about dressing, then the more likely she is to cooperate with you.

By the time your child reaches school age, she should be able to put on most clothes by herself, without your help. However, even at this age, complicated zips and button arrangements may still be too difficult. Likewise, she may not be able to tie her shoe-laces or fasten buckles on her sandals. Choose sensible school clothes that she can manage independently, and put her name clearly on each garment. In particular, give her lots of practice in taking off her coat and hanging it on a peg, and in arranging her clothing neatly after she has been to the toilet – these are tasks she will have to cope with every day at school.

See also **Coordination; Hand-Eye Coordination; Independence**.

Clumsiness Children who are clumsy often grow up to dread physical activities because they see themselves as incompetent at such tasks. They develop a negative self-image about their coordination skills, and avoid any challenge that might test them.

To help a clumsy child acquire a more positive self-image:

- *Remind her that there are plenty of things she is good at.* While admitting she has physical limitations, stress her strong points, such as how well she gets on with others, how quick she is at learning, how good she is at singing. She won't forget her coordination difficulties, but repeatedly emphasising her positive qualities will help strengthen her self-esteem.
- *Give her physical challenges that are likely to lead to success.* Your child's self-confidence will be boosted every time she masters a task involving physical ability – so pick activities that are easy for her. Make the

challenges appropriate to her level of motor coordination.

- *Accept your child's feelings if she gets upset.* Tears at being last in a playground race may seem rather silly to you because you know it's not a very important event in the grand scale of life. However, to a child, crossing the finishing line after everyone else can seem a catastrophe. So listen to her, don't dismiss her emotions as babyish, and tell her you know how miserable she feels.
- *Don't let her avoid physical tasks.* For instance, when wanting a breakable object brought to you from another part of the room, your natural tendency may be to avoid asking your clumsy child. Although this strategy minimises potential damage, it denies her opportunities to learn how to improve her motor coordination. She needs these activities just as much as any child does.

The term 'minimal brain damage' is often applied to an extremely clumsy child, suggesting that there is a small amount of brain damage underlying the coordination difficulties. However, there is no clear dividing line separating a normal child who is clumsy from a clumsy child with minimal brain damage.

The main way of distinguishing which category a clumsy child comes into is by looking at other areas of her development as well. While a normal clumsy child's development is adequate, apart from her coordination, a child with minimal brain damage frequently has additional problems, such as mild learning difficulties, and confusion in identifying left from right. Of course these characteristics are found in many children who do not have minimal brain damage, but when there is a cluster of such attributes in a child, further medical examination is worthwhile.

See also **Cerebral Palsy; Coordination; Hand-Eye Coordination**.

Comforters Most children have a comforter (an object that makes them feel secure when they are tired or unhappy) at some stage in the pre-school years. It could be an old teddy that brings them tranquillity, or a tattered cot blanket. You may be amazed at the importance your child places on such

44

a scruffy object – but it's the familiar smell of the comforter, its familiar appearance, and its familiar texture, which matter to him.

Psychologists claim that the use of comforters originates in the early months of life, when a baby begins to associate particular items with pleasant, loving sensations. A teddy becomes associated with love because your baby hugs it close in the cot as he falls asleep; the cot blanket becomes associated with warmth and security because he is wrapped tightly in it while you cuddle him.

Although he learns how to obtain emotional satisfaction in other ways as he grows up, this does not eradicate the pleasant recall of babyhood. The comforter becomes a way of reliving these earlier happy life experiences, because he still associates warmth and kindness with it. Even though this association is formed early on in your child's life, it remains strong in later years.

A child can have a comfort habit – for instance, thumb-sucking – rather than a comfort object. Adults often become annoyed with pre-school children who thumb-suck because they regard it as babyish. And dentists are aware that continuation of the habit beyond the age of five may result in the child's second set of teeth being pushed out of line.

When this happens, dental treatment to correct the defect is necessary.

If you do want your child to stop thumb-sucking (or any comfort habit):

- *Decrease the habit gradually.* Just as an adult who wants to give up smoking often finds it easier to do it gradually, so too does a child who needs to stop thumb-sucking. Set a time scale of, say, eight weeks, during which time you hope to eliminate the habit.
- *Explain to your child why he should stop the habit.* Use language he can understand – for instance, tell him that his best friend doesn't suck his thumb, or that his teeth will be damaged. A child aged three and upwards will understand this sort of explanation.
- *Select one short occasion, during which he usually sucks his thumb, and use this as your starting point.* It may be when he is watching television, or perhaps when you are reading a story to him. Give him advance warning that you don't want him to suck his thumb on that specific occasion on that specific day.
- *Slowly increase the number of occasions your child has to do without thumb-sucking.* Build up gradually from, say, once every two days, to once every day, to twice every day, and so on. Decide on a clear plan of action, and stick to it.
- *Give him lots of praise when you see progress is being made.* Each day that you see the thumb-sucking decreasing in frequency, let your child know you are pleased. Make a big fuss of his achievements.
- *Don't use techniques based on avoidance principles.* Strategies such as painting your child's finger with a nasty-tasting solution, or covering the offending thumb in sticking-plaster, rarely work. This usually makes a child more determined to persist with the habit. Of course, you may get lucky and have instant success, but if you take an aversive approach you run the risk of heated confrontation.

Excessive use of a comforter can be a sign of insecurity. If your child reaches the stage where he cannot go anywhere without one, then his dependence on it has become too great – this may be the first sign that he is deeply unhappy. There are many reasons why young children become anxious. Failing to get something right in nursery, having a poor relationship with parents, being reprimanded by mum and dad, not being invited to a birthday party, catching a cold, noticing that a pet is unwell, or a family bereavement, can all undermine a young child's sense of well-being.

Rather than getting annoyed at him for behaving in this way – comments like 'You're behaving like a baby, the way you're sucking that blanket all the time' are particularly unhelpful – take a closer look at his life in order to establish why he may be feeling insecure. Sensitive consideration is needed at this stage. Once the reason for your child's unhappiness is identified and resolved, then his reliance on the comforter will ease.

Comforters can be used positively to help a child through a difficult experience. There are situations where the calculated use of a comforter can boost his self-confidence enough to help him cope with stress. For instance, many children end up in hospital as a result of an accident or ill-health. Being allowed to take a favourite toy with him into the ward will make your child feel more at ease. Indeed, he may even be emotionally vulnerable without it, and there is no harm in letting him have the comforter in these circumstances. The same applies to holidays; strange rooms with unfamiliar noises can make your child distressed when he is trying to sleep at nights. Having his favourite blanket drawn over his bed can ease his anxious feelings – it could make his holiday more enjoyable, as well as your own.

See also **Dummies; Masturbation; Teeth; Unhappiness.**

Concentration No matter how keen your child is to discover and explore his surroundings, he needs to concentrate on what he's doing or he will not learn very much. A strong attention span is very important, particularly when he nears school age.

His attention skills change throughout the pre-school years, in the following ways:

– *from passive to active.* Whereas a new baby attends to something only when it captures his attention by moving across his field of vision, an older infant actively searches and explores. His attention becomes more dynamic and controlled, more in line with his desire to discover.

- *from unsystematic to systematic discovery.* Watch a young baby pick up and examine, say, a rattle. You'll notice that he does this in a very haphazard way, and will only look at one or two sections of it. However, an older child explores an object more systematically, which enables him to discover more about it.
- *from broad to selective attention.* Young babies can't filter out information very well – they try to attend to everything they see and hear. Older children are more able to focus their attention on one specific aspect of a situation – e.g.' they can see the flashing 'green man' at the pelican crossing, even though there are hundreds of other objects in their visual field.

Some children have a very short attention span, long after others of the same age are able to concentrate for more than a few seconds. This can cause problems at school, because they may not be able to look at and listen carefully to the teacher. A useful way of extending your child's attention span is to present him with a short activity (e.g., colouring in), and, using a stop-watch, time how long he persists with it until his attention wanders (say, two minutes). The next night tell him to colour in another picture but add that this time he has to spend a little more time on it. Using the stop-watch, encourage him to persist with the activity for 2 minutes 15 seconds; and give him lots of praise when he achieves this. Then gradually increase the amount of time each night, until his attention span is longer.

See also **Knowledge; Learning Skills; Play**.

Coordination   Your child's coordination skills – her ability to move and manage her legs, arms, hands and fingers in a controlled and deliberate way – fall into two categories:

- *gross motor coordination* – her ability to control general body movements involving arms and legs (e.g., kicking a ball, climbing over a fence, walking along a straight line, running quickly, catching a ball, and hopping);
- *fine motor coordination* – her ability to control hand and finger movements (e.g., cutting with scissors, colouring

in, writing, picking up a sweet from the table, making a model with toy bricks, tracing, and using cutlery).

These skills are acquired at the following ages:

3 months   A baby's head no longer flops about like a rag doll when she is lifted or when she lies in the cot; back firmness increases and she shows signs of straightening her back when sitting on your knee; she will attempt to thrust out her hands when the feeding source (whether breast or bottle) comes towards her, but she will not be successful in touching it every time.

6 months   By this age, an infant will probably be able to sit up on the floor on her own without any support; hand and finger control is more organised, allowing her to hold toys, shake them and throw them away when she is bored with them; she can also reach out deliberately to grab hold of something that catches her interest.

9 months   Her leg movements are not fully coordinated but, when put face down on the floor, she will try to propel herself along by crawling; she may even be able to stand up, using a low table or chair for support; coordination between thumb and forefinger starts to show, and she begins to use them together, in a pincer movement, to pick up small objects.

12 months   She can crawl round the floor without much difficulty, pulling and pushing with her arms and legs in unison; she may be able to walk rather unsteadily around the room using furniture as support; hand control may be developed to the point where she can use a pencil or crayon to make a mark on a piece of paper.

2 years   Your child can now walk confidently wherever she pleases; she can go up and down stairs on her own, although she still puts both feet on the same step before going to the next; she can kick a ball without falling over; most toddlers of this age have established a definite preference for using one hand or the other.

49

3 years	She can jump up and down without overbalancing and can walk a few steps on her tiptoes; she can catch a large ball thrown gently to her; she will attempt to tackle outdoor equipment in the local park; pencil control is stronger and she can make circular scribbling marks on the paper; she will also have an idea of how to hold scissors, although she may not yet be able to cut with them.
4 years	She can use pedals to propel a pedal-car or tricycle along the ground; throwing and catching is easier; she can run in specific directions and steer herself round obstacles without bumping into them; she makes a reasonable attempt to thread beads, pencil control is more mature and she can draw a person, or a house.
5 years	Your child can negotiate any obstacle in her way; she will show ability in ball games; she can also manage climbing frames, ladders, and other outdoor play equipment; now she can hold scissors properly and can cut paper with them; she may be able to write one or two letters that appear in her name.

Although some of these abilities develop naturally, your child probably acquires most motor-coordination skills through the process of learning – so your role is crucial.

Do's

● *Do give your child lots of practice.* Most activities for developing fine motor-coordination control can take place indoors without any difficulty. Activities such as colouring in and cutting pictures out of old magazines are easily organised – and extremely beneficial.

● *Do let her have access to outdoor play equipment.* Fortunately, in recent years there has been a huge upsurge in the number of well structured adventure playgrounds for young children. Climbing frames and balancing logs, obstacle courses made out of smooth pieces of wood bound safely together with nuts and bolts, are a child's dream. Your child's confidence in playing with these will increase with experience.

● *Do make these activities fun.* She will learn more quickly in a situation she enjoys than she will in one full of tension. Laughing and joking with her will make her feel at ease and more willing to try to master the challenge.

- *Do break up each task into small stages.* For example, when teaching her to catch a ball, her first goal should be to watch the ball when it is thrown towards her; the next goal should be to put her arms out towards the ball; then it should be to touch the ball with her hand when it is thrown towards her, and so on. Each successive stage moves closer to the desired outcome, until she eventually masters the task.
- *Do give lots of praise.* Each time your child makes progress – no matter how slight this may be – show her that you're pleased. Tell her how well she's doing, how much she had improved.

Don'ts

- *Don't force your child to be too adventurous on play equipment.* It can be very frustrating to watch a timid child tentatively explore the first step of a ladder when you want her to go to the top. But a child should never be encouraged to climb up to a height from which she is unable to climb down by herself.
- *Don't make fun of her because of poor coordination.* She'll be unhappy enough when she realises she can't propel her pedal car along, especially when her friends can do it with ease. She doesn't need you to make sarcastic comments about her lack of skill. And sometimes cajoling is done with the best of intentions – but it rarely, if ever, works.
- *Don't have unrealistic expectations.* Children mature at different rates. The fact that another child of her age can kick a ball while running doesn't mean your child is inadequate because she can't do this. Nor is there much advantage in a child having coordination skills normally found only in older children.

See also **Cerebral Palsy; Clumsiness; Hand-Eye Coordination**.

Cot Deaths The sudden death of a healthy baby is one of

the worst things that any parent can possibly experience. Yet the tragic fact is that every year in the UK approximately one baby in 500 dies suddenly, without any apparent reason. Cot death (also known as 'sudden infant death syndrome') affects babies between the ages of one and five months, (the average age is four months). At least half of all babies who die in this way appear to be in perfectly good health before death, while the other half often have had a minor respiratory infection. Frequently, parents only realise their baby has died when they try to wake him after he has apparently been asleep for a longer period than expected.

Despite a great deal of medical research, the cause of cot death is unknown. However, medical consensus suggests that parents should be aware of the following factors:

- *smoke-free environment*. Try to create a smoke-free atmosphere around your young baby. Don't smoke in her bedroom, don't let others smoke in any room in the house that she uses, and don't take her into smoky places. A baby is at increased risk of cot death if her mother smoked during pregnancy.
- *temperature*. Every parent wants to be sure their baby is comfortable and warm. However, she is at increased risk of cot death if she is too hot in bed, so use lightweight blankets which you can increase or decrease depending on how hot she is; and maintain a comfortable and steady temperature in her room.
- *sleeping position*. Doctors advise parents to lay their baby to sleep on her back, or on her side with the arm positioned slightly forward on the mattress to stop her rolling over on to her tummy. Although parents worry that their baby may be sick and then choke when she is asleep on her back, this does not appear to happen. Cot death is more frequent amongst babies who are allowed to sleep while lying on their tummies. If you are uncertain about the best sleeping position for your baby, discuss it with your health visitor or GP.

Cot death is still a rare occurrence, and few families experience more than one. Aside from these basic general precautions, keep your baby close to you when you think she is unwell – this will enable you to watch her closely, and to notice any abnormality in her breathing. If you are at all concerned about her during the early months, don't hesitate to visit your family doctor.

Creativity Psychologists have compiled a list of features which describe an object or idea that is creative:

- *It must have novelty;* it should be original and unusual (e.g., inventing a skateboard was novel because there was no other object that children could play with offering these qualities).
- *It must be appropriate;* it should be sensible and suitable (e.g., the suggestion that we can travel to work by flying saucer isn't appropriate because we don't have access to flying saucers).
- *It must involve a transformation;* it should involve a change in perspective, a new way of looking at an old problem (e.g., the invention of the hovercraft was creative because it involved the craft hovering above water rather than moving through it, as is the traditional method).
- *It must involve condensation;* it should incorporate many different characteristics (e.g., the invention of the modern video recorder was creative because the video allowed people to record programmes, to play programmes others have recorded, to plan their leisure time more effectively).

History reveals that many famous figures in the world of art and music showed signs of creativity even in childhood. For instance, Mozart composed symphonies before he was five years old, and Leonardo da Vinci demonstrated his artistic ability very early on in life. And creativity, like all human characteristics, is present in every one of us to some extent. Every child has the potential to do something creative.

A 'genius level' of intelligence is not needed. True, most creative people are of at least average intelligence, but beyond that minimum standard there are wide variations in the intellectual levels of creative minds. Nor is forgetfulness a requirement of creativity – there is no evidence to support the stereotype of the creative individual as the absent-minded professor. Research has shown that creative children tend to be willing to take risks, to be less frustrated by their mistakes, self-confident, independent, successful at learning tasks, socially competent, unconventional, and keen to experiment with new ideas.

Tests for measuring creativity are open-ended (they have more than one right answer). The problem with these tests, though, is how to score the answers. Suppose two children are asked to take a blank piece of paper each and make as many different patterns on it as they can. One of the children might make five patterns while the other might make six. Yet that does not necessarily mean that they differ in levels of creativity, because it could be that the first child's five patterns are all completely different whereas the other child's six patterns are all similar. Problems like this have made tests of creativity unpopular.

You can help your child become more creative in these ways:

- *Show respect when he asks unusual questions*. You may have a busy enough day without having to deal with such questions as 'Why don't trains fly like aeroplanes so that they would arrive at the station quicker?' It's tempting to dismiss such inquiries as unnecessary interruptions, but that attitude will discourage your child from developing his creative thoughts further. Treat unusual questions seriously, and take time to answer them. If you can't think of a suitable answer, then be honest and admit that to him.

- *Allow him to express his imaginative ideas freely*. Listen to your child when he suggests that cars should be made with engines that run on water because it's cheaper than petrol. If you show interest, he will not be afraid to voice other imaginative ideas in the future. Don't ridicule his idea or be sarcastic about it.

- *Give your child opportunities to play in unstructured situations*. Resist the temptation to turn all play experiences into some form of learning experience. He needs to be allowed to play freely at times, in order to unleash and develop his creative skills through play.

- *Explain the practical implications of his idea*. Research indicates that tying a child's creative idea into its practical consequences encourages further creativity.

- *Allow your child to solve problems himself sometimes, instead of always showing him solutions*. One study of the problem-solving methods of children aged between three and five involved each child having to reach a piece of chalk on the far side of the table at which he was seated. The materials available to him were two short sticks and a clamp. Before each child was presented with the problem, he was either shown the long stick out of two short ones or allowed free play with the sticks and clamp. The investigators found that children who were allowed free play with the materials were much more innovative and creative in their solutions to the problem than the other children.

See also **Imagination; Intelligence**.

Criticism . No child thrives on criticism, although every child benefits from helpful correction. While both these measures share the same purpose of improving a child's behaviour or learning, criticism is nearly always negative – it tells him what is wrong, without offering suggestions for positive change. A child who is constantly criticised will soon lack self-confidence and have little belief in his own abilities.

Your child cannot improve his behaviour at home, or his performance in class, unless he is aware of his weaknesses and of ways to overcome them. This is part of the learning process. So don't be afraid to point out to him, for instance, that he has put his jumper on back to front – in fact, if you don't let him know his mistake, he's likely to repeat it – but at the same time help him learn how to do it properly, perhaps by explaining that the label goes to the back. These two aspects should be combined.

Parents can become trapped in a cycle of criticism when their child regularly misbehaves – a pattern that is hard to break. The more, say, a child refuses to do as he's told, the more his parents reprimand him. This increases tension at home, which unsettles the child even further, resulting in more criticism. If you find yourself in the situation of constantly criticising your child, think closely about him and try to determine why he has the need to behave this way. Perhaps he has fallen out with his best friend, or is worried about something in school. Perhaps your expectations of him are too high. Dealing with the factors that are causing him stress is a more effective way of improving his behaviour than regularly criticising him. And be careful not to use your child as a scapegoat for your own difficulties – it can be very tempting to blame him when things go wrong, even though he is entirely innocent.

This doesn't mean you should never give your child a telling-off, of course. Every child reaches the point where he needs a reprimand for breaking the family rules. But ensure yours understands the difference between rejection of his behaviour and rejection of himself. He has to learn that you can be angry with him for something he has done and yet at the same time still love him. If he knows this, then your occasional criticism won't do him any harm; if he doesn't know this, then he will fear even a slight negative remark.

See also **Discipline; Scapegoat; Self-Confidence**.

Crying Baby   If your baby cries consistently throughout the night, and doesn't respond to your efforts to quieten her down, consider the following possibilities initially:

- *nappy change.* Your first step should always be to check that your baby doesn't need a change of nappy, or that a nappy pin hasn't become unfastened and is sticking into her. The chances of this causing regular crying throughout the night, though, are remote.
- *health check.* It is always sensible to rule out any physical problems. After all, although your baby may seem perfectly healthy – especially if she is very settled during the day – it is possible she has a medical problem. A thorough examination at your local baby clinic will reassure you on this point.
- *colic.* A term used by doctors to describe a pain in the stomach caused by a spasm in the tummy muscles, and thought to occur only in infants of three months or younger. But not everyone is convinced about the existence of colic. The explanation sounds good, and it's a plausible way to account for a young baby's distress. But it is impossible to verify – you can't be certain that your baby has stomach pains. You can give her gripe-water

(available from your local chemist), though care must be taken to use it only in moderation.

– *wind*. Some people think that a baby's crying may be caused by an excess of wind in her stomach, since a baby who cries constantly releases enormous belches quite regularly. Yet this doesn't mean that it's the build-up of wind that has caused her crying. On the contrary, there is the opposite argument that the very act of continuous crying makes a baby suck in vast amounts of air. So it is just as likely that a loud expulsion of wind has been the result of crying, not the cause of it.

– *additive-free diet*. There are some professionals who claim there is a link between food additives – used as colourings and preservatives – and unsettled behaviour in children, but the evidence on this point is unclear. Even so, it is possible that a crying baby may be allergic to milk formula, for example, so it's worth trying a change.

If you have ruled out these possibilities, but your baby still cries throughout the night, then you may have to broaden your perspective. Crying babies create anxiety in their parents, and this can become self-reinforcing. For instance, parents who automatically assume their baby will wake up crying, will be tense and agitated at the prospect of another horrendous night. The baby may sense this tension, reacting to it by becoming tense and tearful herself. Your own anxiety caused by anticipating your baby's crying, therefore, could actually play a part in causing the very behaviour you dread. That's why calmness is extremely important when managing a crying baby – make a big effort to stay relaxed at night, despite your knowledge of what almost certainly awaits you.

A more likely explanation of your baby's regular crying at night is that it is attention-seeking behaviour, that her tears are about getting you to do what she wants. (She probably enjoys these middle-of-the-night sessions, even though you may be rather unresponsive to her in your sleepless daze.) If this is the underlying explanation for her crying, consider the tactic of ignoring her. Of course, no parent feels comfortable about leaving a baby alone when she is in tears, but you must use your own judgement. (If you do adopt this strategy, use a baby-listener so that you can hear her crying, even though you don't go into her room to see her.) Stick to your plan for at least three weeks, rather than giving up after one or two nights.

Some babies cry constantly for a completely different reason – perhaps because their emotional attachment to their mother (or mother-substitute) isn't as close as it might be. An infant who does not receive emotional warmth from her parents during the early part of her life will be very unhappy and will cry a lot.

Getting short-term relief from a crying baby is always a valuable practical measure. Distancing yourself from your screaming infant, if only for a short while, can make the world seem a brighter place. Do not hesitate to use family or friends as temporary caretakers for your baby. A few hours off-duty can have a very positive effect.

See also **Additives; Attention-Seeking Behaviour; Bonding; Dreams; Nightmares; Sleep**.

Cystic Fibrosis   A scientific breakthrough gave hope to thousands of families with children suffering from cystic fibrosis – a genetically inherited condition in which the mucus glands produce an abnormally thick, sticky mucus in the lungs, pancreas and bowel – when researchers identified the exact gene responsible for the disease. But a cure is still a long way off.

Cystic fibrosis affects approximately one person in 1500–2000. This means that almost 400 cases are diagnosed each year in the UK, making it one of the most common genetic diseases in the Western world.

Estimates suggest that over two million people in the UK carry the gene responsible for cystic fibrosis, but they are completely unaffected. Should their partner also be a carrier – and there is a 1 in 400 chance that pairing will occur – then the couple have a 1 in 4 chance of having a child with cystic fibrosis, a 2 in 4 chance of having a child who is a carrier but who doesn't have the disease, and a 1 in 4 chance of having a child who neither is a carrier nor has the disease. The cystic fibrosis gene is not sex-linked, and so boys and girls are equally affected.

Without treatment, cystic fibrosis can be a killer. The child's bronchial tubes become clogged up, leaving her prone to pneumonia and other lung infections. Digestion is also affected, because the enzymes which normally flow from the pancreas into the small intestine are prevented from doing so. In the 1950s, when effective treatment wasn't available, most children with cystic fibrosis died before reaching adulthood. However, medical advances in the past 30 years mean that more and more children with the disease survive into adult life (roughly 70 per cent), and sustain relatively little damage to their lungs.

Treatment for the condition has two essential components:

- *physiotherapy*. Must be carried out regularly each day, in order to keep the child's lungs clear of mucus. Although initially treatment will be provided by a qualified physiotherapist, eventually it can be carried out by the parents and child working together at home.
- *enzyme substitutes to compensate for the pancreas problem*. These pills – often a very large number – are taken at mealtimes, in conjunction with vitamin supplements and a high-protein diet.

Parents vary in their reaction to the diagnosis. Some become over-protective, and isolate their child from her peers as a precaution against picking up an infection, while others encourage theirs to lead as normal a life as possible. A child with cystic fibrosis is usually able to attend her local nursery or school; the only difficulty may be that she will need physiotherapy around lunchtime, carried out at home. School staff should be aware that a child with cystic fibrosis is not fragile, although they should exercise caution if she becomes breathless and starts wheezing.

See also **Genes**.

D

Discipline The word 'discipline' is often used in a negative way, as though it's something nasty to be inflicted on children against their wishes, in order to control and limit their behaviour. But a caring and sensitive discipline helps a child, because it

- *provides structure and consistency*. We all need a degree of predictability in our lives – that's not to say we need one day to be the same as the next, just that constant change is difficult for us to manage. Imagine what it would be like in your workplace if the rules were changed each day: you wouldn't know what to do or what to expect. That's the sort of feeling a young child has when his environment lacks discipline.
- *sets out clear standards of behaviour for him to follow*. A child does not instinctively know how to behave in a way that is acceptable to those around him. He has to learn this, through guidance and experience. A well defined discipline clarifies what is expected of him.
- *encourages him to consider other people's feelings*. In the early stages of development, an infant thinks exclusively of himself, not of anyone else. Only as he grows older does he learn to think of other people. And discipline helps that process along because it forces the child to realise that his behaviour has an effect on those around him.
- *makes him feel safe and secure*. Defined standards of behaviour benefit everybody. For instance, the rule that says 'Punching isn't allowed' means, first, that he shouldn't punch his friend, and second, that his friend shouldn't punch him. Discipline, therefore, protects each individual child.
- *eventually leads to self-discipline*. In the early years, parents provide discipline for their child; he is entirely dependent on them to set appropriate standards. One sign of this is that he doesn't always behave well when

he's away from his mum and dad. However, this situation gradually changes, until his parents' standards become his own standards – at this point, he achieves self-discipline.

Between nine months and a year, your child begins to understand what you mean when you say 'no'. He may not like you saying it, and he may try to resist you, but he knows what your intentions are. At this point – when he begins to realise that some of his behaviour is acceptable and some of it isn't – the process of establishing discipline properly begins.

There is no specific discipline that suits all children (although there are general principles which are universal). Discipline partly depends on your child's age (e.g., while you may not get annoyed when your six-month-old throws his rattle out of the pram, you probably will when your six-year-old throws his toy on the floor); on his maturity (e.g., an older child is more able to take responsibility for controlling his own behaviour); and on his personality (e.g., one child may be very timid and sensitive, bursting into tears the moment an adult looks angrily at him, while another may ignore this sort of mild reprimand and only respond to more severe measures).

There are two key dimensions to parental discipline. First, 'warmth vs hostility'. A 'warm' parent is defined as one who is accepting, and affectionate, who uses praise and rarely resorts to physical punishment, whereas a 'hostile' parent is defined as one who frequently rejects their child, rarely praises for good behaviour, and regularly uses smacking when he misbehaves.

Second, 'restrictiveness vs permissiveness'. A 'restrictive' parent has very fixed and narrow guidelines for acceptable behaviour, punishes their child for every incident of misbehaviour, and does not encourage him to make independent judgements. In contrast, a 'permissive' parent avoids fixed rules, never punishes for misbehaviour, and lets their child do what he wants irrespective of the effect his behaviour has on other people.

Detailed investigations reveal that behaviour problems and emotional disorders are less frequent in children raised in a warm, loving atmosphere, and delinquency rates are lower. In addition, children raised in a very restrictive

61

household tend to be submissive, over-polite and dependent on others. They may also lack the ability to compete, and to be assertive. Extremes of discipline rarely have a positive effect on a young child – a balanced approach is usually best. The most effective style is one in which a reasonable level of control is exercised, within a framework of love and support.

Inconsistent discipline is as futile as too little or too much, however, because it means that a child is unable to predict what will happen when he does something wrong. It may also make him more aggressive and he may be more prone to emotional disturbances.

Discipline can be inconsistent in a number of ways. For instance, one child in the family may be allowed to get away with misbehaviour that isn't accepted from another child. This only breeds jealousy between the children and leads to resentment. But a more damaging type of inconsistency occurs when each parent in a family applies discipline differently. One may be strict, while the other is more flexible. Problems frequently occur in this situation, especially when the parents begin to disagree about discipline in front of the children – young minds are very quick to exploit divisions of that sort, and soon learn how to play one parent off against the other.

See also **Attention-Seeking Behaviour; Bedtime; Crying Baby; Illness; Self-Confidence; Smacking; Tantrums**.

Down's Syndrome   This condition was first described by Dr John Langdon Down, in 1866, although he couldn't identify the source of the problem because medical science was not sufficiently advanced. However, he was able to list a number of common physical and psychological features, and hence it became known as a 'syndrome'.

Almost a hundred years passed before scientists were able to demonstrate that the defect lies in the child's genetic structure: in 1959, investigations revealed that Down's Syndrome originates in the baby's chromosomes, and that the condition can be diagnosed by analysing a sample of his blood. With Down's Syndrome, each parent has normal chromosomes but their baby has an extra chromosome in pair no. 21, making a total of 47 per cell instead of the usual

46. This form of the condition is known as *standard trisomy*, and accounts for 96 per cent of all children with Down's Syndrome. A small percentage of babies with Down's Syndrome have either *translocation*, in which one of the no. 21 chromosomes becomes attached to another chromosome; or *mosaicism*, in which some of the cells have 46 chromosomes and some have 47. Since this latter form of the condition involves a mixture of affected and non-affected cells, children with Mosaic Down's Syndrome may look less affected than other babies with Down's, and may show a better rate of development.

Down's Syndrome is present in approximately one in 700 babies, and occurs by chance. Research studies have shown that the likelihood of a baby being born with the condition increases significantly when the mother is 35 years of age or older at the time of conception – that's why pre-birth screening techniques are targeted at this particular age group.

The traditional screening technique for detecting Down's Syndrome in the unborn baby is amniocentesis, which involves a fine needle being inserted into the womb so that a small amount of amniotic fluid can be drawn off for analysis. There is a slight chance that this process may stimulate a miscarriage, and so the test is restricted to those women in the high-risk category. A new test – developed by scientists in Britain – has since become available, and is likely to be favoured by the medical profession because it involves the pregnant mother in merely giving a small sample of her own blood. This poses no risk at all to the foetus, and so can be offered safely to women of all age groups. The blood test is also more accurate than amniocentesis.

Children with Down's Syndrome share certain physical characteristics (though not all features are present in every child). As a result, the condition can often be identified in the first few days of a baby's life. Common signs include floppy muscles and loose joints, an extra fold of skin at the inner corner of each eye, a low nose bridge, a protruding tongue, and a small, straight mouth. In the first week, a baby with Down's Syndrome may not gain as much weight as would normally be expected.

There are health difficulties associated with the condition. A child with Down's Syndrome is prone to chest and sinus infections. Cardiac problems may occur – varying from a minor murmur to a more serious defect – and therefore medical specialists always pay close attention to the child's heart development, especially during the first year. Difficulties with eyes and ears are common, and speech may be unclear because of poor muscle tone in his mouth. The average lifespan of someone with Down's Syndrome is shorter than normal, but there are those who live beyond the age of 70.

Virtually all children with Down's Syndrome have some form of learning difficulty, ranging from mild to severe, and they need a stimulating environment in the pre-school years. Language development is frequently delayed, though useful speech is often acquired eventually. (Speech therapy may be helpful). Many attain a purposeful degree of independence, which can extend into adult life.

At one time it was assumed that children with Down's Syndrome – whatever their level of development – had such severe problems that they could not benefit from being educated alongside their peers in ordinary schools. So most pupils with the condition automatically attended segregated special schools with smaller classes and specially trained teachers. However, educationists have begun to question the value of segregated special schooling. Many local education authorities are ready to accept the principle of integration, and are increasingly willing to support pupils with Down's Syndrome in local primary schools. Some local authorities start the process of integration at the nursery stage, which makes it easier at the primary stage. However, provision does vary from county to county.

Parents may fear that, while integration is acceptable in principle, it doesn't work. Yet a study which compared the development of 18 pupils with Down's Syndrome who attended ordinary schools against the development of 18 pupils with Down's Syndrome who attended segregated special schools for children with moderate learning difficulties, found that the children who were 'mainstreamed' made significantly more progress than those who were 'segregated', in terms of numerical ability, comprehension and mental age.

Not every parent wants their child with Down's Syndrome to attend his local primary school. The attractiveness of his being able to move at his own pace, the confidence that special equipment and learning materials are readily available whenever needed, and the knowledge that he can get the teacher's individual attention when necessary, makes many parents still favour segregated special schooling. That's why decisions about schooling should only be made after detailed consideration of the child's educational, social and psychological needs, and of the educational facilities and opportunities provided by the local education authority. At least, now, more parents are being offered a choice.

See also **Integration, Educational; Special Needs**.

Dreams Ask your child what she dreamed about last night. Can she remember? The chances are she can't, but the chances are she did have a dream. Virtually everybody dreams, even though they often forget the content of their dreams when they wake up.

Dreams occur during REM sleep – that phase of sleep in which the eyes move about very rapidly while still shut, as if scanning a picture beneath the unopened eyelids. Experiments have revealed that 80 per cent of people report having dreams when woken during REM sleep, while less than 10 per cent do when woken at other times. In addition, the length of the dreamer's description of her dream is directly related to the length of time she has been allowed to have an uninterrupted period of REM sleep.

Research by American psychologists suggests that:

- three-year-olds give short accounts of dreams, with very little action and feeling in them. Dreams in this age group are often about play sequences which take place in familiar settings, or about animals.
- six-year-olds produce much longer accounts of their dreams, with a lot more movement and activity in them. Their dreams usually feature friends or members of the immediate family, and the dreamers themselves play a passive role in them.
- dreams of six-year-old girls tend to be pleasant, are about friendly people, and often have happy endings. Dreams of six-year-old boys contain more conflict and aggression, and often have an unhappy content. This gender difference disappears when children reach seven or eight.
- 10–12-year-olds usually have dreams which focus on their

home, the play area immediately outside home, or school. Mostly, the people appearing in these dreams are friends or members of the child's family, although boys of this age often dream about male strangers.
- children's dreams mainly centre on play and other leisure activities, and the majority of dreams experienced by young children are not frightening or distressing.

REM sleep is found not only in adults, children and young babies – even a foetus has REM sleep. Ultrasonography has shown that a foetus begins to have REM sleep as early as the twenty-third week of pregnancy. Amazing to think that a being so young – some 17 weeks before leaving the womb – could actually be dreaming. Of course, precisely what is going on in the mind of the foetus at this point is unknown. But we do know, from close electronic monitoring of new-born babies, that during periods of REM sleep they experience intense stimulation through their central nervous system. Almost 50 per cent of a new baby's sleep is REM sleep. Maybe she dreams about vast quantities of milk!

During a baby's first year of life, total sleep time drops from about 16 hours per day to about 13. Since the amount of non-REM sleep stays the same, this means that the amount of REM sleep is considerably reduced between birth and 12 months. This pattern continues until adulthood, by which time approximately 20–25 per cent of total sleep is REM sleep.

Freud maintained that the only way to fully understand a child is to understand her unconscious mind, and that the best way to do this is through interpretation of her dreams. He reached two major conclusions about children's dreams. First, the purpose of a child's dream is to allow a hidden wish to come true: a wish that can never become a reality in the child's real world – or that would get her into trouble if she did try to make it come true – can become a reality in her dream world. Second, a child's dream is usually triggered by something that has happened in the previous 24 hours – e.g., a fight with a friend, a reprimand from parents, an incident involving a particular toy, or a comment from another child.

Analysing the dreams of very young children, from 18 months upwards, is very easy, claimed Freud: since a young child always dreams of the fulfilment of wishes that were aroused in her the day before but were not satisfied, in order to understand her dreams all you need do is ask about her previous day's experiences.

Some dreams, though, require more interpretation than this because they used symbols to represent people and objects in the child's life. For instance, parents are often symbolised by figures of authority, particularly royalty. Other common symbols appearing in children's dreams include falling into, or coming out of, water (representing birth); houses (representing people); and rodents or other small animals (representing brothers or sisters). Very young children rarely use symbolism in their dreams.

To interpret the meaning of your child's dreams, use these principles – you may not get it right every time, but you'll have some fun along the way.

- *Wait until your child is fully awake* before you ask her what she dreamt about last night, because young children can have difficulty knowing when they are awake and when they are asleep.
- *Use a relaxed, casual voice* when asking her about her dreams. If you seem too interested, she may become concerned and not want to tell you.
- *Be satisfied with a short answer*. Don't expect a long description. Most young children will give only a sentence, two at most, about their dreams.
- *Look for symbolism*. Pay particular attention to the people and objects mentioned in the dream, even if you don't recognise them. These objects may be dream symbols that represent something else in the child's life.
- *Look for a central theme running through the dream* which may signify the fulfilment of your child's hidden desire.
- *Try to make a link* between the content of the dream and an incident involving your child that has taken place in the past day or so.
- *Bear in mind related emotions*. Once your child has told you about her dream, ask her how she felt during it. The feeling accompanying a dream can be a good clue about its meaning, because it can reveal whether the dream is happy or sad, worrying or relaxing, etc.
- *Have patience*. If you have difficulty analysing your child's dreams, don't worry – despite what Freud said,

some psychologists spend years in training before they are able to interpret children's dreams accurately.

See also **Bedtime; Crying Baby; Nightmares; Sleep**.

Dummies Sucking dummies is probably the only comfort habit that some parents encourage. A dummy is especially shaped to fit the contours of a young mouth, and is designed so that it cannot be swallowed. Most dummies are made of plastic, are non-toxic, and can be washed and sterilised.

Aside from using teats to feed their baby with bottle-milk, parents usually allow the use of a dummy for three reasons:

- *to silence her*. Placing a dummy in her mouth is a sure way of getting her to be quiet, and this is often preferable to having her screaming while you are trying to talk to someone. The use of a dummy can be a quick and effective way of achieving the desired goal.
- *to help her fall asleep*. A dummy may bring about a state of relaxation in a tired infant – something you may be desperate to achieve. If you take it out of her mouth just before she falls asleep, she is unlikely to become dependent on it for getting to sleep.
- *to soothe her*. A child who is accustomed to having a dummy will be calmed by it when she is distressed or afraid; sucking it will have the effect of reducing her tension.

If you do let your child use a dummy, make sure it is clean and germ-free. Many children take enormous pleasure in throwing their dummies on to the ground, and this runs the risk of dirty objects ending up in their mouth. Sterilise the dummy regularly; otherwise, your child will pick up an infection, and that is hardly likely to bring her peace and tranquillity. And never dip the dummy into honey, or anything sweet – that could cause her teeth to rot even before they emerge through the gums. For the same reason, avoid using a dummy attached to a small juice-bottle, in case you are tempted to fill the bottle with a sweetened drink in order to encourage her to suck.

One of the prices to be paid for using a dummy is that your child's early explorations may be restricted. Young babies learn about the world around them by putting objects (e.g., toys, rattles) into their mouths. This is a natural phase of development in the first year. A dummy constantly in your baby's mouth will prevent her from exploring toys in this way.

Another potential problem with encouraging her to use a dummy is that it can create dependency on an object where before there was none. You may find that your child doesn't want to give up the dummy, even though you think she should. Or she may want it at other times, not just when she is tired or unhappy. The habit can be extremely difficult to eliminate once it has started. You must be prepared to wean your child off her dummy at some point when she is older.

See also **Comforters; Learning through Play; Masturbation; Teeth**.

Dyslexia   Children experience learning difficulties for many different reasons. In some instances, a child is of below average ability and, as a result, is expected to have difficulties with school work – a pupil like this has a general learning difficulty. In other instances, a child is of at least average ability, uses language well in discussion, gives an impression of being bright, and yet has unexpected difficulties with reading, writing, and spelling – a pupil like this has a specific learning difficulty, often referred to as 'dyslexia'.

When a child has dyslexia, there is a surprising disparity between his apparently good ability and his low educational progress. The effects of dyslexia vary from mild difficulties with reading, writing and spelling to complete illiteracy. Some dyslexic children also have problems learning mathematics. Early identification is vital, in order to provide appropriate help.

There is an emotional dimension to dyslexia – a dyslexic child whose condition has not been properly identified may have a poor self-image because he thinks he is not clever. He may lack confidence with any task involving literacy, describing himself as 'stupid'. The longer the child's learning problem goes undiagnosed, then the worse his psychological problem will become. That's another reason why early identification is important.

A child with dyslexia experiences some (or all) of the following problems in learning:

- lack of progress in reading when it is taught in school by traditional methods;
- confusion of letters that have a similar shape – e.g., b/p, p/q, u/n, b/d, p/d;
- trouble with elementary punctuation and grammar;
- difficulty learning even the basic rules of spelling, and misspelling words that he has previously learned;
- failure to learn to write, and producing letters that are frequently reversed or badly formed;
- reversing complete words when reading – e.g., 'was' for 'saw', or 'god' for 'dog';
- confusion between left and right, when asked, for example, to point to his left or right foot;
- poor short-term memory, causing problems when he is asked to follow an instruction containing more than one piece of information;
- trouble remembering sequences of information – e.g., months of the year, or multiplication tables;
- difficulty copying drawings or pieces of writing accurately from the blackboard into his jotter.

In addition, children who are dyslexic often have a history of slow speech development in the pre-school years, and there is often a family history of speech and learning difficulties, perhaps involving parents, aunts and uncles, or other relatives.

These signs, however, are only guidelines, and their presence does not mean your child has dyslexia – many non-dyslexic children also show these features in the early stages of learning to read, write and spell. You should become concerned only if they persist beyond the first year in infant school. A diagnosis of dyslexia can be made only by a psychologist, having fully assessed the child's

- *level of intelligence.* Since one of the criteria for diagnosing dyslexia is that a child should be of at least average intelligence, this must be measured using a standardised intelligence test. Weaknesses with specific learning skills will also be identified (e.g. in auditory or visual short-term memory, pattern recognition, ability to recall sequences, spatial skills).

- *level of attainments in reading, spelling, writing and number*. The psychologist will want to establish the exact level of the child's progress in each of these areas. The first stage will be to find an age level (e.g., a nine-year-old may be reading at a level normally associated with a five-year-old, and hence has a reading age of five).
- *pattern of errors*. Aside from quantifying the child's educational attainments, the psychologist will consider the types of mistakes that he makes in reading, writing, spelling and maths, since this will enable future learning support to be targeted most effectively.
- *learning attitude*. The attitude that a child has towards learning partly determines his level of success or failure. Children with dyslexia often appear to make little effort in any task involving literacy. But they should not be accused of being lazy – rather, it's as though they have given up trying altogether because they expect to fail.
- *developmental background*. A diagnosis of dyslexia can only be made after the elimination of other, external factors which could depress progress in school. These factors could include stress at home (e.g., recent divorce, bereavement), lack of stimulation in the pre-school years (e.g., due to long periods of hospitalisation), and hearing or visual difficulties.

Nobody knows the cause of dyslexia, although most psychologists now accept that it is related to the brain's neurological structure. Neither is there a cure for it. However, dyslexic children can be helped to cope with their difficulties through the provision of multi-sensory teaching methods, which combine hearing, seeing, touch and movement – dyslexic children have problems processing information through at least one of these senses. Effective multi-sensory teaching must be highly structured, moving one small step at a time, so that a pupil can build up his reading, writing and spelling skills in a systematic way. Many local education authorities provide teachers who have been specially trained in these methods. Basic exercises to improve memory skills are also useful.

With proper professional help, a dyslexic child can progress successfully through primary and secondary school, and even through higher education. But his special educational needs call for close consideration at every stage.

This can only be achieved through adequate assessment, appropriate teaching methods, and sensitive understanding from all the adults involved.

see also **Intelligence; Learning Skills; Memory; Self-Confidence**.

E

Eating Sometimes a meal can be unattractive to a child, even though his parents find it very appetising. That's because eating isn't just about the quality of food – it's also about the way the eating experience is perceived by him. Ever paused for a moment to consider how a meal looks from your child's side of the table or high-chair? The world looks different when you are only three years old and 30 inches high. Ask yourself the following questions:

Q. *Is my child seated properly?*
A. Most children can find a comfortable sitting position in a high-chair, because it has been specifically designed for their body length, bottom size and length of reach. But when your toddler makes that transition to the family dinner table, the chairs will be designed for an adult's bottom size, height, and length of reach. Perhaps he would prefer to have a small cushion on his chair, in order to raise the height; and perhaps he would like the plate nearer to the edge of the table so that he can reach it easily.

Q. *Is his cutlery the right size?*
A. Try eating a main course using a garden fork and trowel instead of cutlery. Difficult, isn't it? Well, that's the struggle facing a young child who is expected to use adult-sized cutlery. It won't speed up the rate at which he learns to use a knife, fork and spoon – if anything, it will slow him down.

Q. *What size portions am I giving him?*
A. Your child has a smaller stomach than you and therefore doesn't eat as much. An adult's portion of mashed potatoes can seem like Mount Everest to him, and a large dollop of stew like Lake Windermere. Putting too much on the plate may put your child off his food before he even lifts his cutlery. Smaller portions are better – you can always give him seconds if he clears the first plateful.

Q. *Is the food at the right temperature?*
A. Most adults like food to be piping hot when it arrives at the table. They are capable of coping with such a temperature – they blow on the food, or take a very small amount to start with, or simply wait for a few moments until it cools down. Your child may not be as confident, however, and may be afraid of burning himself. He prefers warm food that can be placed into his mouth without concern about possible injuries.

Q. *What does it taste like?*
A. Everybody is sensitive to five kinds of taste – sweet, sour, bitter, salty and savoury. But our sensitivity to each of these varies with age. For instance, while adults usually enjoy the sharp taste of olives and pickles, children rarely do. The flavouring that you enjoy may not suit your child

– better to cook the food first, and then add salt and pepper to each portion individually.

Q. *Is the texture pleasant?*
A. Children vomit more easily than adults. Food that is too dry can stick to a child's upper palate and make him sick; this is an involuntary action that he can't help – it's not a trick to avoid eating. Greasy food can have the same effect, and chewy meat can be very unpalatable. Avoid textures that your child doesn't like.

Taking these factors into account will give you an insight into the way your child views eating. Remember that the more palatable the meal is from his perspective (not yours), the more likely he is to finish everything that is placed in front of him.

see also **Additives; Eating Out; Fussy Eaters; Healthy Eating; Manners; Overweight; Snacks**.

Eating Out   This should be good fun. For a start, someone else does the cooking – and the dishes – which allows you to relax and give your child your full attention. Then there's the fact that she chooses from a wide range of courses, which means she is more likely to eat the food when it arrives. In addition, you probably relax the rules about her choice of food. All of these factors should go together to make a recipe for a happy eating-out experience – but it doesn't always turn out that way.

Basic principles for a successful family meal in a restaurant are:

● *Let your child see the menu (preferably the children's) before you enter the restaurant.* This way you can be certain there is something available that she likes. Give her plenty of time to look at it.

● *Explain to her that the food may be served differently from the way that same dish is served at home.* Advanced warning will help her cope with a food presentation she has not expected.

● *If there isn't a children's menu, check with the waiter that child-sized portions are served.* Most restaurants provide children's meals – if not, ask for an extra side-plate so that you can give your child some of your main course.

- *Ask the waiter how your child's meal will be presented.* If, for instance, the sight of tomatoes completely kills her appetite, you would be well advised to request that tomatoes are left off the plate, when placing her order.
- *Don't expect her to behave perfectly, or that she'll eat everything she ordered.* Eating out is a thrill for a young child, and she may accidentally spill her drink or drop her cutlery on the floor, in excitement. Ironically, excitement may also deaden her appetite.

See also **Eating; Fussy Eaters; Healthy Eating; Manners; Overweight; Snacks**.

Education at Home Although the majority of children receive their education at a school (either state or public), there is no law that says they cannot be taught at home. Indeed, the 1944 Education Act states: '*It shall be the duty of the parent of every child of compulsory school age to cause him to receive efficient full-time education suitable to his age, either by regular attendance at school or otherwise.*'

And the same Act emphasises the importance of parental wishes regarding their child's schooling: 'In the exercise and performance of all powers and duties conferred and imposed on them by this Act the Minister and Local Authorities shall have regard to the general principle that, so far as is compatible with the provision of suitable instruction and training, and the avoidance of unreasonable expenditure, pupils are to be educated in accordance with the wishes of their parents.' (Scotland and Northern Ireland are covered by equivalent Acts.)

This means that parents are allowed to teach their child at home – and an ever-increasing number are exercising this right. There are many and varied reasons for this. Some parents are simply unhappy about the quality of teaching in schools today; some are concerned about the level of bullying and intimidation their child experiences in school; some teach their child at home because they don't want her to mix with children of a different religion; and some embark on a programme of home education because they think they can do the job better than anyone else. In Britain, approximately 10,000 children are presently being educated at home.

A local education authority is not obliged to monitor the progress of a child being educated at home, unless that child attended a state school at some point. However, most local authorities will be pleased to advise parents embarking on this course of action. Parents are not obliged to produce a written curriculum for their child, although it is often a useful way of clarifying aims and objectives.

There are several self-help organisations, run by parents who are educating their children at home. The largest of these, Education Otherwise, was formed in the late 1970s by a small group of parents who wanted to support each other. This organisation issues a regular newsletter containing practical ideas, and encourages members to join together for social events. It also publishes a selection of very useful booklets.

Education at home can be very successful, providing an environment in which a child thrives academically, and personally. But it isn't a commitment to be taken on lightly. Preparation, short-term and long-term planning, identification of resource materials and a positive attitude from parent and child are all prerequisites of a successful home tuition programme. In addition, the child should be provided with plenty of opportunities to mix with others of his own age.

Emotional Deprivation In 1953, Dr John Bowlby wrote that every baby must have 'a warm, intimate and continuous relationship with his mother', or else he will not thrive. Although this theory of emotional deprivation has been heavily criticised for its assumption that a mother-child relationship must be continuous (there is no proof whatsoever that a child needs to be in his mother's company all the time), Bowlby's two other major assumptions have stood the test of time, namely:

- A close emotional attachment between mother (or equivalent) and baby is essential for satisfactory childhood development.
- A baby deprived of this will show adverse effects throughout later life.

77

There is now a wealth of evidence to support this view.

Your child can become distressed even when separated from you only briefly. Extreme reactions have been observed in children admitted to hospital without a parent alongside them: they usually show an initial period of protest, followed by a period of despair and apathy, which in turn is followed by detachment from others around them.

The effects of this type of short-term emotional deprivation are often temporary, however, as was confirmed by one study which focused on a group of young children who experienced maternal separation when their mothers went into hospital for the birth of another baby. The infants' actions were recorded on video during play episodes before, during and after the mother's stay in hospital; their activity level and heart rate were recorded at night. Mothers also commented on their infants' behaviour. The researchers found that the brief separation did have a marked effect. For instance, while the mother was in hospital, her child was likely to have an increase in night wakings, heart rate, crying and fussiness. He was also likely to be more aggressive, more clingy, and less cooperative at mealtimes. Fortunately, all of these adverse effects eased when the mother returned home.

Given this background of research findings, there are three questions parents often ask:

Q. *Will emotional deprivation be avoided if I spend every minute of the day with my child?*
A. Not necessarily. What matters is the quality of the parent-child relationship, not the quantity. The amount of time you spend with your child does not, by itself, indicate whether or not he will be emotionally deprived or not. Some parents are with their child all the time, and yet don't have a close and caring relationship with him, while others work all day, rarely see their child, and yet have a very strong relationship with him.

Q. *Should I stay at home and not return to work, in case my young child becomes emotionally deprived?*
A. Not necessarily. In fact, a British survey of pre-school children looked at the link between their mothers' working habits and their mothers' mental health. Those who had given up work were most likely to be depressed

78

– and a child looked after by a depressed mother who feels trapped in the house by her parental responsibilities may experience emotional deprivation even though his mother hasn't returned to work. This doesn't mean that you should automatically go back to work when your baby is young. Decisions of this sort are very personal, and depend greatly on individual circumstances. But it does mean that you should not instantly feel guilty about resuming your career early on in your infant's life.

Q. *Will my child be emotionally deprived if I send him to a day nursery, instead of looking after him myself during the day?*
A. No (although the quality of the day-care provision is important). Children who have a high level of day care tend to be more sociable, engage in less solitary play, are less attention-seeking and are more cooperative with other children and adults. Quality day care, therefore, adds to a child's emotional stability and can even compensate for poor parent-child relationships at home.

See also **Bonding; Hospital; Quality Time; Separation and Divorce; Working Mothers**.

Epilepsy A child with epilepsy tends to have recurrent fits (seizures), which are caused by abnormal bursts of electrical activity in his brain. There are several different types of the condition, resulting in over 20 types of seizure. Certain types of epilepsy don't result in fits, but affect the child in other, milder ways. Bear in mind that a single fit is not normally a sign of epilepsy, since some isolated childhood seizures are caused simply by a high body temperature – medical investigation is the only way to identify the condition. Epilepsy affects around 1 in 200 of the population, and 1 in 50 may have an epileptic fit at some stage in his life; every year in Britain, approximately 10,000 children develop this problem, which is neither infectious nor a sign of mental illness.

There are many different causes of epilepsy, including brain damage as a result of a birth injury or accidental injury, infection (e.g., meningitis, encephalitis), tumours, and hormonal problems. In many instances, the specific cause cannot be accurately pinpointed. Epilepsy can start at any age, but frequently it starts in the pre-school years, and most commonly before the age of 20. The frequency of fits varies, from once in a lifetime to several in an hour.

Seizures can be triggered by many different factors, depending on the particular child. Common triggers include, flashing lights, sudden loud noises, lack of food or sleep, stress, anxiety and infection. There are two main types of fits:

– *petit mal*. This mild type of seizure occurs only for a second or so, and although the child loses consciousness momentarily, he remains standing (or seated). During the fit, he will look blank and stare into space; he may also blink or twitch slightly, but as soon as the *petit mal* seizure is over, he will continue as though nothing has happened. Some children have several in one day.
– *grand mal*. With this major type of seizure, the child will lose consciousness, his body will stiffen and jerk, his lips may develop a blue colour, and he will fall to the ground. He may also wet and soil himself. The most important thing you can do is to protect him from injury; cushion his head, don't put anything in his mouth, don't try to prise open his mouth if his teeth are clenched, and turn him on to his side in order to help his breathing. Stay with him until he has fully recovered, quietly reassuring him all the time, although he may want to go to sleep straight away.

Medication can control – but not cure – epilepsy: almost 80 per cent of people with the condition have their fits controlled or greatly reduced by drugs. The choice of drug, of course, depends on the child and the type of seizure he experiences. Doctors prefer to use one drug only where possible (rather than a combination), and most children do not experience side-effects if they take the medication in the way it is prescribed.

Equality Treating each of your children equally is not the same as treating them fairly. Remember that each child is an individual, with her own particular emotional needs and her own particular likes and dislikes; each needs love and attention in varying amounts and in different ways. The idea that the best way of raising children is to treat them identically – by giving them all the same material items (e.g., when one child gets a toy, the others get the same toy) or giving them all the same opportunities (e.g., when one gets skating lessons, the others get skating lessons) – is a mistake, and will not be satisfying for any of them.

You may be tempted to buy each of your children exactly the same toy because that way there can be no complaints about one getting something better than the others. But this tactic takes no account of each child's individuality, and means that one or more of them will get something they don't really want. Treating your children fairly, on the other hand, means taking each child's individual needs into account. For example, if one joins a sports class, the other might be allowed to join a drama class.

Even if parents adopt a policy of equal treatment, the children will find the outside world takes a different approach. Schools, for instance, encourage children to progress at their own pace. Clubs, whether sporting organisations or the Brownies, encourage each member to develop mastery in different areas, depending on her skills. These individual differences make life interesting, and are nothing a child need fear. A child who lives in an environment that tries to create equality in everything will receive an abrupt jolt when she ventures beyond the family home. Far better to strive for a family structure in which every member has equal opportunities to develop her full individual potential, even though this may result in different activities and lifestyles.

See also **Sibling Rivalry**.

Eye　A baby's eyes are large in relation to the size of her head, when compared with an adult. In fact, a baby's are almost 65 per cent the size of adult eyes. This is why some adults find babies so attractive – their disproportionately large eyes can seem very appealing.

The visible part of the eye is covered with a thin, delicate transparent membrane – the conjunctiva – which extends to line the inside of the eyelid. Fluid produced by the tear gland washes the eyeball and keeps it well lubricated. Underneath the conjunctiva, at the front of the eye, lies the cornea, a disc-shaped section which bends the light rays and brings them to focus as they enter. The cornea also protects the parts of the eye lying directly behind it, and is extremely sensitive, with an in-built ability to remove any bits of dirt that land on it. The eye itself is filled with fluid, known as vitreous humour.

The iris – the coloured portion of the eye – lies behind the cornea. This has a dark hole in the middle (the pupil) which is controlled by lots of very small muscles, and light enters the eye through it. Just like the aperture of a camera, the pupil adjusts constantly in relation to the degree of light – in bright sunlight, it becomes smaller, and in dim light it becomes larger.

Immediately behind the iris is the transparent and solid lens, whose muscles adjust its shape in order to focus light rays on to the retina at the back of the eye. When cells in the retina are activated, visual impulses are transmitted along the optic nerve to the brain. At this point, they are transformed into an image. Damage to any part of the eye, or to any part of the nervous system linking the eye to the brain, will result in visual difficulties.

See also **Genes; Vision; Visual Difficulties**.

F

Fathers The typical father of Victorian times would be surprised – and very probably perturbed – by today's typical father. The biggest change to have taken place is the degree to which he is allowed to become involved in matters of childcare. No longer is the man's role rigidly confined to earning money, to making decisions about how it should be spent, to discussing weighty political matters, or to kissing the children goodnight after they have been fed, washed and changed by the mother. A contemporary father is able to play his part in every aspect of his children's lives – if he wants to.

And this possibility for increased involvement starts even before the baby is born. For instance, in the last ten years there has been a tremendous upsurge in the number of soon-to-be fathers attending ante-natal sessions along with their partners. Go along to the 'preparation-for-parenthood classes' at your local maternity hospital; you will be surprised to see the large number of men helping their partners through the regimen of relaxation exercises, or else participating enthusiastically in the breast-feeding vs bottle-feeding debate.

This very early interest in family life signals a pattern which will probably persist throughout the child's life. And at this stage – even though their baby is not born yet – both partners benefit. For a mother-to-be (who may be understandably apprehensive about pregnancy and childbirth), her partner's presence during the ante-natal phase can be very reassuring. For a father-to-be (whose apprehension probably equals that of his partner), participation in the ante-natal preparation stops potential feelings of isolation and detachment. Many men are extremely enthusiastic about this change in their role, and take advantage of the opportunities it affords.

Movies shot in the 50s and 60s often portray scenes in the labour ward in a way that no longer applies today. Typically, the father – wearing a suit and hat and clutching a bunch of flowers – is shown pacing anxiously up and down the hospital corridor, while smoking one cigarette after another. Eventually a smiling nurse comes through to tell him that his wife has just had the baby, and at this point he hugs the nurse, relieved that the process of childbirth has proceeded without a hitch while he stood by passively.

It is now virtually routine for fathers to be present at the birth of their child. Indeed, this has become so firmly institutionalised as part of his role that people show surprise when a man admits he wasn't there. Many women see nothing particularly startling about the father being present at the birth, anyway. They reason that since the woman has to be there, and since she has to cope with the physical strain, the man should share in the emotional strain. This is a difficult argument to contradict.

In Britain nobody looks twice at the man in the supermarket, giving deep consideration to which disposable nappies he should buy. And nobody looks twice at a man spending time in a playgroup or nursery with his child, or pushing a pram. The media, too, promote this image of the father's role. For instance, many advertisements for children's goods show a father with his children, whereas ten years ago it was always the mother who was shown. And it's now fashionable for pop stars to talk openly about their family life, instead of pretending they are unattached.

This very significant change in a father's role inside the family runs alongside his unchanging role in the outside world. In a high percentage of the population – irrespective of the degree of the father's involvement with his children – he is still the only one who works. And this is particularly true when the children are in the pre-school years. This means the man has to accommodate the demands of both these roles, which may not be easy. (Remember, though, that despite these increased possibilities for a father's greater involvement with his children, many men reject the new role. Perhaps there are more of these than most people suspect.)

Another sign of the changing role of the father in contemporary society is the high number of single-parent families headed by a man. Between 1910 and 1960, fathers were rarely given custody of their children following divorce, unless they could prove to the court that their ex-wife was 'unfit'. The situation has changed significantly in the last three decades. Since 1960 there has been a spectacular growth in the incidence of single fathers who are entirely responsible for raising their children. One survey suggests there are at least 1.5 million single-father families in the USA alone, with approximately 3.5 million children.

Psychologists investigating single fathers have found that most feel competent as parents, and consider themselves to be fulfilling that role adequately. They also report a great deal of satisfaction with the relationship they establish with their children.

Many observers anticipate that this trend for fathers to play an increasing part in raising children will become even stronger in future years. There are several reasons for this:

- Couples realise the benefits this brings the children.
- Many men prefer to relate to their children outside the traditional disciplinarian role.
- Women welcome the sharing of household tasks that a father's new role brings.
- Sharing the care of the children is a fairer way of managing family relationships.

See also **Mothers; Older Parents; Parents; Quality Time; Single-Parent Family; Working Mothers; Young Parents**.

Fears   Childhood fears are a normal part of early development – almost 90 per cent of young children experience a mild fear at some point. And these fears may be real, such as a fear of lightning, or they may be imaginary, such as a fear of ghosts.

Children can develop fears about the strangest of things, even though there doesn't appear to be any obvious explanation. But childhood fears – just like adult fears – do not have to be rational. For instance, many adults are afraid of the dentist, even though modern dentistry techniques ensure virtually pain-free treatment. Few adults can logically explain what it is about a visit to a dentist that frightens them so much. Similarly, few children can explain what quality of darkness it is that makes them feel uneasy.

Fears usually emerge around the age of two years. A child at this stage of development has a greater understanding and awareness of the world around him. However, his understanding is not so great that he can fully explain every-thing that goes on. So, for example, a toddler knows that birds fly because he sees it happening quite regularly. But he does not know that a bird will not pick him up and fly off with him, or that a bird will not eat him. Therefore, he may be afraid. If your child is worried by something that is apparently irrational, he needs your reassurance.

Parents can arouse fears in young children by talking carelessly in front of them. Of course, your child needs to be made aware of the routine hazards of domestic life. Electric heaters can catch fire, people can fall down stairs, burglars can break into a house, children can drown in a few inches of bathwater, and so on. These are very real dangers. But they have to be kept in perspective. Continual reminders of what could happen may make your child afraid rather than cautious, and that is not the aim of safety warnings.

Sometimes fears are used as a threat to a child, as a way of making him behave properly. Parents are often tempted to resort to this strategy when all else fails. You know the scene. Dad takes his four-year-old to a children's party, but when they arrive the child will not let go of dad's hand. He pleads with his father to stay a few moments longer, and in a fit of embarrassed rage – because somehow every other child is settled – dad warns: 'If you don't shut up, I'm going to leave you right now.' This only increases the child's anxiety. Threats of this nature, threats which play on a young child's weakness, are only likely to make the weakness even greater.

Always take your child's fear seriously, no matter how ridiculous it may appear. What may seem a minor obstacle to you, as an adult, may seem like Mount Everest through his eyes. And never try to bully him out of his fear. Comments like 'Act your age' or 'You're behaving like a little baby' will only increase his agitation.

Take a planned approach to helping him. First of all, ascertain exactly what it is he is afraid of. For example, a child who becomes anxious when approaching the bathroom may be apprehensive about any one of a number of things. Is he afraid of falling into the toilet-bowl? Is he afraid of the smell when toileting? Is he afraid that he cannot reach the taps to wash his hands afterwards? Ask him what frightens him. You may not reach a direct answer straight away, but eventually, by breaking down the frightening event into small components, you should be able to establish more precisely the area of concern.

Second, show your child that he can manage, that he doesn't really have any cause to be afraid. For instance, he may be afraid of thunder because he thinks it will make the house fall down. You can reassure him that the house cannot be damaged by noise, and demonstrate this by turning your television, radio and stereo system on full for a few seconds. Once the child sees that the house is still standing, even though that was louder than any noise thunder might make, he will probably be less afraid than before.

Third, give him lots of encouragement when he takes a step towards overcoming whatever it is that he is afraid of. Constant praise from you, coupled with your frequent reassurance that he will be safe, is a very effective way of boosting his self-confidence. And lastly, there are story-books written specially for children, to help them overcome fears. You may find that reading some of these to your child is an effective way of helping him tackle his fears.

See also **Hazards; Phobias; Road Safety**.

Fighting   Your child may become involved in a fight for a variety of reasons (e.g., she feels threatened, someone has taken one of her possessions, she can't get her own way). Minor fights are common in childhood. However – assuming that you don't approve of this sort of behaviour – you should try to teach your child other ways of coping with conflicts, ways that don't involve physical assault on other children.

Since fights often start because two children want to play with the same toy at once, an effective way of avoiding conflict is for both parties to reach a compromise. You can help your child develop this skill. For instance, when you see her disagreeing with a friend over what game to play, suggest to them that they play one game first, then the other. Emphasise that this type of compromise is not the same as giving in, because in the end both of them will get what they want. Tell her this is a more sensible way of settling disputes. The best timing for compromises is before the disagreement has escalated into a full-scale conflict.

Fights can also be avoided by discussion (this doesn't

always work, but it is certainly worth a try). Children who are unable to explain their feelings are frequently the same children who get into fights. The more a child is able to tell someone what is troubling her, then the less likely she is to start fighting; and a child who is able to talk her way out of trouble may never have to fight her way out.

Another way your child can avoid a fight is by distracting the child who is threatening her. This technique involves attracting the hostile child's attention on to some other matter, such as telling her that an adult is about to walk into the room, and can be a very effective way of breaking tension.

Before suggesting these alternatives to your child, however, you must first of all clarify your own ideas. Some parents feel quite strongly that their child should be able to stand up for herself and retaliate when struck by others. Although this may appear to be a reasonable point of view, a young child will have a problem differentiating between fighting in order to protect herself and fighting in order to get her own way. If you do encourage your child to defend herself physically, therefore, make sure she knows when fighting is acceptable (i.e., when she is under physical threat from another child) and when it is not acceptable (i.e., when it is merely a way of achieving what she wants).

See also **Aggression; Sibling Rivalry**.

First-Born Jealousy There's nothing like the impending arrival of a new baby to unsettle a first-born child. Until this moment she's had mum and dad all to herself, and she expects this way of life to continue for ever. No wonder, then, that the thought of a new brother or sister fills her with feelings of insecurity.

Look at it from the child's point of view. You and your partner spend all your time with her when you are at home; she is the only child you spend your money on; she gets lots of clothes and presents; and her aunts, uncles and grandparents fight for her love. Then, just when everything is ticking along nicely as far as she is concerned, the adults around her start talking about a new baby. She may have thoughts like 'Why do mum and dad need another baby? Am I not good enough for them?' 'What have I done wrong to make them want another child?' or even 'Will the new baby take my room so that I'll have nowhere to sleep?'

We, as adults, know without a shadow of doubt that loving a second baby doesn't decrease our love for the first. But your first-born doesn't know that. She has to learn by experience, and that takes time. In the meantime, feelings of jealousy towards the new baby may dominate.

Tell her in advance that she's going to have a new brother or sister. Don't wait until the last moment when the contractions are coming every couple of minutes – but don't tell her about the new baby when you are only a few weeks into your pregnancy. A child's sense of time is different from that of an adult; she may see no difference between a week and a month, or between one month and six months. And she may become bored with the long wait.

Start introducing the idea of the new baby when your tummy is so large that even an inexperienced toddler would notice it, probably around the seventh month or so. Tell your child calmly, without feeling embarrassed about it. Pitch the conversation at a level suitable for her age and understanding, and avoid giving too many bits of information at one time. Whatever you do, don't flog the topic to death.

You may find that she reacts with indifference. Or she may seem very interested and want to talk about it further. Or she may simply burst into tears. Be prepared to let her ask you questions, either at the time you tell her or later – and always give her an honest reply. Let her express any anxieties she has, without reacting in a way that makes her wish she hadn't opened her mouth.

When your first-born sees her new brother or sister for the first time, make sure the baby has a present for her (one that you had ready beforehand) and let her have one to give the new arrival. Of course, this exchange of gifts is artificial. But it can help forge an emotional connection between the two children right from the start.

Expect your first-born to feel jealous. She may show signs of this by becoming aggressive towards you, or by being clingy and not letting you out of her sight, or even by regressing and becoming babyish herself. These reactions are natural. Try not to get angry with her when she behaves this way, no matter how irritating and attention-seeking she is. Your anger and rejection at her appalling behaviour will only confirm her worst fears that you love her less than the new baby.

The following strategies will help ease your first-born's jealousy:

- *Get her involved in the practicalities of baby care.* Let her fetch nappies out of the cupboard, or throw dirty cotton wool into the bin. Even a toddler is able to do something to help.
- *Encourage visitors to spend a few moments with her before they go in to see the baby.* The steady stream of visitors to your house has come for one purpose only – namely, to set eyes on the new arrival. But discreetly asking them to give your older child some attention as well will make her feel just as important.
- *Let her help you show the baby to visitors.* It's a new member of her family too. She can take the adults into the baby's room, and can explain to them all about her little brother or sister.
- *Acknowledge her maturity.* If she is upset by the presence of the new arrival, an extra ten minutes of television before bedtime because she is 'a big sister now' will provide some compensation. In fact, any positive change that acknowledges she is older than the baby will help (e.g., spending more time with adults instead of being sent out of play, being allowed to choose what biscuit she eats with her juice).
- *Be honest with her.* There is nothing wrong in admitting to your first-born child that caring for a young baby is very tiring, and that at times you get fed up with all the chores you have to do (though don't overdo it in case she thinks you dislike the baby).

See also **Age Gap; Birth Order; Jealousy; Only Child; Sibling Rivalry.**

Friendships   Children form friendships for many different reasons, and at times it is difficult for parents to understand why two particular children enjoy each other's company so much. Friendships provide psychological benefits, such as giving a child self-confidence, giving him someone to share his secrets with, teaching him about loyalty and sharing, providing someone to compare himself against, and offering emotional support when he feels unhappy. Friendships also provide practical benefits, such as allowing a child to play with his friend's new bicycle – in fact, many friendships in early childhood are motivated more by this type of self-interest than by feelings of personal attraction.

Genuine friendships don't usually start until the age of three because only then is a child able to play cooperatively with others. At this age, children tend to pick friends who have the same interests, and will be happy playing with children of the opposite sex. However, most friendships amongst three-year-olds fluctuate from week to week, because at this age a child is very self-centred. From the age of five or six onwards, children tend to mix more with others of the same sex, and during the next three or four years their friendships become more stable. It is not usually until a child is nine or ten that he begins to form long-lasting friendships. An inability to acquire friends may be an indication that a child has emotional problems.

Most parents would like their child to be popular, to have lots of friends and to be invited out to play. You feel good when you see your child surrounded by friends of his own age. Popularity, however, partly depends on characteristics over which a child has no control. For instance, popular children tend to be quite bright at school, and gain high marks in exams. And a child who is physically attractive, as well as being sporty, is also likely to be popular.

But popularity also depends on characteristics over which a child does have some control, such as social skills. Being able to take turns, to follow rules in games and to share, will help your child get on better with other children. Similarly, he has a better chance of being popular if he isn't aggressive and is prepared to listen to other children's points of view. You can encourage him to develop these features.

Problems arise when parents disapprove of their child's friend because he behaves in ways that are not acceptable by their standards. This requires delicate and tactful handling:

- *Try to avoid banning your child from playing with a particular friend.* This will only make the friendship more desirable. Instead, tell him why you don't like his friend (e.g., he swears, he pushes other children), but don't overdo it or your child will think you are being totally unfair. However, there may be occasions when a straightforward ban on a friendship is your only option – use this strategy only as a last resort.

- *Tell your child why it is that he should not play with his friend.* Give practical reasons: for instance, because he gets into trouble for being naughty.
- *Remind him that although he likes his friend, he doesn't have to behave the same way.* If you find that he plays with the friend you dislike, despite all your efforts, suggest to him that although they play together, they don't have to act like each other.
- *Encourage him to be friends with a different child.* This is a more positive approach, and is especially successful with children under the age of six or seven. Invite children (whom you want your child to play with) round to your house, and do your best to give them an enjoyable time. This strategy may allow the friendship you don't approve of to fade into the background.

See also **Sociable Play; Social Development.**

Fussy Eaters   Every child is a faddy eater sometimes. From an early age, your child will start to have particular likes and dislikes when it comes to food. This phase may pass within a few days, or it may be more long-lasting. Surveys have found that:

- while only 10 per cent of parents worry about their child's eating habits when he is one year old, this figure leaps to 42 per cent by the time he is four;
- 10 per cent of three-year-olds are described by their parents as 'finicky about their food';
- 31 per cent of children who have poor appetites at the age of three still have poor appetites when they are eight;
- parents who voice strong disapproval of sweets are usually the ones who give their child the most sweets.

So you're not alone in having a child who is a fussy eater, who sits and picks at his food as though he's afraid harm will befall him if he swallows it. And a faddy eater can spoil mealtimes – in fact, if your child *is* one, you may find it

92

easier to serve his meal first, allowing the rest of you to sit down peacefully when that particular battle is over.

To change your child's eating habits, try these suggestions:

Do's

- *Do serve meals at regular times*. Routine is especially important with a fussy eater. Having meals at reasonably fixed intervals means that he doesn't get too hungry or over-tired, both of which will upset his appetite.
- *Do keep meals simple*. The more time and effort you invest in a meal, the more upset you'll be when your child doesn't wolf it down – so don't slave over a hot stove for hours.
- *Do make the food attractive*. Some parents expect their child to eat food that they wouldn't touch themselves. Bear in mind that if the sight of a particular meal makes you turn up your nose, then it may have the same effect on your child.
- *Do let him finger-feed*. Table manners are important, but your child will acquire these in time. What matters is that the food should get inside his tummy; it has the same nutritional value whether it arrives at his mouth by hand or by cutlery.
- *Do end the meal when he has had enough*. There's no point in keeping a toddler trapped in his high-chair in the hope he'll eat more. When he has reached the point where he will eat no more, lift him down. And the same applies to an older child who asks to leave the table – there is no harm in some persuasion at that stage, but don't let it build up into a confrontation.
- *Do allow him choice*. He will approach mealtimes with enthusiasm if he has a choice over what to eat. This doesn't mean you should run your house like a restaurant, but it does mean you could let him choose from, say, two items for lunch (e.g., scrambled eggs on toast, or yoghurt followed by fresh fruit).
- *Do be flexible*. The order in which food is served isn't fixed by law! Young children love to experiment with everything, including food. You may not find the thought of soup with baked beans attractive, but your child may. If he wants to experiment this way, let him.

93

- *Do set a good example yourself.* If you come home munching a bag of greasy fish and chips, you can hardly expect your child to behave differently. He will copy your bad eating habits.

DON'TS

- *Don't force-feed your child.* No matter how desperately you want him to finish his meal, you can't force him to eat it – try to, and you'll end up feeling drained, while he'll end up being sick.
- *Don't hover during mealtimes.* There's nothing more likely to make your child anxious about feeding than seeing you hovering about, studying every mouthful he takes. You wouldn't like someone peering intently at you during meals – neither does he.
- *Don't exclude him during preparations.* One way to encourage him to eat a meal is by involving him in its preparation. Of course, you're not going to ask a young child to cook a hot dish, but a two-year-old can put a cup on the table, and a four-year-old can help set out the cutlery.
- *Don't stay silent.* Just as you enjoy a good chat while eating, so does your child. Rather than slapping the food down in front of him and then getting on with another chore, sit down beside him and talk. This way eating becomes a social occasion.
- *Don't be negative.* Work on the assumption that your child isn't going to starve, no matter how little he eats. The more you worry, the more tense he'll be every time you put a plate of food in front of him.
- *Don't use threats.* Out of sheer frustration, you may be tempted to cajole him with threats such as 'You can have some sweets if you eat your spinach' or 'Your dad will be furious when he hears you've not eaten your spinach.' This rarely works, because your child may well think to himself 'The spinach must be really awful or else why would mum try so hard to persuade me to eat it.'
- *Don't concede defeat when he rejects a new food.* Children take time to acquire tastes for unfamiliar foods. When you do try to introduce a new item into his diet,

94

persevere a couple of times a week, for at least a month. He may gradually develop a taste for it.

- *Don't rush through meals.* Food is more easily digested in a calm, unhurried atmosphere. A fussy eater is usually also a slow eater, and he needs lots of time to work his way through a meal. This will be particularly noticeable at breakfast, so wake him up in plenty of time.

See also **Additives; Eating; Eating Out; Healthy Eating; Overweight; Snacks.**

G

Gender Play   Try this: make a list of play activities and toys which you think are suitable for young boys, and another list of play activities and toys which you think are suitable for young girls. (To make this task slightly easier, consider your own children or a particular boy and a particular girl that you know, and think of the games and toys you would want them to play with.) Allow yourself about 10 minutes to compile the lists.

Having done this, consider the following questions:

- *Did you find this easy to do?* Most people have no prob-lem making up these separate lists because they know that boys seem fascinated by one set of play activities (e.g., football, play-fighting, toy cars) and girls by differ-ent ones (e.g., brushing a doll's hair, make-up sets, pre-paring pretend tea-parties).
- *Are there any activities or toys that appear on both lists?* The chances are that you identified a number of pastimes – perhaps art and craft activities, reading books and doing jigsaw puzzles – that you thought suitable for either sex. Most adults agree that this type of activity is acceptable for all children.
- *Are you able to find any common theme running through the boys' play activities (and a different theme running through the girls' play activities)?* It is likely that many of the suggestions in your list for boys are action-based, suitable for releasing aggressive emotions (e.g., toy weapons, toy soldiers, sporting activities), and that many in your list for girls encourage more sedate, domestic behaviour (e.g., dressing-up activities, toy vacuum cleaner, flower press).
- *How do you think the parents of a young boy would react if you bought him one of the girl's toys (and vice versa)?* You would probably find that they would be very con-cerned if you gave their son a Cindy doll as a present, or their daughter an imitation gun.

Those are the easy questions. Now for the difficult ones. Where do these differences in toy and game preferences come from? Are children born with them? Are such preferences created by the media? Do parents inadvertently encourage their child to play with specific toys? Or is it just chance that boys tend to like different toys from those favoured by girls?

Psychologists have considered these vexing issues in detail, but as yet have failed to provide a conclusive answer. There are, however, a number of theories which attempt to explain sex differences in play preferences.

Some theorists claim that men are born with a biological instinct to be aggressive and that women are born with a biological instinct to be domesticated, to have children and to raise a family. These instincts are reflected in children's play preferences, these theorists continue, which is why boys enjoy aggressive play activities while girls enjoy more placid ones.

However, this idea fails to explain why some girls dislike domestic-based play activities and instead prefer to play games traditionally associated with boys.

A more popular view is that sex differences in play stem from social pressures, and from the media. You only need to watch adverts for children's toys at Christmas-time to see this. Adverts for dolls never show boys playing with them, and adverts for football equipment rarely, if ever, use girls. This inflexible presentation influences the views of adults and children alike.

A more covert social pressure on play choices stems from the language that adults use to describe children. For instance, the term *tomboy*, which is still in common usage today, describes a girl who offends normal play patterns by showing a preference for rough-and-tumble activities. The assumption underlying this term is that these activities are the sole province of boys, and that a girl is losing some of her feminine characteristics by playing this way. It's not surprising, then, that such social pressures on children to play in predetermined ways have their effect.

However, as your child's parent, it is you who have the greatest influence on his play preferences, because usually it is you who chooses his toys. Of course, you make these choices partly on the basis of his own interests, but mainly on the basis of your own views about suitable toys. Do you know of any fathers who have bought their three-year-old son a tea-set, or of any mothers who have bought their daughter a pair of boxing gloves? Selection of toys is one of the ways in which stereotyped play preferences are passed down from generation to generation.

There's nothing inherently wrong with girls playing with dolls or boys playing at football – *or* vice versa. Children should be allowed to participate in a wide range of play opportunities, and they shouldn't be limited to preconceived notions of what constitutes 'boy's play' and 'girl's play'.

See also **Learning through Play; Play; Sexism; Sociable Play**.

Genes   Every human body is made up of millions of tiny cells, and usually each cell contains 23 pairs of chromosomes (those parts of the cell that contain the blueprint for the growth and development of the body). Each chromosome has thousands of smaller particles (genes) which carry instructions for physical development. The genes determine the child's sex; body size; colour of eyes, skin and hair; blood group, and so on.

Genes interact to form complementary pairs. However, some genes are 'dominant' (their instructions are recognised by the body in preference to those of the other gene in the pair) and some genes are 'recessive' (their instructions are not recognised by the body unless both genes in the pair are recessive). For example, the gene responsible for brown eyes is dominant and the gene responsible for blue eyes is recessive. At conception, if the gene pair has two 'brown' genes, or has one of each colour, then the child will have brown eyes. On the other hand, if the gene pair has two 'blue' genes then the child will have blue eyes. In this way, it is also possible for two brown-eyed parents to have a blue-eyed child (having inherited a recessive 'blue' gene from each parent) but it is not possible for two blue-eyed parents to have a brown-eyed child (since if either parent had a dominant 'brown' gene then they themselves would not be blue-eyed).

The way in which genes act depends on the characteristics they control. While certain genes show their effect in early life, such as in blood type and skin colour, others act only at specific periods in the child's development. These age-linked genes contain plans for sequences of events, such as the age teeth will appear in the child's mouth, when she will walk, when menstruation will begin, and so on. There is no evidence, however, that genes carry plans for personality development.

See also **Down's Syndrome**.

Giftedness   The cut-off point which separates a 'very clever' child from a 'gifted' child is unclear. Some psychologists regard a child as gifted when she has an IQ of 130 upwards, whereas others require an IQ of at least 140. Estimates suggest that around one or two children in 200 are gifted.

The stereotype of a gifted child is a humourless, precocious and bespectacled young person who is more concerned with knowledge and worldly matters than she is with typical childhood interests. But not all gifted children conform to this pattern. They have the same psychological needs as any other children – the need to be loved, the need to feel secure, and the need to fulfil their potential. What does differentiate a gifted child from others of her own age is her exceptional thirst for learning, whether this manifests itself in one particular area (e.g. music, or language) or whether it shows as general all-round talent.

A gifted child usually shows her ability in the pre-school years, often in the following ways:

– *early developmental milestones*. She may attain bowel and bladder control early, and may walk and talk at a younger age than would normally be expected.
– *more energy than usual*. She may need less sleep at night than other children of her age. (However, this is also a common characteristic of hyperactive children, and therefore should not be used as the sole criterion for assessing giftedness.)
– *an insatiable curiosity*. The child may show great interest in the world around her, asking lots of questions about abstract issues – for example, about life and death.
– *well developed language*. Vocabulary is often extensive, and she is probably able to talk fluently about a wide range of topics, long before other children of her age are able to do so.

- *keen powers of observation and reasoning.* She may be able to see relationships between events, and to understand general principles on the basis of a few examples. Memory is often quick and retentive, and imagination may be unusually vivid.
- *a preference for the company of older children.* The chances are that she enjoys spending some of her time with older children and adults because they are better matched to her intellectual level.

Bear in mind that a gifted child need not be good at everything. For instance, her handwriting skills can lag behind her reading ability. Some gifted children are better at seeing and doing than they are at talking and listening; they may have difficulty expressing themselves in words, yet show exceptional mechanical ability.

In a few instances, parents push their gifted child too far, and become concerned only with her educational achievements while ignoring her personal and social development – they may forget that a six-year-old who has the intelligence of a 15-year-old is unlikely to feel at ease in the company of that older age group. However, this type of pressure is unusual. A Canadian study found that most gifted children have no social difficulties. The results showed that the typical gifted child is a well adjusted individual, able to cope with the social and emotional demands of childhood.

Much depends on the attitude of the child's parents, of course. Parents who attend to all aspects of their child's development, and who don't simply focus on her intellectual needs, are less likely to create psychological hazards for her than are parents who place their child's intellectual skills above everything else.

There are three approaches to the education of gifted children. First, segregation, which involves the child attending separate classes (or even separate schools) for children of exceptional ability. Here, every child in the class is categorised as gifted. The drawback with an approach based on segregation is that the child loses contact with most others of her age. Second, acceleration, which involves a gifted child progressing through the ordinary school curriculum at a faster rate than the other pupils. She may even skip one year group entirely. Like segregation, this approach carries with it the danger that the child is thrust into situations that she can cope with intellectually but not emotionally or socially. And third, enrichment, in which the child has mainstream schooling for most of the week, but in addition attends special classes to enrich her knowledge and understanding. The advantage of enrichment classes is that her intellectual ability is stretched and yet she is still able to spend most of her time with children of her own age.

Unlike in other countries, such as America and Israel, most local education authorities in Britain are reluctant to provide special classes for children of exceptional ability. Any special help available is directed to pupils with learning difficulties. The National Association for Gifted Children runs many local Young Explorer Clubs, at which children can meet others of similar talents and abilities, make friends and share their interests. The children are not required to pass any form of test in order to gain admission.

See also **Creativity; Intelligence**.

Grandparents Becoming a grandparent means that one's own child has become a parent – a point that might seem too obvious to make, except that the combined effect of these two wonderful but emotionally charged events can be explosive.

For the new grandparents, the birth rekindles their own memories of early parenthood, and is an opportunity to relive many of those moments again. For the new parents, the birth is the start of the next phase in their life, a phase usually anticipated with great relish. But the baby is the parents' child first, and the grandparents' grandchild second – the prime responsibility for decision-making rests with the parents. Yet many couples complain that in the first few days and weeks of their baby's life the new grandparents act as if the baby was their own. This undermines the parents' self-confidence, frequently resulting in increased family tension. Grandparents should take a back seat at this stage, allowing the couple to gain confidence in their new role as parents.

The relationship between parents and their own parents changes as the grandchild grows older. In the early years of the infant's life, the parents may rely on the grandparents for occasional advice. But as the child develops, the grand-parents may be asked for more practical help – e.g., looking after the child so that the parents can go out on their own. The grandparents may begin to take on the role of trust-worthy baby-sitters rather than advisers. And there may be resentment, as a result. However, looking after the grandchild in this way helps strengthen the bond between them, and keeps the grandparent-grandchild relationship special.

Grandparents often over-indulge their grandchild, and their rules may be far more lenient than the discipline she experiences at home. Most children, though, are well able to cope with two such sets of standards. Difficulties can arise, though, when grandparents undermine the parents' authority by disagreeing with them in front of the grand-child. You know the scene: the whole family are together for a big occasion, the child is very excited, her parents tell her to behave, and then the grandparents announce that the child should be left alone as she is not doing anyone any harm. At this point, the relationship between parents and grandparents becomes strained.

It's important for grandparents to remember that they are exactly that – namely, the child's grandparents, and not her parents. Matters of discipline are best left to her mother and father. This doesn't mean that everything the parents say and do is correct – nobody is infallible when it comes to looking after children. But it does mean that if grand-parents are concerned about their grandchild's develop-ment, they should raise any worries they may have when she isn't present. And they should be prepared to accept that their advice and opinions may not be heeded.

Sadly, one of the common (though not inevitable) side-effects of divorce is that the child may lose touch with one set of grandparents. This can add psychological stress to a child already distressed by the loss of one parent at home. Where she already has a close relationship with her grand-parents, it would be best for this to be maintained irrespec-tive of the parental separation. The grandchild-grandparent relationship is one that should be encouraged both in intact families and in divorced families.

See also **Parents; Separation and Divorce**.

Grief Few adults come to terms with the concept of death, and so it is not surprising that children can have difficulties coping with their own grief following the death of a relative or friend. One of the problems a child frequently faces after a bereavement is that his feelings are ignored. Adults are usually too busy trying to cope with their own distress to consider the feelings of a young child – but that child will be grieving all the same.

A child under the age of eight or nine does not fully understand death in the rational way that adults do, and his reaction to bereavement is unpredictable. For instance, one minute he may tell you that he knows his grandmother has died and that she has gone for ever, and the next minute he may ask you when she's coming back home. Don't get annoyed when he poses this question – it's simply that a young child can't understand that death is irreversible.

Children (like adults) show a wide range of grief reactions when faced with the bereavement of a friend or relative:

– *shock*. The overwhelming sensation that arises the moment a child is informed of the death. He may become very quiet, or even angry and hostile – it's an instant response to the burst of sadness and confusion that overwhelms him. At this time, he needs your comfort and reassurance.

– *denial*. This reaction usually passes within a few days. Until it does, a child acts as if the death hasn't occurred at all. For instance, he may buy a bar of chocolate for his grandmother, just as he did before she died. Denial is a psychological mechanism which allows the news to filter through slowly; if your child does behave this way, don't continually confront him with the facts – he will face them eventually, when he is psychologically ready to do so.

– *searching*. In this grief reaction, a child may literally look for the deceased person – in the rooms she used, and even in the chairs she sat on – in the hope of finding her. It stems from his deep desire for the death never to have happened. Like denial, this phase will pass within a few weeks.

– *guilt*. Amidst the confusion and despair associated with bereavement, a child may develop a sense of guilt about the death. He may, for instance, believe that the loss occurred as a punishment because he was naughty earlier that morning, or because he didn't tidy up his room the previous night when he should have. He may even blame himself because once, in a temper, he wished that person would die. Guilt isn't rational. However, it still hurts, and can stay with a child for years.

- *fear.* A child's fear arising from bereavement can take many forms – e.g., fear that he himself is going to die very soon, or fear that someone else close to him is going to. As a result, he may be afraid to leave his house or to let you out of his sight. In time, he will regain his confidence, but this sort of fear can last for several weeks.

The most common bereavement children experience is that of an elderly relative, although, sadly, some children do have to cope with the death of a sibling or parent. The closer the child's relationship with the dead person, then the stronger his grief will be. Adults frequently make the mistake of assuming that children can't experience genuine grief, and consequently don't pay enough attention to them at this time. In fact, your child's grief reaction will probably be as strong as your own, even though he can't voice his feelings as clearly as you. So keep an eye on his behaviour in the days following a family bereavement. He may show his distress in unexpected ways – e.g., poor concentration in school, fighting with his friends, bed-wetting, unusual reliance on a comforter. Be careful not to misinterpret this behaviour; his reaction is a sign of grief, not a deliberate attempt to upset you.

To help your child come to terms with his feelings about bereavement:

- *Encourage him to talk about his emotions.* Pick a reasonably quiet time when you and he are together, and ask him how he is feeling. He will probably say, 'Fine', but then you might say that you are feeling upset and you are sure he is too. Sharing your emotions with him will let him know that it's permissible for him to describe his own feelings. Whatever he says, listen respectfully.
- *Give him support.* There is nothing like a supportive cuddle from mum or dad to lift the gloom from a troubled child. It won't bring the dead person back, but

104

it will ease some of the pain no matter what age your child is.

- *Let him express his feelings through play.* Encourage him to play with modelling clay, paints, dolls and building bricks, as these provide a vehicle for him to release his inner emotions non-verbally. In addition, your local library probably has books about bereavement, written especially for young children.

A child may have had to consider death before any family bereavement, if he has looked after a pet. Small pets that are popular with young children (e.g., goldfish, hamster, rabbit, stick insects) often have a short life-span. The passing of these can be used as an opportunity to discuss the notion of death with him.

See also **Play; Unconscious; Unhappiness**.

Guilt A child's feelings of guilt stem from his conscience, that part of his mind which tells him that he has broken a rule and that he should feel bad about it.

But a conscience is not present at birth. A newborn baby has no sense of what is right and what is wrong, and therefore doesn't have guilt feelings. As far as a baby is concerned, if he wants something then he should get it. When he is hungry and desires more milk, he cries. It does not matter to him that he was fed just a few minutes ago, or that his parents are tired and need a rest before attending to him. A baby only thinks of himself.

Parents are the prime influence on the development of their child's conscience. From birth onwards, an infant begins to identify with his mother and father. Quite simply, he wants to be like them and he begins to behave like them. But identification goes further than this. As well as behaving like his parents, a child begins to think like them. He begins to adopt their attitudes and values, their feelings, and their moral views.

By the age of three, a child begins to experience guilt feelings when he does something wrong, because by then he is able to make elementary decisions about minor moral issues – for instance, whether he should play with a fragile glass ornament when he has been warned not to. He feels

bad when he realises he has broken a rule. (Of course, it's not good that he's been naughty, but his awareness of right and wrong – and the accompanying feeling of guilt – is a sign of satisfactory psychological development.)

Within a few years, your child will have internalised many of your attitudes to right and wrong. This means that he knows how to behave even when you are not with him telling him what to do. Your conscience has become his, and one indication of this is that he experiences guilt when he breaks rules.

Psychologists have studied guilt feelings in young children by placing them in situations which tempt them to break a rule. One classic investigation of this type used a large room which had a rabbit in a hutch in one corner and a pile of toys, comics and sweets in the opposite corner. One child at a time was taken into the room and was asked to watch the rabbit while the experimenter left for a few moments.

On no account, the child was strictly warned, should he leave the rabbit to go over to the 'goodies' in the other corner. After several minutes, the inevitable happened – the lure of the toys and sweets became too much. The child abandoned his assigned task of looking after the rabbit, and instead wandered over to the 'goodies'. As soon as he did that, the experimenter (who was observing the child through a one-way mirror) pressed a switch that made the rabbit disappear down a concealed trapdoor.

When the child eventually returned to the corner with the hutch in it, he was shocked to see the rabbit had gone! And at that precise moment the experimenter burst into the room demanding to know what had happened to his rabbit. The children's responses varied from total denial to reluctant admission and tears.

Through studies like this – along with detailed observations of children in a variety of natural settings – psychologists have identified a number of techniques for encouraging the development of a healthy sense of guilt:

- *Explain rules to your child in terms he can understand.* Simply telling him what the rules are will not encourage him to feel guilty when he breaks them; he should also be told why his action is wrong – e.g., because it upsets you.
- *Make moral rules clear and specific.* Instead of saying to a child who has just smashed his best friend's toy car, 'It's not nice to upset people', it would be more effective to say, 'Don't break someone else's toys because they will cry and they might break your toy in return.' Start with specific rules, and as your child matures he will be able to extend them himself to cover more general situations.
- *React reasonably when he misbehaves.* The most effective type of punishment is that which is balanced against the seriousness of the offence. A punishment that is too extreme is likely to fuel your child's resentment, rather than his guilt feelings.
- *Never smack your child when he breaks moral rules.* Research confirms that constantly smacking a child for his wrong-doings doesn't stop him behaving that way in the future. It simply encourages him to be more

secretive, in order to avoid punishment, and it also reduces his feelings of guilt.

- *Don't put him into situations that you know will tempt him.* That only puts him under unnecessary pressure. If you see that he is about to do something wrong, step in right away before he commits the offence.

See also **Discipline; Lying; Scapegoat; Smacking; Stealing; Swearing**.

Hand-Eye Coordination   Watch your young child trying to close a zip fastener on her jacket and you'll soon realise how difficult this is for small, uncoordinated hands. It is a very complicated task requiring a great deal of hand-eye control, a skill which she may not have fully acquired even by the time she reaches school age. Of course, she improves

with practice (so make sure she is given plenty of opportunities), but she will be limited by her stage of development.

The acquisition of hand-eye (visual-motor) coordination occurs gradually, in the following sequence:

3 months   Control over hand movements is very basic, and is only beginning to emerge. Your child may bring her hands together very suddenly, almost as if she doesn't know how she managed to.

6 months   Rather than putting toys straight into her mouth as she did when she was younger, she can now manipulate them more purposefully. For instance, she may shake them, throw them about, or even bang them against the side of her cot in order to make a noise.

9 months   The first signs of mature finger control are seen. When she's sitting in her high-chair, put a small piece of biscuit on her tray, so that she can clearly see it. You'll notice that she uses her thumb and forefinger together to lift the item to her mouth, in a pincer movement.

12 months   Her thumb and forefinger pincer movement is better coordinated by this age. And she may even be able to hold a pencil or crayon firmly enough to make a mark on a piece of paper.

18 months   Place a pile of small (about one-inch) building blocks in front of your child, and then start to build a small tower, one block on top of the other. She will imitate you and may be able to build a tower of up to three bricks before it topples.

2 years   Now, her hand-eye coordination has developed to the point where she can build a tower of at least six or seven bricks, before it topples. Hand preference has probably been established by this age, and she can pick up small objects with ease.

3 years   She will be able to grip a pair of child's scissors, with their specially shaped handles, but may have a problem cutting with them. She will also have improved pencil control, and can make a good attempt at copying a circle.

4 years	Hand-eye coordination has developed to the extent that she can use a pair of scissors capably in order to cut paper, and can manage to thread some small beads on to a thread.
5 years	By this age, she is probably able to cope with large-size plastic zip fasteners, with your help. However, the chances are that a couple more years will pass before she is completely confident with them.

See also **Coordination**.

Hazards   Fear of potentially hazardous events is a healthy reaction. A child who does not want to hurt herself avoids dangerous obstacles, such as holes in the road, boiling water and fast-moving cars.

But some children are fearless, and lack the common sense that tells them to go no further; they go as high as they can on the climbing frame even though they cannot get down by themselves, and they ride around so fast on their pedal-bikes that they often fall off. A child like this has to learn that there must be limits to her death-defying feats, that even though she came through unscathed this time she may not be so lucky tomorrow. Never applaud your child for her dangerous actions. Continually remind her that she is behaving foolishly. By associating her reckless performances with your disapproval, she will eventually realise that her bravado is unacceptable – and hopefully she will learn this before any serious injury befalls her.

Other children are accident-prone, not because they fail to recognise common hazards, but because they are preoccupied with deeper concerns. A young child who is troubled or unhappy about something in her life may be too distracted to observe basic standards of safety. And some children are accident-prone because of their unconscious desire for attention. Injury is one way of guaranteeing mum's and dad's interest, since it always ensures a strong parental reaction. So if your child is a 'walking disaster', spend some time trying to ascertain if she has any deeper worries that could be making her accident-prone.

See also **Road Safety**.

Health   There is a strong connection between health and behaviour in childhood. A chronically ill child suffering from, say, asthma or heart disease, is more likely than a healthy child to have an emotional disturbance. And there is also a link between minor illness and unsettled behaviour. For instance, many children experience a loss of appetite, seem listless, or become uncharacteristically irritable, before the onset of a bout of flu.

A research project followed the lives of 900 children from birth to five years. The investigators compared each child's record of upper-respiratory infections (coughs, colds, sore throats, bronchitis or ear infections) with her record of behavioural problems, and found that frequent upper-respiratory infections during childhood were closely associated with night waking (defined as waking at least four nights a week), poor appetite (especially at the toddler stage), severe temper tantrums, and management difficulties (due to lack of cooperation on the child's part).

One explanation for this finding is that many children are allergic to certain chemicals found in particular medicines; a child who has a cough may be given a drug which she is allergic to, and in turn this may cause her to behave disruptively. This is another aspect of your child's medication that you should discuss with your doctor.

A more likely explanation of the association between health and behaviour, however, is that a child who is physically unwell is more vulnerable to stress, and less able to take everyday problems in her stride. Minor events that she can handle easily while in full health (e.g., losing her favourite toy, having to tidy her room) become major hurdles; the illness weakens her ability to cope, making her fractious and unsettled. Fortunately, a return to good health is usually accompanied by an improvement in the child's behaviour.

See also **Additives; Crying Baby; Illness.**

Healthy Eating   There are several studies which show that young children will, over a period of several weeks, eat a satisfactory diet – as long as they are offered a broad range of nutritious foods.

For instance, one research project presented toddlers with a wonderful array of milk, cheese, eggs, vegetables and so

112

on. The children could eat what they wanted, using their fingers, and they received no advice or interference from any adult. Three amazing findings emerged:

- The children tried everything eventually, and only rarely did they eat a large amount of any one particular food – quite incredible, given a toddler's almost predictable rejection of vegetables when they are given to him by his parents.
- Not one child had a tummy ache, even though the project lasted for several weeks.
- Analysis of the contents of over 35,000 meals revealed that the children had all eaten a perfectly balanced diet (almost as if their meals had been planned in detail by a dietician).

However, these young children were allowed to eat only from a range of healthy, wholesome foods. (Nobody appears to have repeated the experiment using crisps, sweets and cakes!) And this is the point: it's important for you to know the sorts of foods your child should eat. You may well find, when you actually make a note of his food intake over a two-week period, that his eating habits aren't as bleak as you first thought. Everything your child eats contains at least one of these substances:

protein Helps the body grow and keep it in good repair. Children need more proteins than adults because basic body tissue – e.g., brain, muscles, blood, skin – is growing quickly. Animal protein is obtained from meat, fish, eggs and dairy produce, while vegetable protein is obtained from cereals, nuts, pulses and root vegetables.

carbohydrates The main carbohydrates are sugar, starch and cellulose. They provide essential energy, but when too many are consumed the excess is changed into body fat and stored until needed. Carbohydrates are present in sugary foods (e.g., jam, cakes, sweets, biscuits, chocolate) and in starchy foods (e.g., bread, potatoes, rice, lentils, flour).

fat Another source of energy; some fats include

113

vitamins (see below). Fat is present in meat, fish oil and some vegetables, and can also be in solid form (e.g., butter, lard, margarine) or in prepared foods (e.g., crisps, chips, sausages, cream, mayonnaise). Excess fats are converted into body fat.

fibre Encourages good digestion and discourages constipation. Fibre (roughage) is found in fruit and vegetables as well as in wholemeal flour and bread, wholegrain cereals, nuts and pulses. Breakfast cereals incorporating oats, wheat or bran contain fibre.

vitamins Our bodies cannot manufacture vitamins, and so they have to be obtained from food. Main vitamins are:
- *vitamin A*: for healthy skin and night vision (in fish, cheese, eggs, butter, chicken, spinach, carrots);
- *vitamin B*: allows the body to obtain energy from food (in milk, liver, cheese, wholemeal bread, oats);
- *vitamin C*: for bone development and healing (in fresh vegetables and fruit, especially citrus fruits);
- *vitamin D*: builds strong bones and good teeth (in fish oil, liver, dairy produce and sunlight);
- *vitamin E*: strengthens blood cells (in oats, brown rice, liver, nuts, pulses and wholegrain cereals).

minerals Occur naturally in the earth, and present in most foods. Main minerals are:
- *calcium*: forms bones and teeth (in milk, cheese, yoghurt, tinned fish, green vegetables);
- *iron*: prevents anaemia, by building red blood cells (in red meat, eggs, bread, cereals, green vegetables);
- *salt*: maintains the body's water balance (and already present in many foods);
- *fluoride*: important for teeth formation (now in water supplies, but also in toothpaste).

Your child needs a variety of foods every day so that he will grow fit and healthy. But the amount he should eat at mealtimes depends on his particular body size, height, age, daily routine and metabolism. (Episodic growth spurts often cause a temporary surge in appetite which then returns to its previous level.) Give your child portions that you know he can eat – and if he struggles with a main meal, serve it in the form of finger-food.

See also **Additives; Eating; Eating Out; Fussy Eaters; Manners; Overweight; Snacks.**

Hearing Assessment Research into hearing loss has revealed that in three cases out of four the difficulty is first suspected by the child's parents, whereas only 1 case in 20 is first suspected by a doctor. And perseverance may be needed in order to access specialist assessment. Another survey looked at referrals of possible hearing loss to family doctors, and found that half of all such doctors consulted by parents of children who were later found to be deaf did not agree that the child in question was deaf. A third of these doctors refused referral to a specialist for assessment. Once a child reaches a specialist, however, far fewer omissions are made.

Accurate hearing assessment is vital, because a hearing-impaired baby faces specific problems:

- He can't hear what is being said to him by other children or adults. Hearing difficulties impair his ability to interact with other people, and can cause a sense of isolation.
- He gets no feedback from his own speech because he can't hear the sounds he makes. A deaf baby starts to make sounds at around the same age as a hearing baby, but the lack of feedback means he has less encouragement to practise and extend them.

Since babbling and listening to sounds provide the foundation for later speech development, a child who misses these early experiences will find learning to speak is harder than for a child with normal hearing. A hearing-impaired child may be slower to speak, he may not use his first words until long after the age he is expected to, and he may be slower to understand the meaning of words. The sooner a hearing loss is identified and assessed, then the sooner action can be taken to help him.

Routine hearing checks are given soon after birth. These checks are repeated when a baby is around six months, at his local child health clinic, and again at regular intervals throughout the pre-school years. Tests are carried out by a health visitor or doctor. When this very basic screening suggests a child has some hearing loss, he will be referred for more detailed assessment at an audiology clinic, which has specialised equipment available. This involves the child being presented with sounds at varying, but finely controlled, frequencies. Children referred for speech therapy always undergo a full audiological assessment.

Once an initial assessment leads to the diagnosis of a hearing difficulty, the professionals involved need to establish the full extent of the child's residual hearing, which hearing aids would be most suitable for him, and his understanding and his use of language. This enables the hearing loss to be seen within the wider context of his general development.

Children who have been assessed as having a hearing problem may become involved with a number of different professionals, all of whom have an important role to play, including:

- *an otologist*: an ENT (ear, nose and throat) consultant, specialising in diseases affecting the ear, who will be in charge of medical treatment for the child's condition;
- *an audiometrician*: a specialist who measures hearing levels, and who may be involved in fitting hearing aids;
- *a teacher of the deaf*: a specially trained teacher who works with hearing-impaired children and their families, advising on the child's educational needs;
- *an educational psychologist*: a psychologist trained in child development, as well as being a qualified teacher, who will assess the child's progress regularly throughout schooling.

Hearing assessment categorises a child's hearing capacity in two main ways. First, in terms of the loudness of sounds that can be heard: with this system, a mild loss has occurred when a child can't hear a whisper; a moderate loss has occurred when he can't hear a normal voice three feet away from him; a severe loss has occurred when he can't hear a

116

human voice at all; and a profound hearing loss has occurred when he doesn't react to any sound whatsoever. Second, in terms of the sound frequencies that can be heard: with this system, a hearing deficiency may be in the high range of tones, or in the low range, and will impair the child's ability to hear human voices clearly.

See also **Hearing Loss; Language Development; Language Difficulties; Language Learning; Language Stimulation.**

Hearing Loss Whether total or partial, hearing loss is the single most common reason underlying a child's failure to develop normal speech. A hearing-impaired child may be slower to speak, and slower to understand the meaning of words. Approximately 1 child in 10 has a mild hearing loss, and approximately 1 per 1000 has a severe hearing loss or total deafness. Almost 90 per cent of deaf children have parents with normal hearing.

With normal hearing, sound gets picked up by the outer ear, then passes to the eardrum through the ear canal. This activates the small bones in the middle ear, passing the sound on to the cochlea, where it changes into electrical impulses. These electrical impulses are rather like messages which pass along the nerve of hearing to the brain. Problems can arise in any part of this system, and in many instances the cause of hearing defects cannot be traced. Hearing loss can be:

- *conductive*. In this condition, sound is prevented from reaching the inner ear from the outer and middle ear, perhaps because of a blockage of wax. 'Swimmer's ear' – resulting from bacteria and water trapped by ear wax – is another cause of conductive hearing loss, as is middle-ear infection, which often arises from the common cold. Medical treatment from the family doctor usually resolves conductive hearing loss.
- *perceptive*. This condition is much more serious because it usually cannot be cured. It arises from damage to the inner ear, to the hearing nerve, or to that part of the brain responsible for hearing. Perceptive hearing loss is often congenital. Fortunately, the majority of children with this type of impairment have some residual hearing

117

and therefore are likely to benefit from using a hearing aid.

Hearing loss in a baby is difficult for parents to detect, but some of the signs to look out for include:

- *lack of response to your voice.* Your baby should show an almost immediate reaction when you speak to her, either by turning her head towards you or else by showing some change in her behaviour. Failure or slowness to react could signify a hearing loss.
- *not being soothed by your voice, unless you are in her line of vision.* Most unhappy babies will be soothed by a familiar voice. A hearing-impaired baby may be soothed only when she can actually see her parent.
- *being startled when someone comes into her line of vision.* Babies with normal hearing soon learn to anticipate the arrival of another person by the sound they make – e.g., footsteps coming closer, the noise of the bedroom door opening. A baby with hearing problems doesn't have this early-warning system, and hence may be alarmed when she suddenly sees you.
- *restricted sounds after the age of six months.* After this age, a deaf baby's speech fails to develop, whereas a hearing baby's sounds continue to increase.
- *inability to locate a sound source.* By the age of two months, a baby with normal hearing will react to a sound by turning her eyes or head towards it. A baby with a hearing loss, however, may seem confused because she can't tell where the sound is coming from.
- *always turning the same ear towards a sound source, irrespective of the direction of the noise.* A baby with normal hearing will turn the left or right side of her head towards a sound, depending on the sound's direction.

Numerous signals make it easier for parents to detect a hearing loss in an older child:

- *failure to respond to a simple request.* Of course, she may be pretending not to hear you, but if this happens consistently then there may be a hearing difficulty.
- *failure to stop an activity when she is told to.* Again, this behaviour may be a result of her unwillingness to cooperate with you, but repeated instances may be a sign of hearing loss.

- *needing to have questions repeated before she responds.* A child with partial hearing frequently becomes confused when asked a question, because she can't hear it properly.
- *watching the speaker's face and mouth closely during conversation.* A child with hearing loss may rely on lip-reading and other facial clues to help her understand what is said.
- *delayed speech development.* There are several characteristics more common in the speech of children with partial hearing than in the speech of children with normal hearing – e.g., ends of words are missing, vocabulary is poorer, letters are mixed up (t and k, or d and g) and sh and s may sound the same.

None of these indicators by themselves necessarily mean that your child has a hearing loss. But if the above patterns of behaviour are repeated every day, seek a professional hearing assessment.

Techniques for stimulating language development in a child with normal hearing apply just as much to a child with a hearing loss. In addition to these and to any specialist help she is given, you should also think carefully about the sorts of toys that may be suitable. For a young baby, choose a rattle that is brightly coloured and lets her feel vibrations when it is shaken. At six months, a toy music-box or portable radio held close will enable her to feel beat and rhythm. Around 12–18 months, games which present different sounds in different places will be useful – e.g., peek-a-boo using musical instruments. For a child aged two or three and older, most toy shops carry a range of games which stimulate language and listening experiences.

And make sure your child wears a hearing aid if it has been prescribed by her ENT consultant. Hearing aids can make sounds louder for the user, though a deaf child will still not hear words exactly as a child with normal hearing does. She may not be comfortable wearing the aid, and she may feel embarrassed by it, but it should be worn continually at the correct adjustment. Modern hearing aids are extremely powerful, and can offer substantial help to a child with hearing loss.

See also **Hearing Assessment; Language Development; Lan-**

Hospital Going into hospital isn't something that happens only to other people's children – half of all children are admitted to hospital before they reach the age of seven. Sometimes the admissions are planned, while at other times they stem from an accident. But whatever the circumstances, hospitalisation can be a traumatic emotional experience for a young child.

Look at it from her point of view. Hospitals are large, noisy places, where people wear green and white clothes. Some of them even wear masks – in television programmes, only bad men hide their faces like that. The food is different from home, not what mum usually makes, and hospital may already be associated with the death of a relative. Yet all this pales into insignificance in comparison with what actually goes on inside hospital. There are injections, pills, and possibly unpleasant examinations . . . no wonder children are often apprehensive about going in. And this can affect their rate of recovery.

Most paediatricians accept that a child's return to good health depends very much on the way she's managed in hospital – and this management must include due attention to her psychological welfare as well as to her physical welfare. There are very good reasons for this: if a child is unhappy in hospital, she'll not eat properly and she will feel stressed. When this happens, she will not recover from the cause of her being in hospital (whether it's pneumonia or a surgical operation) as quickly as she would if she felt comfortable and at ease.

The foundations for coping with hospitalisation should be laid long before your child has a health problem. You are happy to discuss garages, railway stations, the library and the supermarket with her – so no need to miss out hospitals. There are lots of sensible children's books about being in hospital, which can be read to her at home in a relaxed setting. You can point out your local hospital when passing by; there may even be an opportunity to take your child with you when you visit a hospitalised friend.

If your child has a planned hospital admission, talk to her about it several days in advance. This will give her plenty of time to ask questions – to which you should give direct answers, matching them to her level of understanding. Emphasise how kind the doctors and nurses will be, and reassure her she will be there for only a few days.

Be calm on admission day. Let her take a couple of her favourite toys with her, and ask ward staff to introduce her to some of the other patients. Don't be afraid to tell the nurses about her individual habits (e.g., that she always has warm milk in the morning, that she watches a particular television programme each day, that she says a short prayer before going to sleep). The more the hospital routine resembles her home routine, the happier she'll be.

But actually being with your child while she is in hospital is the most effective way of easing her psychological stress. This elementary fact of child psychology was recognised over 30 years ago by the Platt Report (the findings of a government committee set up to investigate the welfare of children in hospital). It made two important non-medical recommendations: first, that children should be allowed unrestricted visiting when in hospital; and second, that mothers should be allowed to stay with their hospitalised child.

However, these recommendations have still not been universally implemented – the problem is that not every child is admitted to an all-children hospital. A high percentage are admitted either to a children's ward within a large general hospital, or to an adult ward with designated children's beds, where staff have no special training for dealing with young patients. In such institutions, there are unlikely to be residential facilities for parents, and visiting hours for children are likely to be the same restricted times as for the adult patients.

Surveys conducted by the National Association for the Welfare of Children in Hospital (NAWCH) – a voluntary group of parents and professionals aiming to ensure that facilities for children in hospital are of the highest possible standard, and that parents have unrestricted visiting at all hospitals – reveal that many hospital staff think parents simply 'interfere with the hospital routine'!

If you want to be with your child throughout her stay in hospital, even though she's in a ward with restricted visiting:

● *Remember you have a right to be there.* Most doctors

121

realise that it's in your child's best interests to be along-side her when she's in hospital. You are not being awk-ward or eccentric by exercising this right.

- *Don't be put off by the excuse, 'There's no room.'* A chair by your child's bed is not going to take up much space, nor will it inconvenience any of the other patients.
- *Challenge staff who say that they can't work while you're there watching them.* There's no justification for this sort of claim. After all, GPs often treat patients in front of the whole family.
- *Speak to the ward sister – or hospital administrator, if necessary – if you are consistently told you can't stay.* You shouldn't be fobbed off by the first nurse you meet. Ward routines can be flexible, if the goodwill is there. So stick to your guns.

See also **Illness; X-Ray**.

Hydrocephalus Most babies born with spina bifida also have hydrocephalus. In this condition, cerebrospinal fluid – a naturally occurring watery substance in the brain which serves to bathe its surfaces, and to carry essential nutrients – is unable to drain into the bloodstream. Consequently, this fluid begins to build up in the brain, causing it to enlarge. The effects of hydrocephalus vary, but often include visual and learning difficulties, fits and coordination problems.

The signs of hydrocephalus do not usually manifest them-selves until an infant is a few weeks old, or even a few months old. This is one of the reasons why doctors measure the circumference of a new baby's head as a matter of routine – very often these measurements lead to the early identification of the difficulty.

The most common treatment for hydrocephalus is a surgi-cal procedure which involves implanting a device (a shunt) to divert the build-up of cerebrospinal fluid back into the bloodstream. The shunt has a system of tubes with a valve to control the rate of draining, and although the device may become blocked, or infection may develop, usually these difficulties can be resolved. Before the development of this treatment, the majority of children with hydrocephalus died.

See also **Spina Bifida**.

Hygiene Personal hygiene is important for everyone, so do encourage your child to take an interest in his level of cleanliness from an early age. There are three main benefits of good personal hygiene:

- *health*. A child who isn't washed regularly will be prone to infections and irritations, particularly in the genital area and where he has folds of skin. In addition, he may ingest germs and bacteria when he brings his unwashed hands into contact with food.
- *sociability*. Nobody likes a smelly child! It's much nicer to hold a clean, sweet-smelling baby than one who smells of faeces, urine or vomit. And a child who has a strong, unpleasant body odour will soon find that he is alone in a crowd. The only way these problems can be avoided is by regular washing.
- *comfort*. In many instances, poor personal hygiene leads to discomfort. A baby will quickly become distressed when wearing a dirty nappy, and an older child will be uncomfortable wearing dirty clothes that feel stiff and scratchy. Everybody likes the sensations of well-being that arise from putting on fresh, clean clothes after a warm, soapy bath.

Bath-time is the first opportunity for your child to become involved in his own personal hygiene. Even a baby as young as six months can learn to associate cleanliness with pleasure – as long as bath-time is a fun experience for him. Try not to rush your infant in and out of his bath as quickly as possible; let him play with bath toys, or just splash around. He'll learn to enjoy being in the water, especially when you seem to be having fun too.

However, if a child associates it with something unpleasant, bath-time can become a source of conflict. Hair-washing, in particular, can turn out to be a hygiene activity that causes tears. Ask your child what is upsetting him. It may be fear of soap getting in his eyes, or of slipping under the water while his hair is being shampooed. He may even be afraid of sliding down the plug-hole when the plug is removed. Once you have identified the cause of his anxiety, reassure him and offer a solution – e.g., fear of shampoo

123

getting into his eyes can be eased by stroking his hair towards the back of his head when washing it, or by using a shampoo that generates less lather, or by covering his eyes with a flannel. These measures will reduce tension, and will make bath-time a more pleasant event.

Personal hygiene arises again once your child starts toilet-training. Teach him to wash his hands after he sits on the potty. This becomes even more important around the age of three or four, when he is able to wipe his bottom without help. Don't make a big fuss over hand-washing, but do make it standard practice when he uses the toilet so that he adopts the habit without having to think about it. And from the age of three upwards, he should be expected to wash his hands before mealtimes – although be prepared to remind him each time.

In the same way that your child will feel better when he starts the day clean, he will also feel good when he ends the day that way. Develop a bedtime routine which involves him washing his hands and face, and brushing his teeth. Until he is five or six, you may find that he needs constant encouragement to do this; most young children would rather climb into bed straight away when they are tired than waste time getting themselves clean and fresh. You can persuade him by pointing out how nice he is to cuddle when he's clean and fresh, or how pleasant his breath smells after brushing his teeth.

A good standard of personal hygiene can be established in the pre-school years. And a child who has an interest in his own cleanliness at that age will probably maintain it throughout his life.

See also **Independence**.

Hyperactivity   A child with this condition shows an abnormally high level of activity, combined with a short attention span, a low level of concentration, and a superabundance of impulsive and reckless behaviour.

One of the difficulties in identifying hyperactivity is that young children vary considerably in their level of activity. Even during pregnancy, one woman may find her baby moves infrequently, while another at the same stage of pregnancy may find that hers kicks and wriggles most of the time. These differences in activity rates continue after the birth.

However, babies who are genuinely hyperactive are noticeably different from other children in terms of their general day-to-day behaviour. For instance, hyperactive babies often don't like being cuddled, and will struggle in their mothers' arms. They seem uncomfortable and miserable, as if nothing is right for them. Often these babies are poor sleepers and fussy eaters, and they are very difficult and demanding to care for. Researchers have also found other features associated with hyperactivity. For instance, during pregnancy, the mother is more likely to have had high blood pressure and to have experienced vaginal bleeding. Whereas premature delivery occurs in up to 15 per cent of the population, it occurs in up to 25 per cent of hyperactive children. In the period immediately following delivery, a hyperactive child is more likely to have a breathing difficulty.

Perception of the child's behaviour is another factor to be considered in the identification of hyperactivity. Parents who are themselves quiet, withdrawn and bookish may describe their child as hyperactive if he doesn't sit down peacefully to play with his building bricks for, say, 30 minutes at a time. In contrast, outgoing parents who believe children should be allowed to express themselves freely and energetically are likely to be more tolerant of their child's very active behaviour.

Whatever the complicating factors in identifying hyperactivity, there are undoubtedly a significant number of very active children who do cause serious problems for their parents – and it doesn't really matter whether or not they are called 'hyperactive'. Several possible causes of hyperactivity have been suggested (each with its own form of treatment):

- *diet*. One suggestion is that the condition is caused by a child's diet, and that if an over-active, disruptive child eats only natural foods, without any additives, then his behaviour will improve. Some parents find this works, but others do not. Your local health clinic will supply you with an additive-free diet sheet.
- *discipline*. Another theory is that hyperactivity is caused by the way parents behave towards their child. Every child needs structure and predictability in his home life,

125

and this is usually achieved by having a firm and consistent discipline. Yet parents of a hyperactive child often let him break the rules without reprimand, simply because they are too tired to challenge him – but he does need a more structured form of discipline.

– *brain damage*. Some doctors claim that hyperactivity is caused by 'minimal brain damage', which interferes with the child's behaviour. This explanation derives from the medical discovery that there are a few hyperactive children who do have identifiable brain damage. However, the existence of minimal brain damage is impossible to verify using contemporary neurological tests, and consequently many professionals reject it completely.

Explanations which attribute hyperactivity to a physical cause have led to the development of drug treatment. A number of stimulant drugs can have a temporary calming effect on a hyperactive child, but they often have worrying side-effects, including lethargy and appetite loss. And few parents are happy at the thought of their young child taking drugs. This type of treatment, therefore, remains controversial.

Recent research has also suggested that high lead levels in the atmosphere – from car petrol fumes – could cause hyperactivity. Investigators claim to have found a link between blood lead-level and hyperactive behaviour, and conclude that lead at low levels of exposure probably has a small but harmful effect on children's behaviour.

Parents of hyperactive children have a tough time, and should be offered support wherever possible. A psychological approach – such as providing a structured and consistent form of discipline at home – gives them an active role in managing their child's behaviour, and is usually the first suggestion offered to them. A management system like this is not guaranteed to alter the behaviour of every hyperactive child, but it can have a positive effect. And it offers the added benefit of making parents feel that they are beginning to have some control over their child again; this in itself can raise their self-confidence, and consequently decrease family tension.

It's encouraging to know that whatever causes hyperactivity, the problem tends to fade as a child reaches adolescence.

In most instances, a previously unmanageable child becomes more settled during the teenage years.

See also **Additives; Discipline**.

I

Illness Dealing with a sick child is difficult at the best of times. There are so many things to worry about, ranging from the trivial (Who is going to do the school run instead of me?) to the more serious (I wonder what's wrong with her?). After a few days, however, she is usually on the way to a full recovery, and normality is once again restored to your household.

But not all childhood illnesses follow such a brief and predictable course. Some children develop illnesses that can take an exceptionally long time to respond to treatment (e.g., cancer, kidney disease), and chronic ill-health of this sort dominates their lives. However, a child with long-term

ill-health has an instinctive desire to get better, and the more emotionally secure she is, then the speedier her physical recovery will be.

A chronically sick child has the same psychological needs as a healthy one. True, an ill child has additional requirements, such as the need to be reassured that she is going to get well eventually, the need for appropriate medical treatment, the need for lots of rest, and so on. But her basic emotional needs remain the same (though perhaps a little stronger) as they would have been had ill-health not loomed on the horizon. Every child thrives best in a family in which she feels cared for and in which at the same time she experiences structure and consistency. Without these qualities, your child will feel insecure.

The way you manage your chronically sick child depends partly on your views on discipline. For instance:

- If you regard discipline simply as a way of controlling her in order to make her conform to your standards, then you will probably be less insistent on this matter when she is ill. After all, she is less active when unwell and therefore is less likely to break the rules.
- If you regard exerting discipline as a necessary evil of parenthood, that has to be applied for your child's sake even though you would prefer to let her do as she pleases, then her ill-health will give you justification for being more lenient.
- If you believe that discipline makes a positive contribution to your child's development, then ill-health is unlikely to make you reduce your expectations and general standard of discipline.

Although it is perfectly understandable when parents 'spoil' their sick child – and we are all guilty of this at times – there are a number of potential dangers in abandoning family discipline in such circumstances. First, it may confirm the child's worry that something is terribly wrong with her. A sudden change in the rules may increase her unconscious fears that her illness is serious. Second, abandoning family discipline may cause relationship difficulties: within a short time you may find yourself having to cope not only with a chronically sick child, but with a chronically sick child who thinks she can do what she wants. And your other children might also be confused about this relaxation of family rules.

Lastly, adjustment from ill-health to normality can be difficult enough (e.g., restoring self-confidence, becoming independent once again), without the added task of having to
re-learn acceptable standards of behaviour.

Of course, you need to be flexible. There will be occasions
when you 'turn a blind eye' to your chronically sick child's
behaviour. Of course, you should fuss over her, and do
everything you can to make her feel comfortable and happy.
And, of course, you should spend as much time with her as
you can, to stop her feeling lonely and miserable. But this
is quite different from abandoning discipline altogether.

Another way to help your chronically ill child is to establish some form of routine in her daily activities. To a child
confined to bed all day, time can seem to drag. She may
begin to focus on negative aspects of life – e.g., the boredom, missing her friends, worrying about school work.
Make it a matter of routine that, if possible, she gets up
from bed for meals, that at a specific time of the day she
reads a book, that she has a bath every evening, and so on.
Incorporating these routine events into her life may seem
rather tedious from your point of view but, from hers, regu-
larity of this nature can be welcome. It enables her to anticipate the day's events, just as she would during a normal day
when she is in good health.

And give her an occasional surprise. An unprepared visit
by one of her friends can prove memorable; the unexpected
present of a book or game can perk up a dull day.

See also **Discipline; Health; Hospital; Routine; Spoiling.**

Imaginary Friend Many young children have an imaginary
friend, someone who exists only in their own mind.
Although many others go through their pre-school years
without using their imagination in this particular way, it is
a normal part of early child development, and an extension
of symbolic play.

The advantage of having an imaginary friend is that it
gives a child full control over play situations. She decides
when to play with her friend, and what they will play at
together. Freed from relying on other children to be cooperative and pleasant to her, she can do as she pleases with
her imaginary friend and there is no one to interfere with

their game. This makes the imaginary friend all the more desirable. However, the child knows that the friend is not real.

Children have usually passed through the imaginary-friend phase by the time they begin attending school; the peak age for this phenomenon is around four years. Imaginary friends can serve a number of purposes, including:

- *security*. An imaginary friend provides comfort and security in times of stress. When a child is under pressure, she can turn to this friend for support, and the friend will say what she needs to hear. For instance, a child who is afraid of visiting the dentist may be reassured when her imaginary friend tells her that she'll be fine. And once she leaves the dental surgery, her friend can disappear until she is needed the next time.
- *company*. Only children, or children with few friends of their own age, have a greater tendency to play with imaginary friends. The reason is obvious: what a lonely child cannot create in reality, she can create in fantasy. It is far better for a young child to engage in this sort of symbolic play activity than to sit around doing nothing at all, moping because she has no friends.
- *communication*. A child can be very subtle in communicating information to adults, and the imaginary friend can be a useful mechanism for doing this, especially when the child wants to say something that her parents may not want to hear. Telling her imaginary friend (within earshot of her parents) that she's worried mum and dad will be angry when they discover her new toy is lost, is one way of breaking the news gently to them!

Some psychologists argue that when parents teach their child about religion, in a sense they are encouraging her to have an imaginary friend – albeit for good reasons. When introducing religious concepts, parents usually emphasise that there is a deity who looks after the child, who is all around her, and yet who cannot be seen. From a psychological perspective, the imaginary friend is no different from this.

In some instances, the friend starts to play too dominant a role in the child's life and she retains this form of symbolic play long after other children of her age have grown out of it. When it gets to the point that her day-to-day life is impaired by the presence of the 'friend', then it probably indicates that she has a deeper emotional difficulty, of which the need for the imaginary friend is a symptom - e.g., if she won't go anywhere without her, if she absolutely insists an empty chair is left beside her at every meal so that her friend can sit down, if she says she is crying because her friend is unhappy. If this kind of thing is happening with your child, look more closely at her life to see what could be troubling her.

See also **Imagination; Play.**

Imagination   Imaginative play does not emerge until a child is around one year, and continues to develop throughout the remaining pre-school years. This form of play has two features which distinguish it from earlier exploratory play. First, a toddler is now able to use one object to represent another. A brick can represent a car, a cuddly toy can represent mum or dad. He can also use himself to represent someone else – e.g., he can pretend to be his father. Therefore the range of potential play situations is infinitely extended. Second, symbolic play frees a child from the here-and-now. He is not tied to what he can see in front of him: objects, people and experiences are present in his memory, for him to draw on.

   Symbolic or imaginative play develops in stages, although the ages at which children pass from one stage to another vary greatly. The first stage occurs at around one year and involves a toddler using a familiar behaviour in a different context – e.g., when he pretends to feed himself out of a toy cup. The second stage comes at around 18 months, when he himself is no longer the focus of his pretend play: he will act out imaginary sequences on a doll, or another person, instead of always making himself the centre of attention.

   The third stage of symbolic play comes at around three years, when he is able to adopt roles in play. Children at this stage enjoy pretending to be other people, whether it is the milkman, their mother, their father, or the doctor. And elaborately designed clothes are not necessary. The dressing-up box at home requires only a modest collection of old adult clothes, a few hats and headscarves, some cheap jewellery, a couple of shopping bags – that's enough for a child to create any character he wants. Young children love imagining they are someone else.

Symbolic role play serves different psychological purposes. It provides your child with an opportunity to test out roles he may anticipate having to play in later life. He may wonder what it would be like to be an adult, or to be one of his friends, or to be a television character, and role play lets him experience this for a few moments. You may be surprised when you observe him playing like this, especially when you see him acting out the role of 'mum' or 'dad' – he may take great delight in strutting around, pretending to be a complaining parent, bossing everyone else about. Frightening to think that this is how our children sometimes perceive us!

Furthermore, role play allows your child to release his deeper emotions in a socially acceptable way. For instance, a young child would normally be reprimanded for being aggressive and shouting at other children. However, when he delves into the dressing-up box, puts on a policeman's hat and starts issuing orders, nobody bothers. Symbolic role play lets your child release his aggressive impulses without fear of punishment.

This type of play can be called 'imaginative' because the child is able to distinguish it from reality. When he is engaged in imaginary play, he knows that what he is doing is only a symbolic representation of the real world. Of course, he doesn't think of it in these terms, but he does know the difference. You will probably have seen your child apparently having a raging argument with his friend, and when you have gone over to separate them, they will have greeted you with the reassuring remark, 'It's all right. We're not really fighting. We're only playing.'

See also **Aggression; Creativity; Imaginary Friend; Learning through Play; Play; Playing with Your Child**.

Immunisation Although babies who are breast-fed tend to have fewer health problems in the first year of life than babies who are bottle-fed, all children are susceptible to disease. Fortunately, immunisation can protect your child against the major diseases that can be fatal, including polio, diphtheria, tetanus and whooping cough. Medical specialists

133

claim that a fully implemented programme of immunisations could eliminate these childhood hazards completely.

Modern techniques now mean that childhood immunisations are less complicated. For instance, the vaccines providing immunisation against diphtheria, whooping cough and tetanus are combined into a triple vaccine (DPT); this is administered as an injection at the ages of two, three and four months (that is, three times). Infants are now given the polio vaccine in the form of drops in the mouth, usually when they receive the DPT. And the vaccines against measles, mumps and rubella (German measles) are combined into one injection (MMR), administered at the age of 12–15 months. The last stage in the pre-school immunisation programme is between the ages of three and five years, when a child receives booster vaccines against diphtheria, tetanus and polio in order to give added protection for starting school. There is also a vaccine (Hib) which offers protection against meningitis.

Serious side-effects to vaccines are rare, while minor reactions (e.g., temporary irritability) are common. However, the vaccine for whooping cough has come under particular criticism in recent years because some parents have claimed it has caused brain damage. Evidence supporting these claims is not clear-cut, but they have shaken parental confidence in the vaccine's safety. Yet whooping cough remains a very dangerous disease which can itself result in brain damage, and most doctors agree this is a greater risk than possible serious side-effects from the immunisation itself.

Certainly, if you have fears about this, discuss it with your health visitor and GP before the immunisation; they are fully aware of your baby's health record and will be able to provide you with reassurance. There are some medical reasons for delaying immunisation, or for cancelling it altogether – e.g., if your baby is unwell, if he has ever had any convulsions or a severe allergic reaction, or if he has had a bad reaction to previous immunisations.

Independence One minute your child is determined to prove that she can undress herself without your help, and the next minute she desperately wants you to cuddle her because she's afraid of going upstairs in the dark. The early years are characterised by these two conflicting trends –

your child's increasing dependence on you for love and security (which gives her a strong psychological foundation for later life), and at the same time her inborn desire to be independent.

There is no specific age when your child should be independent, when she should be able to do things without your help. True, there are some milestones of independence which are important for all children, such as being able to walk, being able to talk, having bladder and bowel control, and so on. But apart from these obvious skills, much depends on your own view as a parent.

Training your child to be independent at home is hard work because of the demands that it makes on you. And don't leave it all to chance; take a planned approach. Have specific goals that you want her to achieve ('putting on a jumper by yourself' is a clearer goal than 'getting dressed by yourself'), and tell her what each goal is. She'll have more success in increasing her independence if she takes small steps rather than large jumps. Whatever you want her to achieve, break it down into small stages and then tackle one stage at a time. Give her lots of praise when she succeeds, and lots of reassurance when she doesn't.

Parents sometimes inadvertently instil in their child conflicting sets of expectations about self-reliance. For instance, a child who learns to tidy her room may want to extend this degree of independence to choosing what clothes she should wear, and what television programmes she should watch. During the process of becoming independent, most children have difficulty knowing when to assert their individuality and when not to. Be prepared to explain carefully what is acceptable to you and what is not.

Children often take a step backwards in their striving for independence precisely at the time when they should be moving forwards. So, for example, a four-year-old who is learning to eat with a knife and fork may suddenly seem 'handless' just when her parents thought she had mastered that skill. These moments of regression are normal and allow her to gather the emotional strength needed to move on to the next stage of independence, rather like an athlete who turns away from the high-jump moments before she takes a run at it. When your child does seem to be going backwards instead of forwards, be patient with her. It is a natural part of development.

At times, independence training can be inconvenient for the whole family. For instance, your household routine is probably hectic first thing in the morning when everyone is rushing to get out to work or to school – and a young child struggling valiantly to dress herself without any help may slow down the rest of the family. Temptation to assist her can be strong. So if you are in the process of encouraging your child's competence at a particular task, make sure you give her plenty of time. The atmosphere must be relaxed, or her desire for independence will quickly evaporate.

A balance between over-reliance on you and total independence needs to be struck. Your expectations should be realistic – just as it is inadvisable to 'baby' a child, so it is inadvisable to expect too much from her. Don't push her to achieve at a level more advanced than that normally expected of a child her age. There is no advantage, for instance, in a five-year-old being able to do some things that only eight-year-olds usually do.

Breaking away from a state of total independence begins early on and continues throughout a child's life. Often a painful process, it is a necessary aspect of any parent-child relationship, and benefits the child. The confidence that comes from having control over the immediate environment is a tremendous boost to her self-esteem – that wonderful moment when she bursts into the room, telling you excitedly, 'I put my vest on all by myself – I did it on my own', says it all.

See also **Playgroup/Nursery, Starting; Self-Confidence**.

Integration, Educational Until the late 1980s, it was assumed that the best way to help a child with special needs was to place him in a segregated 'special' school, where he would mix with other children at the same level of development and with the same sorts of difficulties. The theory underlying this outlook is that the child's needs can best be met in that type of establishment because it has small classes, is staffed by specially trained teachers, and has additional services (for instance, speech therapy) available on site. Yet the wisdom of placing children into segregated special schools, separate from their 'normal' peers, has been challenged. There is now a drive away from segregation towards integration (known as *mainstreaming*, in the USA).

In Britain, The Warnock Report (*Special Educational Needs*), published in 1978, emphasised the need for integration and expressed '*determined opposition to the notion of treating handicapped and non-handicapped children as forming two distinct groups, for whom separate provision has to be made*'.

This report formed the basis of the 1981 Education Act (England and Wales) which specifies that '*where a local education authority arranges special educational provision for a child . . . it shall be the duty of the authority . . . to secure that he is educated in an ordinary school*', subject to the conditions that '*educating the child in an ordinary school is compatible with (a) his receiving the special education provision that he requires; (b) the provision of efficient instruction for the children with whom he will be educated; and (c) the efficient use of resources*'. (This Act applies only to school-age children, but the principles regarding preschool children are the same.)

Integration is not an all-or-none phenomenon: it develops along a continuum. And it does not happen simply because a child with special needs is placed in an ordinary school. There are three levels of integration:

– *locational integration*. Occurs when a child with special needs attends an ordinary school, but where there is very little social contact between him and the rest of the pupils. Some parents are satisfied with this type of provision because it does at least mean that their child attends his local school, albeit in a restricted way. Other parents, however, reject locational integration on the grounds that it is no better than segregated provision.
– *social integration*. Occurs when a child with special needs attends an ordinary school, and where there are planned opportunities for him to mix with the others (e.g., during breaks). Most parents of children with special needs view social integration positively.
– *functional integration*. The fullest level of integration, which occurs when a child with special needs is not only located in an ordinary school and mixes with the pupils, but also joins in the same activities. Functional integration means that a child with special needs participates

fully in school life, just as much as anyone else. This point on the continuum of integration is the most conducive to the child's overall development.

Integration has gained prominence as an educational policy through the increasing awareness that segregated special schools do not *per se* benefit the children who attend them. Indeed, there is evidence that these children are disadvantaged educationally and socially, and that they do not necessarily make greater educational gains than children with special needs who attend their local school. In addition, many parents of children who have attended segregated special schools admit at the end of their child's schooling that, while they have been delighted with the care and professionalism of the school, they are deeply concerned about the child's inability to cope outside. He is so accustomed to daily living in a sheltered environment that he has problems managing independently in society.

Bear in mind that integration can go wrong. A child may be rejected by the other children, and this is likely to make him unhappy and resentful. Even where he does not meet such peer-group barriers, he may find it stressful if, for instance, he is working at activities that are vastly different from those of his classmates. He may regard this as a constant daily reminder of his differences.

Then there are the parents of the other children. Not everyone is sympathetic to the aims of integration. Other parents may become concerned that their own children will lose out because of all the individual attention focused on the child with special needs. They might also be worried that their own children will imitate his less mature behaviour. These potential problems, however, can usually be overcome through sensitive management by school staff. Integration means attending to the needs of all the children, not just to those of the child with special needs.

See also **Cerebral Palsy; Down's Syndrome; Physical Disability; Special Needs**.

Intelligence Many people think of intelligence only in terms of school performance, and judge a child's intellectual ability on the basis of his scores in educational tests and exams. Yet this is a very narrow perspective, because some intelligent children don't do very well at school. From a broader viewpoint, intelligence is a child's ability to make sense of what is going on around him, his ability to adapt to (and cope with) new experiences and his ability to find solutions to novel problems.

There is heated debate over whether intelligence is inherited, or whether it can be affected by the environment. Those who adopt the former view maintain that every individual has a fixed level of intelligence, and therefore should be taught in a school with pupils of the same level of ability. And those who think intelligence can be affected by the environment advocate an educational system which gives every pupil as much stimulation and encouragement as possible, in order to develop his potential to the fullest level.

A psychologist may use an intelligence test to assess a child's intelligence. The test consists of a number of different items which measure intellectual skills such as language, auditory memory, visual memory, comprehension, and speed of information-processing. Once one of these tests has been administered (usually taking one to two hours), an IQ (intelligence quotient) score can be calculated. The average IQ is 100, and around 70 per cent of all children have an IQ lying between 85 and 110. One criticism of intelligence tests is that they are unreal and don't actually indicate how a child will perform in a real-life situation. Another criticism is that the results of an intelligence test don't lead to practical suggestions for helping a child with learning difficulties.

See also **Creativity; Giftedness; Knowledge; Learning Skills**.

J

Jealousy This is such an unpleasant trait, isn't it! It's a mixture of resentment, fear, insecurity, possessiveness and suspicion – not feelings we would willingly admit to. At best, jealousy makes a child unhappy and dissatisfied with what she's got, and at worst it makes her behave in a hurtful way towards someone else. Sometimes feelings of jealousy between children in the same family can be so strong that they last well into adulthood. Many psychologists take the view that children are instinctively selfish and possessive, and so jealousy is shown by every child to some extent; and that development in the pre-school years involves her moving away from thinking only about herself to thinking and caring about others.

Jealousy begins when your baby first realises, usually around the age of six months, that she doesn't have you all to herself all of the time. You may find at this age that she becomes upset when she sees you cuddling another baby, even if you do so for only a few seconds. The brief instant of having to share your attention with another child is enough to make her feel a surge of jealousy. And at six months she will make no attempt to hide this fact from you – she will cry and cry until you put the other baby down and pick her up.

Of course, she becomes more able to handle these feelings as time passes. A growing child learns to cope with this type of jealousy when she eventually realises through experience that your attention towards someone else doesn't detract from your love for her. By the age of two or three years, she probably won't become upset when she sees you with others of her own age.

Your child will inevitably feel jealous at some points in her life, and the following tips will help you and her cope with it:

- *Don't make her feel ashamed of being jealous.* Saying things to her, like 'You should be ashamed of yourself

140

for being jealous', or 'Only nasty children feel jealous like you', will simply make her feel even worse, and then she'll hide her true feelings from you.

- *Let her know that you've been jealous.* There's no harm in admitting to her that there are occasions when you are jealous of other people – but make sure you add that you never let these feelings upset you or spoil your fun. Once she knows that you understand how she feels, she won't be so upset.

- *Accept that jealousy varies from child to child.* Just because your older child is not the jealous type, and is prepared to share her possessions with others, doesn't mean your younger child will be the same. If one of your children does appear to have a jealous nature, try to avoid comparing her with others who appear to be less jealous – that will only make her even more jealous, because it points out to her how disadvantaged she is in comparison with them.

- *Remember that very intense jealousy can be a sign of a child's deeper anxieties.* Constant jealousy may be a symptom of deep-rooted insecurity and a lack of confidence. If your child feels this way, try to identify the underlying cause.

See also **Age Gap; Birth Order; Equality; First-Born Jealousy; Sibling Rivalry**.

Jokes   Listen to some children's jokes – e.g. 'What did the big chimney say to the little chimney?' 'You're too young to smoke!' – and you'll probably find it hard to believe that these are the early signs of a more sophisticated adult sense of humour. Yet the foundation of the ability to see the funny side of things is laid down in the pre-school years.

A baby will probably show her first smile around the age of six weeks. This is usually in response to a familiar face smiling at her, but it is also the first sign of the psychological mechanism by which a child can derive amusement from her environment. As she grows older, different jokes make her laugh, although what amuses a young child depends entirely on the individual concerned – anyone who tries to make a living out of entertaining groups of youngsters at parties will confirm this!

Children around the age of 18–24 months typically enjoy jokes which involve familiar objects used in an unusual way: for example, when dad sticks teddy up his jumper. It is the incongruity of the situation that makes the child laugh. By the age of three or four years, a child's greater use of language means that she now prefers jokes involving words rather than objects, although it is not always clear to an adult what exactly she finds amusing. And even at this age, she'll still chuckle merrily at the sight of a custard pie being thrown in someone's face.

The more subtle the joke is, then the harder it will be for a child to identify the humorous aspect, even though her ability to laugh at jokes is not directly connected to her level of intelligence. Indeed, every child is capable of laughter, irrespective of her intelligence. A sense of humour is, after all, one of the characteristics that differentiate humans from animals.

See also **Intelligence**.

K

Kibbutz This type of communal farming or industrial settlement, found in rural Israel, has always attracted the attention of child psychologists because of the unique way in which the children of the kibbutz members are raised. Although the precise method of childcare varies from kibbutz to kibbutz (and nowadays, systems tend to be very flexible), the traditional method has been to place the children in a nursery on the kibbutz, both day and night, in order to free their parents for full-time work. The children play together, eat together, and sleep in communal dormitories each night, and are looked after by specialist childcare staff. They return to their parents' houses at weekends and holidays.

One of the interesting findings to emerge from research studies on kibbutz children is that they still tend to form a close emotional connection with their parents, and not with the childcare workers with whom they spend most of their time. This probably occurs because the time that the children spend with their natural parents is highly valued by all of them.

Another psychological effect of children being brought up in a large group on a kibbutz is that they have an unusually strong community spirit. They are more able to get on with each other than would normally be expected, and are more willing to support one another through personal crisis. This social bond and a sense of community often persists throughout life. Statisticians point out that although only 7 per cent of Israel's army during the 1973 war were kibbutz-raised, 90 per cent of those killed were from that group, suggesting that they had a greater determination compared with others in the army, as well as better leadership qualities.

See also **Bonding; Quality Time; Social Development**.

Kindness Human beings have an inborn tendency to be kind to others. You only need to look at very young children

to see evidence of this. For instance, when a new baby hears another baby cry, he bursts out crying himself (and psychologists have also proved that he cries more in response to a human cry than he does to a computer-generated cry). This suggests that babies, even at a very early stage of their development, are sufficiently concerned about other people's distress to become upset themselves by it.

This inclination to be considerate becomes clearer as the pre-school years unfold. By the age of 12 months, an infant no longer cries when he hears someone else cry, but instead will have a troubled look on his face; and by the age of 15 months he will probably go over to a crying child or adult, in order to offer a comforting cuddle. A typical three-year-old will take positive action to help someone in distress – for example, by giving his crying friend a teddy to cuddle.

So what happens in the years between childhood and adulthood to transform us into the inconsiderate individuals we see all around us each day? Perhaps this change occurs as parents – and schools – encourage children to carve a niche for themselves, to compete against each other for first place. Often, success in these circumstances can only be achieved at the expense of others. In such an atmosphere, a child's innate tendency to show kindness and consideration is gradually pushed into second place in preference to self-interest. It's almost as if children are taught how not to be caring.

Yet it's just as easy to teach a child how to be kind to others as it is to teach him how to think only of himself. All it takes is a little bit of careful thought, preparation and self-awareness.

Your child models himself on you – that's why he shares your attitudes, behaviour and mannerisms. So stop for a minute, and consider how you behave in front of him. You can't expect him to care for other people if you don't. This does not mean that you should be gushingly loving all the time, but it does mean you should be seen to treat children with respect. Your individual acts of consideration will motivate your child to behave in a caring manner towards his peers.

Aside from scrutinising your own attitudes and behaviour, there are direct strategies for teaching children to be more caring. One simple method is based on the elementary principle that children learn to be helpful by being helpful – in other words, practical involvement in caring for others increases a child's tendency to be caring. Your child can be given caring responsibility at home in so many different ways. Assigning him a few daily chores (e.g., helping to clear the cups and plates after a snack, tidying away his crayons at the end of the morning) gently directs him towards caring behaviour; even though he may not be keen to do any of these things to start with, he will probably enjoy such tasks eventually if he persists with them.

However, some children are unwilling to become involved with any helping task, because they tend to be selfish. Role play is an effective way of overcoming this barrier. A small group of children (even as young as three years) can act out a basic scenario in which some of them pretend to be in need of help, while the others pretend to be the helpers – and then they can reverse the roles. The effect of this type of role play is more intense when children are encouraged to talk about what happened during it, and to talk about the feelings they experienced when playing the different roles. Role play can also be used to help children understand what it is like to experience bullying; this may encourage more positive behaviour in the playground and in other unsupervised play situations.

Another useful way of teaching kindness and consideration to a young child is by asking him to explain to another child (his own age or younger) how to be caring. This task of 'tutor' benefits the learner *and* the tutor, probably because it forces them both to think about the reasoning underlying their actions.

See also **Bullying; Modelling; Sociable Play**.

Knowledge   A young child is like a scientist – she gathers knowledge by exploring the world around her, making one new discovery after another. And this process, which starts when she is born and continues endlessly throughout her childhood, is a constant source of excitement for her. It involves her actively using movement, vision, hearing, taste and touch in an increasingly sophisticated way to explore her surroundings. Through this process she gains knowledge about herself, her skills and abilities, and about the world.

Your baby is pre-programmed at birth to gain knowledge through discovery. Proof of this comes from research which shows that babies are born with an impressive range of sensory and perceptual skills, enabling them to interact with their environment by various means:

– *vision*. Research findings demonstrate that, within hours of birth, a baby can differentiate her mother's face from that of a stranger; and another study revealed that when a baby as young as nine minutes is shown a picture of a normal face and a picture of a mixed-up face (i.e. the eyes are where the nose should be and so forth), she looks more closely at the normal face, indicating her preference for it. A newborn can also discriminate red, green, yellow and blue, and can see the difference between drawings of a triangle, cross, circle and square.
– *grasping*. Place your finger in the palm of your newborn baby's hand and you'll find that her fingers encircle it in a grasp that is so tight that you may be able to pull her to a sitting or standing position.

146

- *reaching*. A newborn reaches out purposefully for objects placed in front of her, although her hand may be closed by the time it makes contact with the object. In one study, young babies wore special goggles which presented the illusion of a reachable object. The investigators found that the babies reached for the illusion (proving that they expected it to be there), and then cried when they discovered they couldn't grab hold of it.
- *touch and balance*. Soon after birth, a baby reacts differently to the touch of brush hairs of different thicknesses. She will also respond to puffs of air which even an adult has difficulty in detecting. Although she doesn't have a well developed sense of balance, she will become sick if spun round rapidly (say, on a roundabout), and she'll try to right her head if placed in an awkward position.
- *taste and smell*. New babies make distinct facial expressions when they experience sweet, sour and bitter tastes, and these expressions match those of adults experiencing the same tastes. A sense of smell is also present soon after birth; a baby makes a positive expression when smelling a fruit odour, and an expression of disgust when smelling fishy odours. Research has also shown that a newborn will turn towards the smell of her own mother's breast pad but not towards the smell of a breast pad from someone else.
- *hearing*. A newborn baby cries at the sound of another baby's cries, but stops when she hears a tape-recording of her own cries, suggesting she can tell one cry from another. She also prefers the sound of a human voice to any other type of sound, and has a particular preference for her mother's voice. A newborn baby can also discriminate between the noise of a buzzer and the noise of a rattle.

With all these elementary inborn skills, your young baby is ready to start immediately on her never-ending quest to extend her knowledge. Although many of her reactions are automatic at first, within a few months she will explore toys and other objects more purposefully.

Her strategies for discovery change with age and experience. For instance, she will develop different forms of hand grasp once she has had the opportunity to handle different shapes; she will learn to look at different parts of an object rather than look at the whole thing; and her hand-eye movements will become better coordinated. The more she tries to extend her knowledge, the more sophisticated and elaborate her discovery skills become.

Jean Piaget, a Swiss psychologist, was the first to propose a comprehensive theory about the way children acquire knowledge of the world around them. His theory is based on four stages of development:

- *sensori-motor period (birth to 18 months)*. In this early phase, an infant uses overt behaviour – such as sucking, licking, touching, grasping, smelling – to learn about objects with which she comes into contact. This is a time of continual exploration and discovery.
- *pre-operational period (2–7 years)* A child at this stage has the ability to use one object to represent another, and this means she can engage in symbolic play; she can also use language, which is simply a system of shared symbols that allows people to communicate knowledge and ideas to each other. Drawings become possible, because she can represent her ideas on paper.
- *concrete operational period (7–11 years)*. Now a child is able to organise her thoughts, ideas and information in a more logical way. She can cope with more complex numerical operations, such as addition, subtraction, multiplication and division, and she uses these to gain a deeper knowledge of the way things work. A child of this age can also reason out general principles from specific incidents in her own experience.
- *formal operational period (12 years +)*. At this stage of development, a child can extend her reasoning skills to objects and situations that she hasn't seen or experienced first-hand. Problem-solving skills are more advanced, and she is more able to take another person's perspective.

See also **Concentration; Imagination; Intelligence; Language Development; Learning Skills; Play**.

L

Language Development It's amazing that children all develop language in the same way, progressing through the same stages in the same order. (Bear in mind that the suggested ages are only approximate, and that normally there are wide individual variations between children.) At each stage, the infant uses language in a new and more sophisticated format:

- *cooing*. This stage begins around the age of eight weeks, and then disappears some 12 weeks later. Although at times a baby's cooing sounds like words, it has no meaning whatsoever.
- *babbling (random)*. By the age of five months, an infant's vocal chords have matured to the point where she can begin to experiment with pitch, voice range and breathing, in order to produce a range of different sounds. Every child has her own distinctive patterns of noises at this age, and she uses them to communicate with any adult who pays attention to her. Psychologists have found that infants tend to produce the same kinds of babbling sounds, irrespective of their parents' native language.
- *babbling (controlled)*. In the next couple of months, an infant gains more control over her sounds. Babbling becomes more conversational, and her sounds become related to the language used by her parents. She may repeat strings of sounds (e.g., 'lalalalalala'), and may have a favourite sound which she uses consistently in the same situation.
- *early speech*. Towards the end of her first year, an infant begins to use her sounds as if she is engaging in conversation. She may have an earnest expression on her face, and make sounds using tones and emphasis found in adult speech.
- *first word*. By the age of 12–15 months a child will probably have used her first word – i.e., she regularly uses a

particular sound-structure to refer to the same object or the same person. Very often this first word is intelligible only to people who know her, but it is her first word all the same.

- *vocabulary growth*. From the age of 15 months onwards, an infant's vocabulary increases spectacularly. Many two-year-olds are able to use upwards of 200 words (while understanding a lot more).

- *sentences*. By 18–21 months, a typical toddler begins to combine two words together to make a short phrase or sentences: e.g., 'Dada gone' or 'More juice'. From this moment on, throughout the remaining childhood years, her ability to use sentences with more words and more complex meanings continues to increase.

This similarity amongst children in terms of stages in the growth of language has enabled psychologists to plot key 'milestones' of language development – i.e., significant points that most children pass at about the same age. The following milestones should be regarded only as a guide, but will help you to judge your child's progress:

1 month   A one-month-old baby will respond to words directed at her, by turning to the source. She will try to synchronise her sounds with those of an adult talking to her, and she is able to make a range of cries, each of which indicates something different.

3 months   She begins to listen more closely when she hears noises; for instance, when a bell gently rings, she will become quiet and attend to it. She can probably make at least two distinct sounds, such as 'goo' and 'la', and will enjoy listening to music.

6 months   Her babbling sounds are consistent. She can produce at least four different sounds, and can accurately turn her head towards the source of sound. Listening to music may cause a change in her mood.

9 months   Place a ticking watch beside your child's ear and she will immediately turn round to look at it. She will use two-syllable babbles, such as 'alah' or 'egeh'; her first word may appear at this age (usually 'mama' or 'dada').

150

1 year	She may be able to use up to three clear words, and will be able to follow very basic directions. Hearing is usually sharp at this age. Your child will talk to herself when playing on her own or when she is concentrating on a game or toy.
15 months	Although she can't say her own name, she'll recognise it when someone else uses it. She will respond to basic commands, such as 'Leave it alone', and will try to join in with familiar songs and rhymes.
18 months	Your child's vocabulary will be at least a dozen words (though probably a lot more), which she uses properly. However, she can understand more words than she can say. She is able to use language to communicate her basic needs.
21 months	She now uses an increased range of single words, and may begin to combine them to form two-word phrases or sentences, such as 'Mummy car' or 'want sweet'. She can also identify familiar objects if shown them in a picture book.
2 years	A child of this age seems obsessed with people's names, and constantly asks what someone is called. She can use a lot more words now (possibly even hundreds), and when asked to identify certain body parts, she can reliably show hair, eyes, nose, mouth and feet.
3 years	She talks confidently in three- or four-word sentences, and may, for the first time, use adjectives in her speech. She loves having her favourite story read to her. The number of 'who', 'what', 'when', 'how', and 'why' questions increases.
4 years	She now has a broad vocabulary, which includes pronouns and adjectives. Nursery rhymes are very popular, and she may be able to identify several basic colours. She will also be able to give a reasonably accurate account of a recent experience.
5 years	At this stage of development, a child is able to speak clearly and has little difficulty making herself understood to other children and adults.

Most five-year-olds can give their first name, their last name, and their address, when asked.

See also **Hearing Assessment; Hearing Loss; Language Difficulties; Language Learning; Language Stimulation; Questions.**

Language Difficulties There is so much variation in the rate at which children acquire speech that slow progress in language growth at the toddler stage is often within the limits of normal development. However, the situation becomes worrying if the gap in language skills between one child and others of his own age persists beyond the age of three years. If you suspect your child's use of language is delayed – and you have had his hearing tested properly – then ask your GP to refer him to an educational psychologist or to a speech and language therapist.

Speech and language therapists are specially trained in human communication skills and are able to identify and treat problems with speech and language. At the initial visit, the therapist will assess many aspects of a child's language development (e.g., articulation, use of grammar, listening ability, concentration), using both observation and formal assessment techniques. Having diagnosed the difficulty in this way, the therapist will then decide on a suitable course of treatment. For a younger child, this might mean a series of language games which can be integrated into his play routines without any special arrangements. Older children may be seen regularly for speech therapy, either in a small group or in a one-to-one situation at the local clinic. Parents are always expected to give full support to the treatment plan.

A child with a language disorder – particularly in the preschool years – is prone to tantrums. This occurs because his inability to communicate his feelings and wishes gives him a strong sense of frustration, which he can only release through temper. He has no other way to express his annoyance. Parents often find that their previously frustrated child becomes more settled once he can use language more effectively.

A child may have a speech difficulty, even though all other areas of his development are satisfactory. In such

152

cases, the speech difficulty is the child's sole problem and either clears up spontaneously, or else responds to help from a speech therapist. Minor speech difficulties include:

- *lisping*. A child often develops a lisp in the early years. He begins to make letter substitutes, such as 'the' for 's', 'f' for 'th', and so on. Fortunately, these speech patterns pass as he matures, usually by the time he reaches school. A child may acquire a temporary lisp when his first teeth begin to fall out. A lisp can also be caused by misuse of the tongue, or by a cleft palate. Speech therapy can help this condition.

- *mispronunciation*. Learning to speak takes time, and making mistakes is part of the learning process. Many children experience difficulty with certain sounds, causing their speech to become unclear. Again, this defect usually disappears spontaneously. However, if your child's speech is still unclear by the time he is nearing school age, then speech therapy may be required.

- *inadequate stimulation*. Speech development partly depends on a child's interaction with others in his family. By listening to others talking to him, he develops an interest in language. But some children lack this essential stimulation. The remedy for this is lots of individual attention using discussions, stories, songs and poems.

- *stammering/stuttering*. With this defect, a child talks very hesitantly, perhaps repeating the first letter or first part of a word several times. Many children in the early stages of language acquisition develop some form of stutter, probably because there is so much they want to say all at once. This temporary form of speech impediment clears up as a child becomes more confident in his use of language. When talking with a stuttering child, never make fun of him, never imitate him, and never become impatient with him. Speech therapy can help stutterers gain more control over their speech.

More serious speech and language difficulties can involve:

- *general developmental delay*. With this problem, a child will also be slow in other aspects of development, such as learning to walk, learning bladder control, becoming independent, and learning to socialise with other children. The earlier this type of difficulty is detected, the sooner the child will be able to receive help to stimulate his development.

- *hearing loss*. The most frequent cause of serious language difficulties, since adequate hearing is crucial for a child to learn language – if he can't hear the sounds of speech, then he won't be able to reproduce them in his own speech. A child referred to a speech and language therapist will always undergo a hearing assessment as well.
- *autism*. An autistic child uses language in a bizarre way, such that normal communication with him is not possible. In addition to social and emotional difficulties, he has delayed language development and impaired comprehension. Treatment for this condition is usually a multi-professional approach, in a special school setting.
- *brain damage*. Specific areas of the brain are responsible for specific functions, and if the areas responsible for language is damaged, then the child will have a language difficulty. The seriousness and extent of the problem depends on the degree of brain damage that has occurred.
- *severe articulation disorders*. A child may have problems in actually producing speech sounds, even though he may know what he wants to say and how it should sound. Mild articulation errors are a normal part of development: e.g., many young children miss out parts of words (saying 'at' for 'cat', or 'do' for 'dog'), or may substitute one sound for another (saying 'toat' for 'coat' or 'foon' for 'spoon'). However, severe articulation disorders lasting well beyond the age of five may render an older child's language totally incomprehensible. Speech and language therapy is appropriate in this instance.

See also **Autism; Cerebral Palsy; Hearing Assessment; Hearing Loss; Language Development; Language Learning; Language Stimulation**.

Language Learning Spoken language is a child's main means of communication. Of course, a baby is able to communicate his feelings and desires non-verbally, long before he can speak. For instance, when a new baby cries, his parents know there is something troubling him, and when he smiles, they know he is happy. It is at around the age of two months, though, that his desire to communicate verbally emerges – when he starts cooing (happy, gurgling sounds) – and it continues from then on.

One of the most remarkable features of language development in the pre-school years is that it takes place at all! Think about it for a moment. Suppose you were a native French-speaker and you had to learn English. There are thousands of words to be remembered, seemingly endless grammatical rules (for which there are so many exceptions), and a long list of words with more than one meaning. Then there are words which sound the same but have different spelling patterns (e.g., their/there), and words which have similar spelling patterns but yet sound different (e.g., cough/ bough). You would probably think it an impossible task – yet most young children manage to cope without any special help.

That's why most psychologists claim that the ability to learn language is innate, that babies are pre-programmed to recognise certain types of words and grammatical structures when they hear them. This does not mean, of course, that the child's environment is unimportant: on the contrary, a child who is raised in a family with a low level of language stimulation will probably have a limited range of speech himself. And a child who is raised by English-speaking parents learns to speak English, a child raised by French-speaking parents learns to speak French, and so on. The environment, therefore, does play a part in language development.

The best way to view the growth of language skills is in terms of an interaction between a child's inborn ability and the environment in which he is raised. Each affects the other, and the combined effects determine the level and quality of a child's speech

See also **Body Language; Hearing Assessment; Hearing Loss; Language Development; Language Difficulties; Language Stimulation; Questions**.

Language Stimulation At every age, you can stimulate your child's language development. Some parents feel

155

embarrassed talking to their baby, because she can't respond verbally. Yet talking to your baby is important because it

- *will encourage her interest in language*, even though she can't understand what you say. And she'll begin to imitate some of the sounds you make.
- *promotes communication*. Slow-motion replays of filmed mother-baby interactions reveal that a baby appears to fit her vocalisations into the gaps between her mother's sentences, almost as if she's listening to what is being said and then replying to it. Talking to a baby, therefore, involves her in this pre-speech 'conversation'.
- *ensures your close attention* – this shows her that language has positive dimensions.

Many mothers use 'motherese' when talking to their baby – i.e., they speak slowly, in exaggerated tones, using short sentences with clear gaps between the words. Recent research has proved that a baby will pay closer attention to an adult speaking to her in motherese than to one speaking to her in a normal style, so it's worthwhile adopting some of these qualities in your speech when talking to your baby. But this doesn't mean you should use 'baby talk'. Your child has as much chance of understanding the meaning of the word 'dog' as she has of understanding the word 'bow-wow' – baby talk has no advantage over normal words.

To encourage your baby's language development:

- *Name everyday objects involved in her regular routine.* When you dress her, for example, tell her what you are doing ('This is your jumper', 'Here is your milk').
- *When she makes sounds, give a response.* For instance, if she makes a cooing, gurgling noise, you might say, 'Good, you seem to be happy today.' And use lots of facial expressions when talking to her.
- *Play action rhymes that are basic and that physically involve her.* Elementary rhymes such as 'Round and round the garden' or 'This little piggy' will have her chuckling with delight.

One of your main aims at the toddler stage should be to improve your child's listening skills. This can be achieved in two ways. First, listen to her when she talks to you – if you don't, she will have no incentive to use speech. Second, encourage her to listen to you – when you give her instruc-

156

tions (e.g., 'Please come over here'), make sure that she acts on them, even if she appears to ignore you.

Broaden your child's use of words, grammar and sentence structure, by means of the following strategies:

- *Don't constantly correct her speech mistakes.* While there is no harm in doing so occasionally, continually harping on about errors will reduce her self-confidence and may make her reluctant to talk at all.
- *Model appropriate language.* For instance, she might say, 'More juice', to which you could reply, 'I can see you would like to have some more juice.' This provides a model for your child to imitate and is quite different from correcting her.
- *Use the same language in different contexts.* For instance, she will learn the significance of 'on' more quickly if you say, 'I'm sitting on a chair', 'Your biscuit is on the plate', 'Your toy is on the floor', rather than using it in one context only.

Try these activities:

- *Ask her to give an account of something that has just happened.* This forces her to concentrate, to recall details of a previous experience, and to find the words to describe it to you.
- *Play lots of word games with her.* She will still enjoy action rhymes and songs, singing along with you, and may be able to recite a simple nursery rhyme. Let her listen to songs and music – she will probably want to join in when she hears a familiar tune.
- *Let her look at picture books.* This is a marvellous way of increasing her vocabulary, while at the same time developing her early reading skills. Children of this age love to hear the same story read over and over again.

Between three and five years, your child's language becomes even more sophisticated. Now, she chatters away endlessly and asks you lots of questions, which you should try to answer at a level appropriate to her age and understanding. And remember that every child should be given plenty of opportunities to speak. Family life is hectic, and you may have more than one child eager to have her say. But each needs a chance to express her thoughts, not just the talkative ones. So make sure the quiet child also tells you her news, no matter how many others want to speak ahead of her.

These activities will encourage your pre-school child's language:

- *Teach her useful concepts, such as colour, shape and size.* Pick one concept at a time (e.g., colour) and work on this for a few weeks. Begin with matching activities: e.g., 'Which one of these blocks is the same colour as the jumper you're wearing?'; then sorting activities: e.g., 'Put blocks of the same colour in the same pile'; then identification activities: e.g., 'Find me all the green blocks'; and lastly, naming activities: e.g., 'What colour is this?'
- *Play memory games with her.* For instance, bring out a tray with perhaps a dozen common objects on it (ball, scissors, pencil, doll, spoon etc.). Tell her you will take the tray away, and that she has to remember as many as she can. After two minutes, cover the tray with a cloth – then ask her to tell you the objects she can recall.
- *Watch a children's television programme together and then talk about it.* Most programmes broadcast specifically for children can help broaden a child's world because they can give her access to events she may not have experienced herself (e.g., a visit to a factory). And she will derive more benefit if you spend a few minutes discussing the programme's content with her.

See also **Hearing Assessment; Hearing Loss; Language Development; Language Difficulties; Language Learning; Questions**.

Learning Skills Your child's learning skills change frequently during the pre-school years, each stage allowing her new ways to learn about her environment (the following ages are only approximate):

0–1 month   Most of your baby's responses are reflexes – e.g., she turns her head towards anything that gently touches her cheek, she sucks automatically when a nipple is placed in her mouth, her toes fan out when the outside of the sole of her foot is scratched, she grasps any slim object placed in her palm. But she soon learns from experience how to modify these reflex responses.

1–4 months   She no longer gazes passively, but looks around her more purposefully and makes specific responses to specific objects – e.g., smiling at a familiar face. She repeats basic actions involving parts of her body, such as thumb-sucking or twiddling her fingers.

4–9 months   Her explorations continue but now they are directed towards objects other than herself. You may find, for instance, that she becomes determined to whack the mobile dangling above her, or that she tries to hit the activity centre attached to the side of her cot. Reaching out and grasping is more frequent at this stage.

9–12 months   Now your infant can combine two or more strategies in order to make more discoveries. She will, for instance, be able to knock away a cushion which conceals her favourite toy; and when she has done that once, she will be able to apply this same strategy to any similar situation confronting her.

12–18 months   Experimentation is the order of the day, as your child tries out new ways of playing with objects. For example, she may slowly push her spoon off the high-chair, then hit it away quickly, then drop it gently off the side, and so on, each time finding new ways of making the spoon hit the ground. She's not being naughty – just naturally inquisitive. Her ability to walk means she can venture further than before.

18–24 months   At this age, your toddler begins to develop the ability to use symbolism, which means she can now use one object to represent another. This is a completely new skill which opens up a vast array of play opportunities. A building brick can 'become' a dog, and a doll can 'become' mum or dad.

In the remaining pre-school years, these learning skills

expand and develop further. But until the age of five or six, a child's thought processes continue to be significantly different from those of an older child, in two main ways.

First, a pre-school child tends to be egocentric (i.e., she can only see things from her own perspective), and she may not realise that there are other ways of viewing situations. Try this: sit your child at one end of a table, so that she faces her favourite teddy, which is positioned in a chair at the opposite end. Put, for example, a ball and a building brick side by side – exactly in the middle of the table – with the ball nearest to your child and the brick nearest to the teddy. Then ask her, 'What toy does teddy see first? The ball or the brick?' If she is still egocentric, she will tell you that her teddy sees the ball first – because this is what she herself sees.

This limitation on a young child's learning skills means that you have a better chance of getting her to understand something when you explain it to her in personal terms. Psychologists have found that young children understand sentences in which their own name occurs more easily than equally complex sentences without their names. So remember to include your child's name when explaining something to her.

The second characteristic of the learning skills of a child under the age of five or six is that she tends to focus on one part of a problem only. Try this: show your child two drinking glasses, one short and fat, the other tall and thin, but each capable of holding the same amount of liquid. Fill one of the glasses with water. Let her see you pour the water from this glass into the other, and then ask, 'Which glass had the most water?' She will probably focus on the height of the glass and tell you that the tall glass had more water in it than the fat glass did. Only when she is five or six will she realise that although the glass is taller, it is also thinner.

Your child's learning skills expand and develop naturally, but you can nonetheless encourage the process along in the following ways:

- *Make sure she has plenty of opportunities to practise her learning skills.* She can explore and discover without your help, but her curiosity will be increased by interesting surroundings, such as an attractive mobile above her cot, a colourful array of teething rings and rattles, and a varied range of toys, games and books.

- *Get involved!* Your child will derive much more enjoyment from exploratory play if you are involved and if you look as if you're enjoying yourself. This doesn't mean you should take over – in fact, you should definitely not do that. But she will be more interested if you are with her, giving her your attention and encouragement.
- *Give her lots of repetition.* Just because your child has completed a jigsaw once doesn't mean that you need to give her a new one the next time; she'll discover something new every time she solves the same jigsaw. So encourage her to play with toys more than once.
- *Show by example.* Of course, she wants to discover things by herself, but sometimes she needs a helping hand. So if she's struggling to fit a shape into the shape-sorter, don't be afraid to show her how to do it – though make sure you don't do this all the time.
- *Don't push too hard.* The important point to remember, when choosing a toy to encourage your child's learning skills, is to pick one that is at a higher level of complexity than the ones she has, but that isn't so complex that she'll quickly give up trying. She will make progress gradually, step by step.
- *Set limits when you have to.* Much as your child would like to go exploring wherever she wants, to touch whatever attracts her attention, and to discover the qualities of the most fragile objects, you have to set down some rules about what she can and can't do. Explain clearly that certain objects, or areas of the house, are out of bounds, and redirect her interest elsewhere.

See also **Concentration; Knowledge; Learning through Play; Play; Playing with Your Child**.

Learning through Play Play and learning are connected in three ways. First, learning can occur directly through play. In exploratory play, for instance, a child deliberately manipulates a toy in order to find out its qualities. This type of play allows him to discover aspects of his immediate environment. And in play with such things as jigsaws, form-boards and matching activities, he learns skills associated with solving problems.

Second, learning occurs incidentally through play. A typical six-month-old will want to play with any toy given to him. And while he is discovering how to play with it, he will probably put it in his mouth, bite it, lick it, smell it, and even bounce it off the wall. Although the infant's main attention is to play with the toy, these subsidiary actions teach him incidentally about texture, shape, weight, size, etc. And this incidental component of learning has a major influence on a child's learning ability, particularly in the first few years of life when exploratory play is most common.

Third, learning occurs instrumentally when, for instance, while playing, children are suddenly faced with a particular problem that they have to solve before their play can continue (e.g., learning how to climb a tree in order to look out for enemy pirates).

The following guidelines will help you choose suitable toys for stimulating your child's learning ability through play:

6 months   He will enjoy playing with rattles, activity centres and small toys that he can pick up in his hands – but they must not be *too* small, because at this age an infant still tends to put toys in his mouth. He will try hard to get hold of an object that is put just outside his reach.

12 months   A child of this age can imitate adult actions (such as banging two small wooden bricks together to make a loud noise). He will be fascinated by any object that rattles. Put a couple of wooden beads inside a small box, and shake it – he is likely to open the box in order to find out what's inside. This type of activity stimulates a child's interest in puzzles.

18 months   He will begin to show an interest in elementary form-boards. Most good toy shops sell form-boards with just one or two shapes in them. If an adult demonstrates to him how the shapes fit into the board, he may then be able to imitate this action.

2 years   He enjoys stacking building bricks, one on top of the other; he may be able to build a tower

	of up to six or seven bricks before it falls over. And he will enjoy playing with a set of plastic toy barrels, the type that come in two halves that have to be fitted together and then fit inside one another in a fixed sequence.
3 years	His interest in form-boards (with up to seven or eight pieces in them now) and jigsaws (with up to four pieces) continues. Games in which he has to sort objects (e.g., building bricks) according to colour, size or shape may attract his attention – and broaden his learning skills at the same time.
4 years	Jigsaws with up to 20 pieces often fascinate a child of this age. He will also benefit from using crayons and paper, and his drawings of 'mum' or 'dad' will probably include details such as eyes, hair, hands or mouth.

See also **Gender Play; Knowledge; Learning Skills; Play; Playing with Your Child**.

Left-Handedness   We live in a 'right-handed' world. Since most people use their right hand for manual tasks (e.g., opening doors, cutting with a knife, using a pair of scissors, lifting a cup), we tend to forget that this doesn't apply to everyone. Yet around 1 boy in 10, and 1 girl in 12, is left-handed.

Hand preference is not present at birth. When a baby starts to explore the world with his hands, he will show no preference for one over the other and will be able to use them with equal competence. It is only towards the end of the second year that toddlers begin to develop hand preference, although you may find that even at this age your child will use one hand for months at a time, then switch comfortably to the other. Hand dominance is usually firmly established, however, by the age of three or four. Some children remain ambidextrous throughout their life.

Psychologists are unable to say whether left-handedness is innate or whether it is learned. There is evidence to support both points of view. Parents who are concerned about their child's possible left-handedness can gently encourage him – up to the age of 12 or 15 months – to use his right hand. But this does not mean pressurising him into using his right hand all the time. Rather, it means providing opportunities for him to use his right hand – for example, by handing things to his right side. If he appears agitated or uneasy about it, allow him to use whichever hand he feels more comfortable with. After the age of 12 to 15 months, the choice of hand should definitely rest with the toddler.

The significance of left-handedness must be kept in proper perspective. True, being left-handed can make life a little difficult for a young child, especially when he is trying to learn new manual skills such as cutting and sewing, or when he is learning new sports such as racquet games. But it is not a handicap; it is not something that parents should lose sleep worrying about. A child learns to adapt to his world, whether he is left-handed, right-handed or ambidextrous.

Never force your child to use his right hand when his left one is dominant. This could cause difficulties in other areas of development, since hand preference is controlled by the same part of the brain that is responsible for speech, writing and reading. Forcing a left-handed child to use his right hand may result in problems when he starts learning to read, and can be linked to stuttering. Furthermore, undue emphasis on making a child use his right hand will only lead to confrontation and will reduce his self-confidence.

A left-handed child will have difficulty learning to cut with a pair of scissors, since standard scissors are made to fit on to the right hand, not the left. Fortunately, left-handed scissors can be purchased from most educational suppliers, and every nursery class and school should have at least a couple of pairs readily available. Aside from making life easier for the child, this strategy will help him achieve success. And there is no greater boost to self-esteem than that.

The idea that left-handed children are likely to do less well at reading is a complete myth. Reading surveys have confirmed that there is no difference in reading scores between children who are left-handed and children who are right-handed. (The only instance where left-handedness and reading problems can be linked is where a left-handed child has been forced to use his right hand from an early age.)

Learning to write is the biggest hurdle for left-handed pupils to overcome. English writing patterns, going from left to right, favour a right-handed pupil because they involve movements that are natural for that hand preference. A left-handed pupil learning to write faces a number of difficulties:

- *smudging*. His hand holding the pencil moves across the words after he writes them, which (if it's a soft pencil) can smudge the writing – fountain pens and felt-tip pens are therefore not suitable for him.
- *blocking*. While writing, he can't see everything that he has already written because the hand he continues to write with conceals part of the page.
- *awkward direction*. Whereas a right-handed child sweeps the pencil across the page from left to right, a left-handed child has to push it across; this is not an easy task – rather like pushing a rake across a lawn instead of pulling it.
- *cramped position*. A left-handed writer has to hold his arm closer to his body when writing than a right-handed person. This is an unnatural pose for a left-handed child and he may feel restricted. He would be much happier writing from right to left – that's why left-handed children have a head-start when writing languages in which the words go in the opposite direction – e.g., Hebrew.

When teaching writing to a left-handed child, observe these basic principles:

- *Suggest to him that he holds the pencil a little further away from the tip than right-handed children do*. This will give him a clearer view of written work as it is completed.
- *Make sure he does not imitate his right-handed classmates by pointing the pencil in the same direction as they do*. He may want to do this because he does not want to be different – but his pencil should follow the line of direction of the arm that he is writing with.
- *Encourage him to find a comfortable seating position for writing*. He should be allowed to swivel his body slightly to the right if he feels more comfortable in that position.
- *Don't give him a very sharp pencil*. When he pushes it across the page, the point is liable to catch in the paper and snap off.
- *Discourage him from using a fountain pen or a felt-tip*

pen. Apart from the fact that his writing will be instantly smudged, his shirt cuff will be smeared with ink.

Left-handedness need not be a source of difficulty for a developing child, and he will cope well as long as the adults around him show some understanding. A sense of humour also helps – as one child replied when asked which hand he ate his cornflakes with, 'None. I use a spoon!'

See also **School Readiness; Self-Confidence**.

Lying If you ever catch your two-year-old in the middle of an act of destruction, the chances are that she'll deny doing it – even though both you and she know she has been caught red-handed! Most toddlers will deny misbehaving in these circumstances, either because they genuinely wish they hadn't committed the offence (and at this age children have difficulty distinguishing fantasy from reality), or because they know they are in deep trouble and just want to get out of it any way they can.

Yet this isn't lying, in the true sense of the word. A child should only be accused of lying when she is able to tell right from wrong, and when she deliberately tries to conceal or distort the truth – these two features are not usually present in very young children. (Of course, this doesn't mean that mischief and misbehaviour should be ignored by parents – but they should be kept in perspective.) By the age of three or four, however, a child begins to develop moral awareness and has the ability to tell lies.

Studies of child development have established two important principles:

– *Every child is capable of lying, depending on the circumstances*. Most children will try to hide their wrong-doings if they think the consequences of discovery will be very unpleasant. (Be reassured, however, that there is no evidence to suggest that a child who tells lies will grow up to be a fraudster.)
– *A child who is too frightened of confessing will make even more of an effort to justify her initial lie*. If you severely punish your child every time you think she has told a lie, she will soon learn to become a better liar in order to avoid the inevitable consequences. Strike

166

a balance between being too punitive and too lenient. Smacking her for telling lies only encourages her to lie even more, because her fear of discovery becomes even greater.

Not all childhood lies involve concealment. A child might, for instance, tell greatly exaggerated stories about how well she's getting on at school, or how much the other children want to play with her. This type of bragging isn't lying, though – it is more likely to be a sign of lack of confidence. Don't ridicule your child for telling this sort of boastful tale – in this situation, she will benefit more from your support and attempts to boost her confidence than she will from your mockery or reprimands.

There is also the make-believe lie – often a normal part of imaginative play – in which a child embellishes her everyday experiences with fantasy. So don't be alarmed when your four-year-old insists she was chased by a monster; she's just trying to make her life more interesting. She'll grow out of it within a few years.

Your child models much of her own behaviour on yours – that's why if you tell lies in front of her, the chances are she'll do the same sometimes. Although you probably don't tell lies as a matter of course, you may occasionally be guilty of 'white lies', those little untruths designed to protect other people's feelings (e.g., when you told your mother-in-law you liked that horrible vase she brought you back from holiday, or when you completely forgot an appointment and later gave the excuse that you were unwell). Don't be surprised when your child imitates this – only she won't be able to tell the difference between serious lies and white lies.

Dealing with a child who persists in telling lies can be extremely frustrating. You will find these guidelines helpful:

- *Stay calm.* Spend time considering why your child is lying, instead of instantly reacting in temper. Bear in mind that some lies stem from a child's lack of self-confidence.
- *Explain why she shouldn't lie.* Give her reasons she can understand. For instance, 'If you tell lies, other children won't want to play with you' will be more effective than 'Telling lies is naughty.' Children who are taught the difference between right and wrong, rather than simply

167

being punished for lying, are less likely to tell lies in the future.

- *Make punishments reasonable.* Far better to deprive your child of her sweets for that day, or to put her to bed ten minutes early that night, than, for example, to tell her she's not allowed out to play for two months – punishments that are too extreme rarely have much positive impact on a child's behaviour.
- *Reassure her that you still love her, even though she tells lies.* A child who is afraid of losing her parents' love for being naughty will lie fiercely to cover up whatever she's done wrong.

See also **Boasting; Guilt; Scapegoat; Self-Confidence; Stealing; Swearing**.

M

Manners Ever had to sit next to someone who belches loudly, or who picks her nose? Revolting, isn't it? Yet a young child usually takes great delight in the sort of habits that adults regard as bad manners – first, because they usually ease feelings of discomfort, and second, because of the response that greets them. Belching and farting are guaranteed to raise a laugh, spitting out half-chewed food causes onlookers to squirm, and nose-picking (and flicking) makes others feel sick. Other examples of bad manners, such as interrupting a conversation or barging to the front of a queue, also have a positive effect as far as a child is concerned, in that they ensure that she quickly gets what she wants.

But consistently displaying bad manners like this will, in the long run, have two psychological effects. First, the child will become unpopular. Of course, she'll get a laugh from others at first. We've all seen a group of young children burst into squeals of delight when one of them passes wind. But eventually, the joke will wear off, and others won't want to sit beside her during mealtimes because they think she is disgusting. And a child who constantly pushes others out of the way is unlikely to be well liked.

Second, the child herself will feel uncomfortable because she'll be following one set of social rules while everybody else is following another. Suppose, for instance, you tried to join in a game of cricket but played as if it was football, and kicked the ball instead of batting it. You'd feel strange because you'd be aware that what you were doing wasn't in harmony with those around you. This is the sort of feeling a bad-mannered child will experience.

What's interesting about habits that adults regard as 'bad manners' is that children don't start out in life being fascinated by them. On the contrary, a baby does these things with complete indifference – she passes wind without embarrassment, she explores her body cavities quite naturally, and she shouts out as soon as she wants something. These habits are normal, from her point of view. And her parents positively encourage most of them because they know she feels more comfortable afterwards.

Adult perceptions change as a child matures, however. What was considered acceptable from a baby is no longer tolerated when the toddler or pre-school stage is reached. Adults expect a child of that age to have greater understanding of the world around her and to be more aware of social rules. And a child's perception also changes. Somewhere between birth and the next five years, she begins to realise that there is behaviour that adults consider to be 'good manners', although she doesn't know precisely how this distinction is made.

Later on, she'll discover that many of these rules are only a matter of social convention, and that they are not universal. For example, in some Middle Eastern countries, queues don't exist – everyone just pushes their way to the front! She'll also learn that there are very subtle aspects of good manners. Some people, for instance, think that it is good manners to leave a small amount of food on their dinner plate because that lets their hosts know that they've had enough to eat; other people think it is bad manners to leave food on the plate because it suggests to their hosts that the meal was not tasty enough to finish.

In the meantime, though, the child becomes aware that adults start to frown when she makes a 'rude' noise during mealtimes, or that she is reprimanded for picking her nose while watching television. And that's the exact point when she becomes fascinated by these habits. Tell a young child not to do something – particularly if you don't give her a good reason for the veto – and you can be sure she'll want to do it even more. It's the forbidden-fruit scenario all over again. And the more you giggle when you hear your child passing wind, the more she will continue to do so. Positive adult responses like this simply reinforce her behaviour. The more you over-react to nose-picking, the more provocative the act of nose-picking becomes in your child's eyes. And the more you screw up your face in disgust when you watch her eating with her mouth wide open, then the more pleasurable the action becomes for her.

Of course, children do find these habits intrinsically enjoyable – just as adults do – because in most cases they do relieve a feeling of physical discomfort. But it is certainly not the habits *per se* that fascinate the children – it's the adults' reaction to them that give children such joy.

If you want to discourage your child from persisting with actions that you regard as bad manners:

● *Set a good example yourself.* You can hardly expect her to stop picking wax out of her ear and then flicking it across the room, if she sees you mindlessly drilling deep into the side of your head throughout the day. Make sure you are not asking her to follow a set of rules that she knows you ignore yourself.

● *Don't laugh at your child's behaviour.* You may be tempted to giggle furiously when you see her confidently striding towards the front of the queue at your local supermarket, but once she thinks you regard her behaviour as funny, you will have a hard time convincing her otherwise. Better to discourage it right from the start.

● *Keep things in perspective.* The chances are that some of your child's bad manners will make you feel genuinely disgusted. By all means use a firm voice and a scowl to indicate your displeasure; but try not to be extreme. A balanced reaction is more appropriate.

● *Use meaningful explanations.* Tell her why you think good manners are important, and be very explicit about the benefits of being well mannered. Always use explanations that she can understand (e.g., 'You won't get invited to parties if other children know you are rude').

● *Reinforce good manners.* Praising your child for behaving appropriately will encourage her to repeat this behaviour in the future. So let her know that you are pleased with her for showing good manners. Again, make your comments quite specific and clear.

See also **Eating; Eating Out; Modelling; Politeness**.

Masturbation Interest in the genitals is normal in childhood, even in the pre-school years. Boys that age can have erections (although they don't ejaculate), and nearly all boys and girls explore their genitals at some stage, just as they explore their noses, ears, and other body parts. You may be embarrassed when you see your child masturbating, but the habit is not harmful.

Manipulation of the genitals to bring pleasure and relaxation is a phenomenon found in every layer of society. Research has revealed that almost half of all children under the age of five engage in genital handling – and this is probably an underestimate, since some mothers would be reluctant to admit to such behaviour and also since many children masturbate in secret. Most parents find the habit embarrassing because they associate it with sexual pleasure, but pre-school masturbation (unlike adult masturbation which ends in orgasm) gives comfort, not sexual stimulation. Like other comfort habits (e.g., thumb-sucking, hair-twiddling), masturbation soothes a child, providing a feeling of relaxation and security.

Don't be tempted to use old wives' tales to discourage a young child from masturbating. Threats of blindness, or warts, or whatever, will only frighten him, and he will learn to associate his genitals with fear. Similarly, avoid smacking him when you see him fondling himself – that will cause him to associate sexual activities with punishment. The stronger the reaction that you show to his masturbating, the more likely it is that the habit will intensify.

Instead, take a more low-key approach, by gently informing him that you don't want him to masturbate in front of you. Use terms he can understand, such as, 'Please don't rub yourself like that.' Do this calmly. And try to divert his attention away from himself on to another activity, such as playing with a toy or listening to a story. However, if he masturbates frequently, it may be a sign of stress, and you'll only stop the habit by discovering, then eliminating, the source of the stress.

See also **Comforters; Dummies; Sexual Curiosity.**

Memory The means through which we store information and then retrieve it later when we want to use it again. Learning cannot take place without memory, because an individual who cannot recall previous events has no basis on which to build further understanding of the world around him. Children who have difficulties with memory may have problems learning in school.

Psychologists are unable to specify what actually happens in the human brain when memory is used, but they have proved that memory skills are present even before birth. In one investigation, mothers who were six months pregnant read a children's story out loud, three times a day for several weeks. Soon after their babies were born, they read this same story along with two others, and the researchers found that the babies made a greater response to the story they had 'heard' while in the womb! Memory capacity increases from this moment on, and major changes occur even in the first year:

I week	A baby can recognise his mother's voice, and shows preference for the smell of his mother's breast-milk.
1 month	Memory improves to the point where a baby can remember specific speech sounds if he has heard them often enough.
2 months	In an experiment involving two-month-old babies, a mobile hung above each baby's cot was attached to his foot with a ribbon. After a while, he learned to move the mobile by kicking. The mobile was then taken away, but replaced after a few days or a few weeks. Would a baby of this age remember how to make the mobile move? Observations confirmed that memory of his previous exposure to the mobile lasted up to four weeks.
3 months	An infant will respond positively when familiar feeding objects are brought to him. He will recognise them immediately and possibly thrust out his hands in the general direction of the food source; he will also show anticipation of familiar situations, such as bath-time.
7 months	He remembers people he hasn't seen every day – e.g., a family friend, a baby-sitter.
9 months	A child of this age is able to use his memory more purposefully. When sitting in his high-chair, if he accidentally drops a toy from his tray, he will look for it in the right direction. And if he sees you putting a sweet under a cup, right in front of him, he will instantly lift the

cup because he remembers that the sweet is
there.

From then on, an infant demonstrates his memory in play.
He begins to show pleasure at hearing familiar songs and
rhymes, and may want them to be repeated over and over
again. He can remember where his toys are kept, which
means he can access them on his own without having to
depend on someone else. This ability allows him a much
wider variety of play and learning experiences, all of which
provide him with endless opportunities to improve his
capacity to remember even further.

The memory of an adult is greater than the memory of a
young child. This difference is not so much in the size
of memory as in the techniques used to store and recall
information – adults tend to have more efficient strategies
for remembering than children. You can help your child,
aged five years upwards, improve his memory by encouraging him to use the following techniques:

- *rehearsal*. A young child can increase his recall through
  the use of rehearsal (repetition of the information over
  and over again). He is more likely to remember a group
  of objects, if he has spoken their names out loud several
  times while trying to memorise them. Test this for yourself: place a tray of twenty common objects in front of
  your child, let him look at them for a minute; then
  remove the tray and ask him to tell you any he can
  remember. Repeat this activity with another set of
  objects, but this time encourage him to say the name of
  each object loudly many times, while the tray is in front
  of him. He will probably remember more from the
  second tray than from the first.
- *organisation*. Information is easier to recall when it has
  been stored in memory in an organised way. Try this:
  compile a list of twenty objects (e.g. five foods, five
  articles of clothing, five modes of transport, and five
  pieces of furniture), putting them in a random order.
  Give your child this list, let him look at it for one minute,
  then remove it and ask him to tell you how many he can
  remember. Then repeat the activity with a similar list,
  only this time put the objects into their categories, so
  that he sees four groups of items. The chances are that

174

he will remember more of the second list because he stored them in his memory in a more organised way.

- *retrieval*. A child's ability to recall from a previously learned list can improve when categories are suggested to him, even though he may not have been aware of the categories at the time he learned the list. To demonstrate this, give your child the first jumbled list of objects (as above) without mentioning any of the categories, then note how many he can remember. Do the same with a second jumbled list of the same objects, but this time – at the point when you ask him to recall the list – suggest to him that the objects can be grouped into 'furniture', 'transport', 'food' and 'clothes' and that he should try to remember them in these categories. His efforts with the second list should be more successful than with the first.

Practising these strategies for a few minutes each week will benefit your child's memory. Such activities are suitable for a child as young as four or five, as are memory games such as 'lotto', 'correspondence' and 'When I went on holiday I took with me a . . .' Don't get annoyed with him if his recall isn't as sharp as you would like – just keep practising with him, for a few minutes at a time.

See also **Concentration; Intelligence; Knowledge; Learning Skills**.

Milestones Detailed study of child development by doctors, psychologists and other childcare professionals has shown that there are a number of 'milestones' – significant points of development – that most children pass through at around the same age. For instance, most are able to sit independently at the age of six months, most start to put two words together at around the age of 18 months, and most are toilet-trained by the time they are five. Milestones like these are important because they provide guidelines for a child's expected rate of development.

Yet every child develops at her own pace. Milestones are only approximate points, nothing more, and there is often wide variation amongst children. One baby might show her first smile at around six weeks, while another may not do so until around 12 weeks; one may be up on her feet at 12

175

months while another may not walk independently until 16 months. These variations are normal, and are not a cause for concern.

Some differences in the rate of achieving developmental milestones are worrying, however. Sometimes the gap in levels of progress between one child and others of her age does indicate a deeper problem. A severe difficulty is rarely indicated if only one aspect of development is slow – in most instances, there has to be a combination of several delayed milestones before more substantial investigation by a qualified professional is needed.

Determining the significance of developmental difficulties is not clear-cut, and requires detailed consideration of a child's strengths and weaknesses. If you are worried about your child's progress, speak to your health visitor or GP. The chances are that you'll be reassured to hear she is progressing well, but if there is a problem, then the earlier it is detected the better.

See also **Coordination; Language Development; Learning Skills; Normality**.

Modelling When you look closely at parents and their children, you will virtually always see similarities between them in terms of their attitudes, behaviour and mannerisms. This could mean that these personality dimensions are inherited – but psychologists offer 'modelling theory' as a more plausible explanation to account for this link between adult and child behaviour.

The theory proposes that, as a child becomes closely attached to her parents, she begins to adopt some of their personal characteristics. For instance, she starts to use phrases that they use, facial expressions that they use, and may even walk with the same gait. This makes her feel more secure, closer to her parents, and her self-confidence increases as a result. As modelling (also known as 'identification') intensifies, a child gradually absorbs the attitudes and beliefs of her mother and father, selecting the characteristics that she finds most desirable.

But a child does not only model herself on her parents – she partly models herself on other significant adults in her life as well. A young child who spends a great deal of time

with say, a childminder will begin to model some of her behaviour. And one who attends nursery regularly will model herself on some of the nursery staff she feels attached to. It is very important, therefore, that you are aware of the images presented by all the adults in your child's life (including you) – she is just as likely to model an adult's unpleasant features as she is to model their more attractive ones.

Mothers A woman's role within the family has changed considerably. Two decades ago, or perhaps even one, many women would have had to give up their careers when they had children. But changes in legislation mean that having worked for a specified period for her employer, a woman is usually entitled to have her job held open for her for up to six months after the birth of her baby. Most people regard this new mother-cum-worker role as a forward step in freeing a woman from a tightly defined role which tied her to domesticity irrespective of her wishes.

Changes in attitude towards women are also reflected in other ways. For instance, in the 1950s and 60s, single-parent families headed by a father were rare, and almost always arose through bereavement. But the increasingly flexible role available to women in recent years means that it is no longer unique for a mother to break away from the family home, leaving the children behind in the care of her ex-partner.

Women who take on this newly available role of estranged parent frequently receive a mixed reaction from other adults. There are those who deplore such behaviour, claiming that children need a mother more than they need a father, that a woman should stay with her children at all costs. And there are those who make the counter-claim that a woman has as much right as a man to break free of a stifling relationship, and that the concept of 'children needing their mother' is a myth created by a male-dominated society in order to perpetuate existing family structures.

Neither argument can be proved conclusively. What is known is that a woman may love her children very much, yet at the same time feel unable to develop her full potential while harnessed to the responsibility of motherhood. As a result, she may see her departure from the family home as the only step to take. However even though this avenue is more acceptable in contemporary society than previously, it still carries significant emotional consequences for all concerned. Just as being an estranged father can be heartbreaking for a man who leaves his wife and children, so too can being an estranged mother.

A mother's role within the house has also changed. In earlier decades she was expected to fulfil very specific aims, such as feeding, changing and cleaning her child, and keeping the home clean. A mother took great pride in achieving high standards in these areas. As her child grew older, her goals were equally clearly defined – encouraging him to get good marks at school, to be polite and helpful, and so on. A mother today does not have such clear-cut goals. But she is certainly more concerned with ensuring that he achieves his full potential than she is with the whiteness of his shirts. Most women prefer to spend time encouraging their child, for instance, to develop mastery in playing a musical instrument than they would spending the same amount of time cleaning the house, or ironing.

This means, though, that today's mother has to have a better understanding of her child's individuality than was required in previous generations, and has to be able to identify the best way of maximising his talents. This is not always easy. In this sense, a mother's role is more challenging than ever before.

See also **Bonding; Fathers; Older Parents; Parents; Quality Time; Single-Parent Family; Working Mothers; Young Parents**.

Moving House Psychological surveys have proved that moving house is a very traumatic life event for adults, ranking third in terms of stress after the death of a spouse and divorce. It is also a very stressful life event for young children.

By the age of two, a child is comfortable being in familiar surroundings, and has organised his life around the predictability of his home environment; he knows where his toys are kept, what ornaments he mustn't touch, where the juice is kept and so on, and a break from this familiarity caused by moving house can be very unsettling. For a child aged four or five, a house move can have a more complex emotional effect because it may also involve a change of nursery or school, and probably a change of friends. No wonder, then, that he may be troubled by the prospect of changing address.

Another reason why this event is stressful for a young child is that he doesn't play an active role in it. Choosing a house is something that adults do, not children. Decisions about area, type of house, size of garden, use of rooms and so forth are made by adults. A child has to rely entirely on his parents' judgement, and hope for the best. As well as this, not all house moves are for positive reasons, such as gaining more space or living in a more desirable area: some moves are a result of divorce, bereavement or unemployment, and consequently are conducted in a negative atmosphere.

When considering moving house with a child aged five or under:

179

- *Be positive about it*. No matter the real reasons for the move, talk to your child about it in a positive way. Explain to him that it will give you all a chance to enjoy a new home, with new surroundings. He'll be happy about the move if he thinks you are happy about it.
- *Don't take him with you when initially viewing houses*. A young child soon becomes weary when trailed through one house after another while his parents discuss lots of boring details, and this doesn't make your task any easier. Another reason for not taking him with you is that he will probably like most houses he sees, which means that every time you see a house but don't buy it you will have to explain to him why it's not suitable.
- *Once you've purchased your next house, take him to see it*. Emphasise the advantages to him – e.g., he has his own room, there is a bigger garden, he is nearer shops – and talk about decorating and furnishing his room. This will help him see it in a positive light.
- *If the move causes a change of nursery/school, take him to see it before he starts*. Naturally, he will be apprehensive about having to get to know new children and adults, so the sooner he meets them the better. Do this once you have bought the house, but before you have moved in.
- *Remind him that he'll be able to keep in touch with old friends*. His biggest fear may be that he will lose contact with his pals. Reassure him that won't happen, and let him make an advance arrangement to play with his friends after the move has taken place. This will generate a feeling of continuity.

The few days before moving, and removal day itself, will go much more successfully if your child is settled. Allow him to help with packing some of his own clothes and toys, and let him keep out his favourite cuddly toy if he wants. If possible, send him to a friend or relative on the day of the removal, or even the night before – this leaves you free to concentrate solely on the move, without having to worry about him. As soon as the move is over, organise your child's bedroom before you bring him back to the house; a

180

few of his toys and some familiar bedding will be sufficient
to make it seem like home to him.

See also **Routine**.

N

Nightmares Bad dreams occur most frequently in young children between the ages of four and six, although research indicates that at least 25 per cent of children between six and twelve years still have nightmares. Don't be concerned if your child has an occasional disturbed night, even though she may become upset by it.

Bad dreams can be due to many different factors, some of which can be avoided:

- *eating specific foods late at night*. Some children are more prone to nightmares after they have had a late-night snack of cheese or chocolate, or a drink with a high level of colouring and additives. Cut out these foods.
- *television programmes*. Most children have vivid imaginations, and a particularly action-packed television programme or video just before bedtime can cause nightmares. A child who is allowed to stay up late at night shouldn't be allowed to watch these sorts of programmes.
- *ill-health*. When your child is incubating an illness, before the symptoms have fully emerged, her sleep at night may become unsettled. A sudden run of restless nights, coupled with nightmares, can be a warning that she is about to develop an illness. Watch out for this.
- *worrying about something*. What may seem trivial to you (e.g., not being able to sit beside a friend during juice time at the playgroup) can seem momentous to a young child. Anxiety over small incidents like this can cause nightmares.

If your child does wake up distressed in the middle of the night, comfort her and stay until she has settled down again. She needs your reassurance that it was only a dream, that it didn't really happen, and that she is perfectly safe now. In a calm, unhurried voice, tell her that the dream is over, that she'll soon get back to sleep and that she won't have another bad dream like that one. She may calm down more quickly if there is a change of situation: for instance, taking her to the toilet, or downstairs for a drink of juice, will help. Remember that she will be all right in a few moments – don't let your anxiety show.

Repeated nightmares, however, can be a sign that there is something wrong. Once you have made sure that all the factors mentioned above have been ruled out, you should consider the possibility that your child has a deep-rooted worry. Maybe she's not getting on well with friends, or perhaps her self-confidence is low because she is not as good at games as she wants to be. A child may have nightmares if she thinks her mum and dad are not getting on well. If your child is regularly having bad dreams, talk to her about what's happening in her life. Try to find out what's troubling her. You may want to seek specialist psychological advice if the problem persists.

A night terror (*pavor nocturnis*) is an extreme form of nightmare, in which a child screams in her sleep and may even jump out of bed. Or she may sit up, with her eyes wide open and yet still be convinced that she can see something frightening. Twenty minutes may pass before she accepts that she is awake, that the night terror is over.

Always stay with your child during a night terror, all the time reassuring her that she's safe. Do this until she calms down. She will probably have forgotten all about it by the following morning. Night terrors are rare, but frightening, both for a child and for her parents who see her so distressed. As with nightmares, there is no cause for concern unless they become regular, in which case there will be something worrying her.

See also **Crying Baby; Dreams; Fears; Self-Confidence; Sleep**.

Normality There is no clear dividing line between normality and abnormality in childhood, although some aspects are easier to define than others. Professionals know the physical, intellectual, social and linguistic skills expected of each child at each age. But when it comes to identifying normal behaviour the position is less clear, because a child's behaviour by itself does not necessarily indicate whether she is abnormal or not. Bed-wetting, for instance, is the commonest early-warning sign that a child is under emotional stress, but there are many who wet the bed simply because they have not been properly toilet-trained.

Most types of behaviour found in children who are disturbed – including jealousy, aggressiveness, shyness, attention-seeking, withdrawal, excitability, tearfulness and boisterousness – are found in normal children at some time in their lives or to a minor extent indefinitely. Before a child is judged to be normal or abnormal, her actions should be examined in the broader context of what is happening in all areas of her life.

Calculating the incidence of psychological disturbance in childhood is therefore quite difficult. Those studies that have used acceptable criteria for making such judgements confirm that most pre-schoolers have emotional or behavioural problems at some stage in their development. But these difficulties are often only temporary, and can be alleviated by timely intervention from the child's parents. Surveys estimate that at most only 15 per cent of children experience psychological problems that are severe enough to interfere with their development. And of these, only a few require specialist psychological help.

See also **Aggression; Bed-Wetting; Comforters; Jealousy; Manners; Milestones; Modelling; Shyness; Unhappiness.**

O

Older Parents In previous decades most couples married in their early twenties, and usually had their first child by the age of 30. But things have changed. People have different expectations about marriage and family life.

A woman is no longer considered to be 'on the shelf' if a wedding ring isn't on her finger by the time she reaches her thirtieth birthday – there is widespread recognition that an early marriage isn't the only way to fulfil one's potential.

And there is less social pressure on couples to have children in the years immediately following marriage. Added to this, many couples who married young have separated and are now in their second marriage. The combination of all these factors means that it is no longer rare for couples to have their first child when they are both over 40.

There are, though, health considerations that older couples should take into account when planning to have a first child. Medical research reveals that women who conceive for the first time after the age of 35 are more likely to have a child with a developmental problem: for instance, a pregnancy between the ages of 20 and 35 runs a 600:1 risk of having a baby with Down's Syndrome, whereas the risk increases to about 100:1 for mothers between the ages of 40 and 45. Advanced medical techniques, however, allow for the early detection of such conditions. First-time pregnancy over the age of 35 also carries a higher risk of stillbirth, and there is a greater likelihood of having a longer and more difficult labour. Fortunately, the incidence of these problems is reduced when the mother is in good physical health – so older mothers must make a particular point of looking after themselves during pregnancy.

Leaving aside these potential health hazards, the next hurdle that older first-time parents have to tackle is the massive disruption that accompanies the arrival of a baby within a previously well organised household. People get set in their ways as they become older. While change can be hard at any age, it can be especially so for an older person – and there are few events more likely to involve change than the birth of a baby. A couple in this situation discover that they can no longer go out when they want, eat when they want, sleep when they want, go on holiday when they want, or spend what they want. True, every couple faces these circumstances when they have their first child. But a couple in their early forties will be more accustomed to their freedom, and consequently may miss it more.

Giving up the role of career woman for that of mother is more difficult for an older woman than it is for someone 15 or 20 years her junior, because an older woman will probably be on a higher rung of the promotion ladder. Despite advances in employment legislation, few women are able to guarantee a return to their pre-motherhood employment status unless they are back at work within six months of the birth. An older first-time mother who is in no hurry to return to full-time employment could pay a high price in terms of her future employment prospects.

This change of role may also mean that she experiences a sudden shift from, say, being the manager of a group of adults to being the carer of one small child, from making major financial decisions to budgeting for the next load of disposable nappies. The first-time mother who is over 40 may find the contrast between her former lifestyle and her present one much more extreme than a younger mother may, and the danger is that anxieties over loss of status may turn into resentment towards her new baby.

Age can have advantages, however, when it comes to parenthood. One benefit of maturity and life experience is increased self-confidence. Older first-time parents are more likely to be at ease with themselves, more able to handle the pressures of life which often overwhelm younger parents. They have already enjoyed many years of having responsibility only for themselves, and don't have such a strong need to prove themselves personally or financially. A couple's pleasure in caring for a child can offset any of the disadvantages of being older parents.

Young babies have a tremendous capacity to tax their parents' stamina to the full. Before you become a parent, you will be amazed to see even some apparently highly competent adults – people who held positions of high responsibility in their working life – have their self-confidence dramatically reduced by the presence of a baby in the house. After you become a parent, it won't surprise you at all! The physical demands of sleepless nights and never-ending days of washing, changing and cleaning, make first-time parenthood at the age of 40-plus particularly exhausting. No wonder some people argue that parenting – like skateboarding and all-night parties – is a younger person's pursuit.

The so-called 'generation gap' (the difference in outlook between successive generations of parents and children) can occur with parents of any age – some couples behave as if they are old even when they are in their twenties, while some older couples have a very young outlook. However, although much depends on the individuals concerned, a generation gap is more likely to occur between older parents and their children.

There is another generation gap of a different sort. Most people mix with others who have similar interests. Likewise, most tend to have friends with children around the same age as their own. This gives them the opportunity to share ideas and to discuss common problems with each other. But older parents may not have this type of peer-group support; instead all their friends may have grown-up children, and they may find that these friends have forgotten the everyday worries of first-time parents. This lack of common ground with others can increase an older couple's sense of isolation.

See also **Parents; Working Mothers; Young Parents**.

Only Child   Even though the tendency nowadays is towards smaller families, a single-child family is still not the norm. Some say that too much fuss is made about a child not having any brothers or sisters, and claim that only children are the same as first-borns. The main difference, however, is that only children rarely have to compete with anyone else for their parents' attention. Unlike an oldest child who is forced out of his central position in the family, an only child enjoys the limelight throughout his childhood. He never has to wait his turn in a queue of brothers and sisters, and he doesn't often have to share his toys.

Being an only child has obvious advantages – a strong feeling of security, a sense of ease in the company of adults, and a higher level of material comfort than children in larger families. Yet it can also have disadvantages such as a tendency to be selfish, difficulty when it comes to sharing, lack of confidence when mixing with other children (especially when he first starts attending nursery or primary school). Life can be lonely for an only child.

Only children do tend to be more self-interested than other children of their own age, and they frequently need approval from authority figures (this extends into adulthood – many only-child employees rely heavily on the approval of their managers). But they usually relate better to older people: being raised in the company of adults makes them feel comfortable with more mature individuals. And only children also make better leaders, which can be a tremendous asset in situations where initiative is needed.

An only child will not automatically turn out to be selfish

and over-indulged, but if yours develops these characteristics, concentrate on the following strategies:

- *Encourage him to share his toys with friends, neighbours
  and classmates*. Since an only child has little opportunity
  at home to share, at first he will probably have difficulty
  doing this when he is with others. Your encouragement
  will be helpful.
- *Try to involve him in team games*. Where possible –
  usually at playgroup, nursery or school – make sure he
  joins in team games that involve sharing and turn-taking.
- *Let him mix with other children of his own age*. The best
  way to do this is to send him to playgroup or nursery;
  if you can't manage this, then invite other children round
  to the house for him to play with. When he has company, discourage him from making excessive demands
  for attention from the adults.
- *Give him responsibility*. Some only children expect
  everything to be done for them. As parents, you have
  to encourage your child to take more responsibility for
  the everyday events in his life, such as washing, dressing,
  feeding himself and tidying up.
- *Don't always make him the centre of attention*. Learning
  to share adults' time with others is not easy. The onus
  is on you to help your child solve any problems he may
  have in this respect – for example, by playing games
  where he and his friends take turns, or by having small-
  group discussions where every child is given a chance to
  speak.

See also **Birth Order; First-Born Jealousy**.

Over-Organised You probably recognise the importance
of your child using his leisure hours purposefully. Watching
a young child fritter away hour after hour in front of the
television – gazing at a video he has viewed dozens of times
already – is extremely frustrating for parents, especially with
the plethora of extra-curricular opportunities available for
children nowadays (e.g., music, skating, swimming, ballet,
drama, youth clubs, pre-Brownies, pre-Cubs, pre-Boys
Brigade, gymnastics, football, athletics, majorettes, disco

dancing). This type of leisure class can play an important part in your child's life.

Learning to produce a few notes from a descant recorder at four years of age, for example, can stimulate a lifelong interest in music. And there are other benefits too. Being a member of groups that involve interaction with other children can help develop your child's social skills; learning to swim could save his life; appearing on stage for the end-of-year drama show is a great boost to self-confidence. The list of potential advantages is endless.

As well as these activities, you probably encourage your child to be occupied when he's at home, perhaps by making sure he regularly has a friend over to play after school, so that he is never bored. Most children enjoy this sort of arrangement.

But a limit should be placed on the amount of free time your child has organised for him – he also needs time to himself. A child with an over-organised day may:

- *lose his independence*. Every child wants to become independent, to be able to do things for himself. And part of the process of establishing this independence is making decisions about how free time is spent. An over-organised child is denied such decision-making opportunities, and his independence will suffer as a result.
- *have a low self-esteem*. Psychological research confirms that a child's self-respect takes a tumble when he is not involved in making decisions about basic aspects of his life, such as what he eats, what clothes he wears, and who he plays with. A child who has all his leisure time organised for him by his parents may experience similar feelings.
- *be unable to make decisions*. An over-organised child will be so used to having his parents make all the choices for him that he won't know what to do when he has any free time. Quite simply, when left to his own devices, he may not be able to decide how to make his own amusement.
- *be a 'jack of all trades and master of none'*. Logic dictates that your child has only so many hours in the day to devote to leisure pursuits. Involvement in too many means that he doesn't have time to become skilled in any of them.

190

- *appear more tired than usual.* A child who spends most of his time actively engaged in leisure pursuits may not have sufficient opportunity to become settled and relaxed; he may become over-tired.
- *lose interest in his toys.* An over-organised child may not have the chance to play with his toys at home because he is so busy doing something else. He may even start to feel that there is nothing of interest at home, and that he can only enjoy himself when he is somewhere else or with another child.

These disadvantages outweigh any benefits a child may derive from having an exceptionally busy life. So think about your child's leisure time and the way it is spent.

To help you judge whether his day is purposefully organised or over-organised, ask yourself these questions:

- *Is he making progress in all of his activities?* If he has been in a gymnastics class for three years and is still as ungainly in his movements as he was when he first started, then perhaps it is time to consider whether he is deriving any benefit from it. Of course, he may enjoy the class for other reasons (e.g., his friends go there), but you are justified in looking for something more than that.
- *Does he look forward to going?* Most teachers will tell you that there is nothing worse than an unenthusiastic pupil who gets pushed along every week because mum and dad have high hopes for him. Your child should anticipate the activity with at least some spark of enthusiasm.
- *Is he being kept busy in order to suit your needs?* Perhaps you have organised your child's day in order to give yourself free time to pursue your own interests. There is nothing wrong with that on an occasional basis, but don't let it become standard practice.
- *Does he bicker a lot with his friends when they come to play?* Having friends over to the house to play with after school can be tremendous, but it may mean that he doesn't have enough time on his own. His dissatisfaction may show itself in irritability with the children who come to visit him.
- *Is your child able to structure his free time?* One test of whether you are over-organising him is to put him in his room and tell him, 'Find something to do.' You may

191

be horrified when he approaches you after a couple of minutes, complaining that he can't think of anything.
- *Do you spend enough time with your child?* Add up the amount of time he spends in the company of other children and adults (excluding nursery school), and then add up the amount of time he spends just with you. If the total time spent on out-of-home activities is substantially more than the time he spends with you at home, then he may be over-organised.

It's all a question of balance. A child who is never allowed to participate in extra-curricular classes, or to have friends over to his house, is just as disadvantaged (although in different ways) as an over-organised child. One of your tasks as a parent is to ensure that your child's full potential is maximised. Structuring his day can be one way to achieve this, but over-structuring it is not.

See also **Friendships; Independence; Self-Confidence; Supervision**.

Over-Protectiveness   Just as animals have an instinct to protect their newborn, humans instinctively protect their child from any danger or threat to her health. This is a natural tendency found in all parents, and ensures that a child will remain in good health until she is mature enough to look after herself. But some parents are over-protective – for instance, they continue to do things for their offspring long after she is capable of being independent, or they fuss over her when she is playing, or they worry constantly about her diet and sleeping habits.

Parents sometimes become over-protective when the child has had a serious illness in the early years. The stress and worry brought about by ill-health make them extremely cautious about letting her face routine hazards. Or they may become over-protective as a result of family bereavement, the death giving them a feeling of insecurity, which they redirect on to the child. Whatever the cause, over-protectiveness artificially restricts a child, and the effect can be to impair her development.

However, insufficient concern for your child's welfare is more harmful than too much. You have to find a balance in your style of management, so that she is allowed a degree of autonomy and yet is not allowed to put herself in danger. Only then will she learn to tackle everyday challenges confidently.

See also **Illness; Independence; Spoiling; Supervision**.

Overweight Despite intensive medical research over many years, nobody knows whether a child's tendency towards fatness is inherited or whether it is due to food consumption. It is probably a bit of both. However, the following is known:

- About 40 per cent of children who are overweight during their primary-school years will continue to be overweight in adulthood.
- Although a high proportion of parents worry that their child is fat, only between 2 and 15 per cent of children are obese.
- Very few plump babies grow into plump children.
- If you and your partner aren't fat, there is a 1 in 10 chance your child will be fat; but if you are both fat, then there is a 4 in 10 chance.

Height and weight are directly linked. If your child gains weight faster than she gains height, she will become fat. But remember that assessment of her correct body weight for her height can only be made using standard growth charts, which are available from your doctor, health visitor or local child-health clinic. Table 1 provides a rough guide to average growth rates, but it doesn't take into account acceptable individual variations.

Table 1 Average Growth Rates

age (years)	average height (cm)		average weight (kg)	
	Girls	Boys	Girls	Boys
1	74.3	76.1	9.5	10.2
1.5	80.9	82.4	10.8	11.5
2	84.5	85.6	11.8	12.3
2.5	89.5	90.4	13.0	13.5
3	93.9	94.9	14.1	14.6
3.5	97.9	99.1	15.1	15.7
4	101.6	102.9	16.0	16.7

If your child is overweight, don't put her on a rigorous diet to reduce the *amount* of food she eats, unless you are medically advised to do so. But do exercise more control over the *type* of food she eats. Common problems causing fatness during the toddler and pre-school years are:

- *too many sweets and crisps*. You may not be able to cut out sweets altogether, but try to reduce them – your child might not even notice that you gave her two sweets instead of her usual three.
- *too many sugary drinks*. Try watering down fresh fruit juice, and encourage her to drink milk instead of lemonade. Milk consumption should be one pint a day – no more, no less.
- *too many fats*. Spread butter and margarine more thinly (or give her toast without any at all), serve boiled instead of roast potatoes, and reduce the amount of fried food.
- *too many snacks*. There is nothing wrong with snacks as long as they are nutritious and infrequent. But don't give her a snack every time she asks for something to eat.
- *too little exercise*. We are in danger of becoming a chair-bound nation. A toddler can push her buggy along the street; a four-year-old can run, jump and climb – this decreases the opportunity for fat to build up.

See also **Additives; Eating; Eating Out; Healthy Eating; Snacks**.

P

Parents Most couples experience mixed feelings at the prospect of becoming parents, especially when it is their first child. First comes excitement at the thought of having a baby in the family, someone extra to love and care for. Then comes apprehension: won't a baby cause an enormous disruption to their existing lifestyle? It's also the time when many of us realise that the ability to be a good parent – beyond the basic instinct to protect – is not innate.

Animals seem to be better equipped than humans, when it comes to being natural parents; they are very capable of protecting their babies. Yet nobody tells animals to behave in this way, and they don't attend animal ante-natal classes. Neither do they have health visitors, maternity nurses or psychologists advising them. All the same, they instinctively do a good job.

Animals, though, are not concerned with the higher issues of parenting, such as giving their offspring toys to play with or ensuring that he fulfils his potential. Animals, in fact, are not concerned with many of the issues that we regard as central to our role as parents. The main goal of animal parents is to make sure their babies survive until they have learned enough skills to hunt for themselves and to avoid danger. Our own concerns are far more complex, for while you too have a natural desire to protect your child from danger, you want much more than that for him, including a good education, a happy home life, a suitable career and, probably, a satisfactory marriage. These higher-order goals are not instinctive.

There are, though, some inborn tendencies that pull parents and child together. For instance, when a baby comes into the world he is pre-programmed to interact with his parents – e.g., his hearing is tuned to human voices, his vision is set to focus best on his parents' faces when they feed him, and he can use his voice to let them know when he is unhappy. And there are other biological forces acting on parents which encourage them to look after their child, such as the mother's natural production of breast-milk following birth. In addition, the minimum delay before the mother can have another child – at least nine months – means that their baby doesn't have to share their attention with other babies in the family (although the arrival of twins, triplets or more throws this particular natural plan into disarray!).

Aside from these basic tendencies, most aspects of parenthood have to be learned. Your starting point for deciding how to act as a parent probably stems from your own experiences (either negative or positive) in childhood. Some people have such a miserable time as children that they are determined to raise their own child in a totally different way, while others find their childhood so satisfying that they replicate the same style of parenting with their own children.

Think about your own childhood. What do you think were your parents' main priorities when they raised you? Make a list of them – it might contain answers such as 'keeping me clean and tidy', 'encouraging me to be well behaved', 'taking me to music classes so I could learn to play the piano', 'teaching me to read before I started primary schooling' or 'helping me to be friendly to other children'. Write these down, and cover up the sheet of paper.

Then take another sheet, and make a list of the priorities you have for your own children. Compare the two lists. Are there similarities, or are the lists completely different? How much do you consider that the priorities in the second list have been influenced by those in the first? The chances are that you will see a connection between your parents' skills as mother and father and your own views on how you would like to be as a parent.

Previous generations of parents had one substantial advantage over today's – namely, they were often part of a large, close-knit family network. A host of helpful – and experienced – relatives and friends were always close at hand to give advice on matters of parenthood. Those earlier generations had less need to ask for advice and help on day-to-day matters, since they already had a bank of 'folk-wisdom' immediately available. This made parenthood easier to cope with.

The current generation of parents does not have that luxury. The basic concept of the extended family has broken down, and there is no longer the family support for new parents that there once was. This has happened for a number of reasons. First, the increase in separation and divorce means that links between generations cannot be taken for granted. One of the many effects of divorce is that one entire side of a child's family may no longer be accessible. And many divorced parents cite this feeling of isolation as the main distress factor when bringing up their children.

Second, even when a family is intact, a child's grandparents may not be on hand to give advice. In previous decades, grandparents would probably have lived close to their married children, ready to help out whenever called upon. Today, it is highly likely that the grandparents live in a different city or that, even if they live nearby, they may have outside employment for at least part of the day.

This loss of access to caring family support is felt keenly by many mums and dads who want to be good parents but who also know that parenting doesn't come altogether naturally. So don't feel guilty or insecure when you find you don't have all the answers to questions about child-rearing. You're no different from anyone else. Ask your friends and family, read books like this one, and if necessary talk to child care professionals.

See also **Bonding; Fathers; Grandparents; Mothers; Older Parents; Separation and Divorce; Single-Parent Family; Working Mothers; Young Parents**.

Personality   Psychologists define 'personality' as the sum of all the emotional and behavioural attributes that combine to form a unique individual. Every child has personality, whether he is quiet or talkative, confident or insecure, sociable or solitary. Right from birth, a baby shows that he has a personality of his own and responds to his parents in a unique way.

There is little evidence to suggest that personality is genetically transmitted from parents to child. Studies of identical twins (who have the same inherited characteristics) have found that each child develops a distinctive and individual personality – there are few signs that identical twins ever have identical personalities. However, there is probably a small inherited component in personality.

There are numerous psychological theories that explain personality development in terms of upbringing. For instance, Sigmund Freud proposed that personality is formed in early childhood as a result of parents' attempts to control their child's natural self-centred instincts. And B. F. Skinner's theory of behaviourism claimed that personality is formed as a result of conditioning: e.g., a child who is rewarded for behaving in a certain way will repeat that behaviour until it becomes part of his personality, and a child who is punished for behaving in a certain way will learn not to repeat it.

On balance, it is probable that your child's personality develops from an interaction between inherited characteristics from you and your partner and environmental factors (including the way he is brought up). So he is not the way he is simply because 'he was born that way', *or* because 'you made him like that' – both sets of influences combine to determine his eventual personality.

See also **Genes; Unconscious.**

Phobias Similar to normal fears, but more pervasive. For instance, a child who is afraid of cats may cross to the other side of the road to avoid one – this will probably be the extent of his difficulty. But a child who has a phobia about cats will have a much more serious problem. It is not just that he avoids coming close to them: he cries when he sees one on television, when he sees a picture of one in a book, or even when another child casually mentions one.

To judge whether your child's fear is a harmless phase that he is likely to grow out of, or whether it is a phobia, consider the following pointers:

- *fear at the mere thought?* A child who has a fear will show anxiety only when he actually experiences the dreaded event, whereas a child with a phobia will become terribly upset even at the thought of it.
- *intensity of his fear?* In most cases, a child's fear will pass within a few minutes, and he will then settle down. But a child with a phobia will remain terrified for much longer, perhaps for several hours.
- *impact?* Fears usually have very little impact on a child's

life, except for the few minutes when he has a face-to-face encounter with the object of his fear. On the other hand, phobias are more sweeping and may take over his life, to the point where he is too afraid to cross the threshold of his home.

- *resistance?* Most children can be helped to overcome their fears quite quickly, and welcome their parents' support in this; phobias, though, are much more resistant to change, tending to persevere despite all efforts to remove them.

If you think your child's anxiety is a normal childhood fear, then (if you are right) it will almost certainly pass as he grows older and more confident. If you think his anxiety is a phobia, then (if you are right) it may have greater psychological significance, and merits closer consideration. Such fearful behaviour may be a symptom of a deep-rooted insecurity. You need to look closely at his life, in order to establish the underlying cause of his behaviour. Fortunately, genuine phobias are rare in childhood. Sometimes psychological advice may be necessary to help the child overcome the difficulty; this can be arranged through your health visitor or GP.

See also **Fears; Unhappiness**.

Physical Disability Any physical problem which affects a child's mobility can also have a significant effect on her psychological development. There are a number of reasons for this:

- *A child's self-confidence is affected by her physical appearance*. Disabled and non-disabled children share the same system of values about personal attractiveness; both groups have the same ideas about their ideal body shape. Therefore the self-confidence of a child with a physical disability can be particularly low.
- *She may be forced into adopting roles not normally associated with childhood*. She may, for instance, have to take the role of 'someone who misses class because she has to attend physiotherapy', or 'someone who sits out during the PE lesson'.
- *She may be denied roles that are usually accessible to*

children. Most children take for granted their role of 'someone who runs around in the playground' or 'someone who moves around the school without help'. A child who has physical difficulties can't access these roles, and this can make her unhappy.

Most children with a physical disability are integrated into ordinary primary and secondary schools, unless the difficulty is so severe that the child has no independent mobility whatsoever. Practical arrangements, such as ensuring the availability of ramps for access to the school building and access to a toilet suitable for a disabled user, can usually be made by the local education authority before the child's school placement begins. Some ordinary schools designate a teacher with specific responsibility for supervising the welfare of pupils with physical disability.

See also **Cerebral Palsy; Clumsiness; Coordination; Integration, Educational; Self-Confidence; Special Needs; Spina Bifida**.

Play   There are many different types of play, each stimulating the development of a different aspect of your child's life. The particular form of play that she engages in at any one time will depend on her level of maturity, her individual interests, and the toys she has available. The following categories of play are not mutually exclusive, and any one sequence can have more than one psychological purpose:

– *exploratory/discovery play*. Most commonly seen in infants up to the age of 18 months to two years, because it is through exploratory play that a growing child discovers the world around her. Only by reaching out and exploring does a baby begin to make sense of her surroundings. That's why toy activity centres, attached to the side of the cot, are so popular – a baby is fascinated by the different reactions she gets from it. And the more discoveries your child makes, the more she wants to explore further.
– *physical/energetic play*. Once your child is able to move around independently, she can play more adventurously. This type of play involves her moving her entire body, unlike exploratory play which may involve only her fin-

gers. Physical play – whether crawling, running, jumping, balancing, climbing or kicking – encourages a child's independence and boosts her self-confidence.

- *creative play* and *imaginative play*. Often regarded as two separate kinds of play, because the former involves a child making something out of materials (e.g., a model, a picture, a puppet), while the latter involves her in play-acting (e.g., pretend-play at home, play in the nursery's dressing-up corner). But there are two points common to these activities. First, they involve symbolism – i.e., the child pretends that an object represents something else – and, second, they allow her to express inner feelings (feelings that she may not even be aware of).

- *social play*. Occurs when children play together. The earliest stage is known as solitary play, because at this level (often until the age of 18 months to two years) a child is content to play on her own. Then comes parallel play (usually between the ages of two and three), in which two children play in the presence of one another, although they do not actually interact. And the last stage in the development of social play is cooperative play (usually at the age of three or four upwards), which takes place when two or more children play together. Through genuine cooperative play, children learn how to get on with each other, how to take turns, how to follow basic rules, and how to be fair.

- *manipulative/cognitive/problem-solving play*. Play of this sort includes activities in which a child learns by solving a puzzle. Jigsaws, form-boards, building bricks, lotto and other matching games, and memory games, all involve this type of play. Problem-solving play encourages a child to think about her actions and their consequences, to plan strategies for tackling new problems, and to learn through trial and error.

In understanding these different types of play, and the varied benefits they bring your child, don't think that she can be engaged only in one type of play at a time. Any single action can serve several purposes. Throwing a ball to another child is social play because it involves cooperation; it is physical and manipulative because her hands and limbs are involved; and it may also be imaginative, if the ball becomes an entirely different object in her mind. Try to ensure that your child has play experiences that cover the whole spectrum.

See also **Coordination; Gender Play; Imaginary Friend; Imagination; Knowledge; Learning through Play; Playing with Your Child; Sociable Play**.

Playgroup/Nursery, Starting Breaking away is a two-way process – as hard for you as it is for your child. A parent who has been looking after a child for several years is used to her company. True, every parent wants their child to stand on her own two feet. But feelings of regret that she is growing up are only natural, and both parent and child need time to adjust to this phase of development.

When she attends playgroup/nursery is probably the first time that parents let their child go out into the world on her own. Although playgroup provides a child-centred environment, it can be a daunting challenge all the same. Watch the first day of a new term. Some children cling tearfully to their parents at the playgroup doorstep, not wanting to let go; and the parents may be just as upset, though trying not to let it show. At the same playgroup, on the same day, other children arrive full of enthusiastic anticipation, happy to wave goodbye to their parents without so much as a backward glance.

You can take positive steps to help your child through this stage. First, prepare her for the event by talking about it beforehand. Visit the playgroup before the start of term to familiarise her with the staff and the building. Second, be calm and relaxed when taking her there each day. If she appears anxious, reassure her that there is nothing to worry about. Third, don't linger on the doorstep. Make the separation brief, even if she appears upset. Finally, talk about the day's activities with her when you collect her at the end of the session. All these measures reduce the pressure.

One of the advantages that a playgroup can have over nursery is that parents may take turns managing the group. This can have a settling effect on a child, especially if she is anxious. But it can work the other way as well – a manipulative child can use her parent's presence to draw attention

to herself. We all know of children who behave perfectly with everyone except their parents.

Should your child seem agitated at the thought of being away from you, do not panic. She needs you to be calm. Some parents feel embarrassed when they realise that other children are settling down while their own is not; but there is no need to be, because she will settle down in time. You'll find that after a couple of weeks she no longer needs you to be with her, and, with her new-found independence she will be a stronger, more mature individual. When, at a later stage, she attends school, the experience of having coped with playgroup/nursery will have given her extra confidence.

Preparation for leaving you can be made in other areas of your child's life as well. Attendance at leisure classes, or any type of structured, supervised recreational activity where parents are not constantly present (e.g., dancing classes, Tumble Tots, swimming lessons), provides her with an opportunity to cope on her own.

See also **Independence; School Readiness**.

203

Playing with Your Child   When you see your child playing happily with his toys, are you tempted to join in? Probably not. The chances are that you become involved only if he begins to make a terrible mess. Apart from that, you are probably reluctant to join in his play for two reasons – first, because you think he wouldn't want you to 'interfere', and second, because you think that your joining in would reduce the spontaneous nature of his play.

But adult involvement in a child's play need not be detrimental. Research into the effect of mothers' involvement in the play of their children (aged 18 months to two years) at home has revealed the following patterns:

- A child is likely to play for longer spells when his mother plays with him than when she stands by and watches.
- Although most pretend-play sequences are initiated by toddlers, few of them are actually completed when a child plays on his own; but the mother's involvement seems to ensure that pretend-play sequences are followed through by her toddler.

It has also been shown that adult intervention can improve the imaginative quality of children's play. A group of five-year-olds took part in a number of 20-minute demonstration sessions, in which an adult introduced a theme based on the children's interests and then used pipe-cleaner figures to act out a story around the theme. They were then encouraged to make up their own role-play situations, using a range of materials (Playdoh, pipe-cleaners, fabrics, etc.). The researchers found that these children (compared with a matched group of children who hadn't received this form of tutoring) showed more imagination and creativity in their play, as well as greater concentration. These improvements were still present more than two months after the demonstration sessions had ended. So sensitive adult participation can facilitate and enhance a child's play.

There are three principal ways, or styles, in which parents can become involved in their child's play.

- *by prestructuring*. With this style, a child's play is to a great extent prescribed by his parents, usually because they have given him toys which can only be played with in a specific way. For instance, a jigsaw only has one use, and by its nature determines what a child can do with it; on the other hand, building bricks can be used in many different ways. Parents sometimes also prestructure their child's play by telling him exactly how he has to play with a particular toy, rather than letting him discover for himself. A prestructuring style can inhibit imagination and creativity.

- *by redirecting*. With this style, the parent lets the young child initiate the play activity, but then takes over and redirects the play in a predetermined way. This often happens in an infant class or nursery, when the adult in charge subtly changes a child's original play activity into one which apparently has greater educational value. For instance, a child may be happily playing with water – thoroughly enjoying the fun of filling up empty containers and then emptying them back into the basin – when an adult suggests that he should count the number of small containers he can fill from the contents of the large container. That redirection shifts the nature of the child's play.

- *by extending*. This one differs from the two previous styles in that it is primarily concerned with stimulating the expressive and imaginative dimensions of play. The extending style requires parents to evaluate the play activity from their child's point of view, and then to elaborate and extend its key features (e.g., when your child is forming shapes from modelling clay, you can suggest other items he might make).

The next time you feel tempted to join in with your child's play, pause for a moment to consider which style of involvement you might adopt, think about the reasons for choosing that particular style, and try to anticipate the possible effect it might have. There is room for all three types of parental involvement: the prestructuring style can give a disorganised child some direction in his play, the redirecting style can make a dull play sequence more interesting, and the extending style can be helpful for a child who lacks self-confidence.

See also **Gender Play; Learning through Play; Play; Sociable Play**.

Pocket Money Most children aged five and over receive a small sum of pocket money each week from their parents, to spend or save themselves. (A child under five doesn't have an understanding of money and so there is little point in giving him a regular amount.) Pocket money allows a child a limited amount of responsibility over minor purchases, as well as giving him a sense of independence and teaching him the value of money.

Despite what you child may tell you, there is no fixed amount that he should receive at any specific age. You will soon learn that there is a universal law regarding pocket money . . . no matter how much you give your child, his friend always gets more! By all means, conduct a brief survey of other parents to determine the average amount for someone of your child's age, but expect to find a broad range. Some parents give a larger amount and expect their child to buy sweets, comics, etc. with it, while others give a smaller amount but give the child extra money for such everyday purchases. It really doesn't matter which system you operate, as long as you make the rules clear to your child. Tell him what things you expect his pocket money to cover.

Parents often use pocket money as a way of introducing their child to the concept of saving. And that's perfectly reasonable, as long as the saving element doesn't become so extreme that the child has nothing left to spend! Probably the best strategy is to encourage your child to save a proportion of his pocket money each week (e.g., a third) and to spend the rest in a planned way. A child aged five or six will need his parents' help in budgeting his money, because his natural inclination will probably be to spend it all as soon as he gets it. Explain to him why he should save (e.g., because he will eventually be able to buy a larger item normally outside his purchasing power), and discuss with him how and when the remaining sum might be spent.

You may be tempted to use the threat of withdrawing your child's pocket money as a way of discouraging misbehaviour. While this is reasonable on an occasional basis, it's not a good idea to use such a strategy regularly. First, you may find he is being punished on pocket-money day for something that happened four or five days earlier, and this is unlikely to have any effect on his misbehaviour. Second, it makes your system of family rules more like a penal

206

system and less like a loving, structured discipline. Third, once he realises he has lost his week's pocket money, he has no incentive to alter his misbehaviour. Far better to keep pocket money separate from any punishments you might want to use.

See also **Independence**.

Politeness The way a child behaves towards others – and politeness is part of this – has a direct effect on the way others behave towards her. Politeness, however, assumes less significance nowadays than it did in previous decades, and what is accepted by many contemporary parents would have been frowned upon by strict Victorians. Middle class children are no longer expected to stay silent until they are spoken to, to call their fathers 'sir', or to knock on the door of the family sitting-room before entering – thank goodness these ridiculous rules governing children's social behaviour have fallen by the wayside.

But this doesn't mean that all forms of politeness in children should become a thing of the past. On the contrary, politeness brings a child a number of benefits. For instance, it is likely to make her popular with others: a child who says 'please' when she wants to borrow a toy from her friend will be more liked than one who simply snatches it out of her friend's hand without asking. It has practical benefits, too – e.g., a child who says 'thank you' for being given a piece of chocolate is more likely to receive another piece than a child who takes it without comment. And her politeness can help put others at ease, because they will probably assume that she will also be well behaved (although this is not always the case).

Your child's attitude towards politeness stems directly from you and your behaviour; if your family values include being polite and respectful to others, then her behaviour will reflect this. Hearing you say 'please' and 'thank you' provides her with an appropriate model to imitate in her own relationships. And do show politeness towards her as well, not just to other adults – there's every reason why children should be treated politely. Encourage your child, from the age of three or four, to begin to use 'please' and 'thank you'.

Don't get angry with her, however, when she isn't polite, especially if she is not yet five. The chances are that she has simply forgotten what you told her, or that she didn't really grasp the rule in the first place. She may not pick up social conventions easily, and so you may have to specify the rules clearly – e.g., that she should say 'please' when she wants something, that she shouldn't barge in front of others in a queue, that she should apologise when she realises she has made a mistake. She will understand and follow your rules eventually.

See also **Manners; Modelling**.

Post-Natal Depression New mothers experience mixed emotions immediately after the birth of their baby. Some women are very excited at having a healthy baby to care for, and can't wait to shower love upon him. These women slip comfortably into the role of motherhood; their dream has been realised. Others, though – perhaps the majority – are more apprehensive. Thoughts such as 'Will I manage all the changing, feeding and washing?' or 'Will I learn to love him in the way that all my friends love their children?' run through the minds of many new mothers.

In addition to these typical worries, a new mother may still be recovering from the exhaustion and physical strain of the birth process itself. This too takes its toll on her stamina. Increased tiredness resulting from her baby's regular feeding schedule is a further pressure, and there may be additional stresses, including lack of privacy with her partner (because visiting hours are packed with friends and relatives), and unhelpful comments from other people ('I don't know how you manage with a baby screaming all the time like that').

Small wonder, then, that almost 80 per cent of women have mild feelings of depression and anxiety in the first few weeks following their baby's birth. Known as the 'baby blues', these emotions are so common as to be regarded as normal, and are an almost predictable first reaction to the onerous responsibility of caring for a baby. Like most stresses caused by fear of novel situations, the baby blues soon pass, as the mother gains self-confidence.

Many women with the baby blues are too embarrassed to

admit their feelings to their partner or friends. The image of motherhood promoted in the media is one in which the new mother sits in supreme serenity in the maternity ward, holding a silent, contented baby in her arms, while she chats proudly to her admiring husband. It takes courage for a woman to accept that the reality of motherhood is different from that rosy picture, and to admit to herself and to others that not everything is going according to plan. As a result, she may hide her true feelings.

But pretending that negative emotions do not exist isn't the answer. Denial of the baby blues won't make them go away. So if you are experiencing anxiety and depression – however mild – in the post-natal period:

- *Speak candidly to your partner*. Tell him exactly how you feel, no matter how irrational your worries may seem. Or talk to a close friend. Discussion with your health visitor will also be useful.
- *Talk to other new mothers*. You may be surprised and reassured to find that your experience is not unique. Sharing worries with other women in the same situation can have a very supportive effect.
- *Don't feel guilty*. Harsh comments, such as 'You should be ashamed of yourself, behaving like this when you've got a lovely new baby', are totally unhelpful, only produce pangs of guilt, and should be ignored. This pull-yourself-together approach falls short of the sensitivity required to help someone cope with anxieties.

'Post-natal depression' is a more severe and long-term condition, occurring in approximately one in 10 new mothers. Symptoms can include inability to sleep, appetite loss, episodes of tearfulness, loss of sex drive, and anxiety attacks. The significance of post-natal depression has only relatively recently been acknowledged by professionals as a genuine psychological disorder. Yet it has been given special consideration under the British legal system for many years – the Infanticide Act of 1938 states that a woman cannot be found guilty of the murder of her baby within a year of his birth because '*the balance of her mind was disturbed by reason of not having fully recovered from the effects of giving birth*'. (She can, however, be charged with the less serious offence of manslaughter.)

The cause of post-natal depression is disputed. Most

209

medical practitioners emphasise the role that hormones – natural chemicals that control bodily reactions – play in the condition. The marked chemical changes which occur throughout the pre-natal and post-natal periods, claim medical scientists, are directly linked to the appearance of post-natal depression. Some women seem relieved to be told their problem is 'physical rather than psychological'. Drug therapy aimed at resolving the hormonal difficulty is an increasingly popular form of treatment, with new advances being made all the time.

Yet there are other professionals who reject this explanation of post-natal depression. Many psychologists maintain that the baby blues and post-natal depression are linked to a woman's personality and the pressures in her life. Evidence for this comes from studies that have found that many women experiencing this form of depression had a depressive nature before their pregnancy, or were subject to pre-pregnancy stresses (e.g., money worries, marital difficulties).

The true explanation is probably somewhere in between. Effective management of post-natal depression combines both the psychological and the medical approaches, and should (depending on individual circumstances) include:

- *drug treatment*, prescribed by a general practitioner after detailed medical examination;
- *psychotherapy*, from a qualified therapist who is able to help the mother gain insight into her anxieties and concerns;
- *contact with self-help groups*, organised by other mothers who have experienced similar problems. Local health clinics have the relevant contact numbers.

Hospitalisation is necessary only in the very extreme form of post-natal depression (puerperal psychosis) which affects approximately 1 in 500 new mothers. This psychological disorder results in a new mother losing contact with reality; she may become confused, thought-disordered, and almost certainly unable to care adequately for her baby. Treatment for puerperal psychosis is lengthy, and a full recovery may take more than two years.

See also **Bonding; Fathers; Mothers; Parents; Working Mothers**.

Potty-Training

Although children vary in the ages at which they gain bowel and bladder control – girls usually achieve success with potty-training more quickly than boys, and bowel control is usually achieved before bladder control – you will find the following 'ages and stages' helpful in planning your child's training:

1 year   A baby of this age cannot possibly be potty-trained because the nerves and muscles involved are not sufficiently mature for another two or three months. But there's no harm in letting him play with a potty, just as long as you don't expect him to be able to use it.

15 months   By now, your baby begins to sense when his bowels and bladder are emptying, but he isn't yet ready to retain the contents. You can try asking if he needs to use the toilet, but don't be surprised when he says 'no' or else looks rather puzzled by your question.

18 months   Although a toddler of this age usually knows when he is wetting or soiling his nappy, this doesn't mean that he has sufficient muscle control to regulate the flow. However, since he shows some of the signs of readiness, you can begin to sit him on the potty – after meals is the best time. He'll have a few successes, but mostly failures. He'll probably have a sense of pride at having his own potty.

21 months   Potty-training is well under way. You find that he seems to want to use the potty a lot, sometimes only a few minutes after he last used it. That's perfectly normal, and occurs for two reasons. First, he has an increasing awareness of bowel and bladder sensations. Second, he is as keen as you to avoid accidents, and isn't fully confident about his own skills. He likes to talk to you about his successes with potty-training.

2 years   He is happy to sit on the potty, perhaps for up to half an hour at a time, and he gets upset if you try to remove him before he is fully ready.

A typical two-year-old is fiercely independent, determined to pull his pants up by himself. And he will love being praised by you when he uses the potty.

2½ years   Even though he has the occasional 'accident', he wouldn't thank you for giving him the opportunity to wear a nappy during the day. You probably find that the nappy he wears during a short sleep is still dry when he wakes up.

3 years   At this age, most children have full bowel and bladder control during the day, and 75 per cent are trained at night as well (90 per cent are by the age of five). He likes to have a potty by his bed (or a light left on in the toilet) so he can use it during the night. He can retain the contents of his bowel and bladder for up to four or five hours.

STARTING POTTY-TRAINING

Putting on that last nappy is a magic moment. For your child, it signals a new stage of independence: no longer reliant on you to change him and clean him, he can now take responsibility for himself when using the toilet – that's a great feeling of achievement. And for you, there's a sense of pride in your child's progress, as well as relief in knowing you'll have no more dirty nappies to deal with.

But do remember that there's no point in trying to start potty-training too early, because an infant younger than 15–18 months simply isn't mature enough to make a conscious decision to use the potty properly.

Take bladder control. The bladder is made of stretchy material which allows it to become half full of urine before we even know about it – only when it is almost 75 per cent full do we begin to have a feeling of discomfort. However, in young children the bladder empties automatically, long before that stage of discomfort is reached. Elementary control of bladder muscles doesn't begin until 15 months at the earliest.

Your child is ready to begin toilet-training when he shows one or more of the following signs, most of which emerge around 18–22 months:

- *He watches you, or others in the family, use the toilet.* This alone does not mean he has the necessary muscle control for toilet-training, but his interest is a very positive sign.
- *He lets you know his nappy is wet or soiled.* Once he can draw your attention to the fact that he has used his nappy – either by gesture or by words – then he is probably ready to start potty-training.
- *He knows when he is wetting or soiling his nappy.* When he deliberately indicates to you that he's filling his nappy, then he has a level of awareness that means potty-training can begin.
- *He indicates that he's about to fill his nappy.* There is no doubt that your child is ready to learn bladder and bowel control when he is mature enough to let you know that he needs the toilet – at this stage, muscle control is well developed.
- *His nappy is dry even though he has worn it for several hours.* If his nappy is still dry late in the morning even though you put it on first thing, then he almost certainly has some muscle control. The same applies if you find that his nappy is consistently dry after being worn during a short nap.

There isn't one particular 'right' moment to start potty-training, although statistics confirm that your child will probably be fully potty-trained by the age of two. (Resist pressure from grandparents/mothers-in-law/aunts who insist that they potty-trained children at a much younger age.)

Starting potty-training too early, before a child is ready either physically or psychologically, always causes problems. For instance, parents who think that their six-month-old infant is toilet-trained because he eventually uses the potty after sitting on it for several minutes, are likely to become angry with him at a later stage when he is able to get off the potty by himself and walk away without having used it. Frustration and confrontation will be the outcome, and this bad feeling may re-surface when potty-training begins in earnest at a later date.

How to Potty-Train

Between the ages of 18 and 22 months, your infant will show some signs of readiness for potty-training. But before

you begin, make up your mind never to smack him. Potty-training rarely goes smoothly, and few parents can honestly say they have never felt like smacking their child when he wet their new carpet. No matter how strong this feeling is, though, ignore it. If you do smack your child for struggling with toilet-training, he will become worse.

Remember that you can't force him through potty-training – like eating, it's one of the few things in childhood that parents cannot do without their child's cooperation. Of course, you can frighten him into remaining seated on the potty, but you can't force him to empty his bowels and bladder on demand. He should be encouraged, not bullied.

To begin potty-training in earnest:

- *Familiarise your child with the potty*. You may have done this already in the preceeding months, but you should now make a point of explaining to him what a potty is for and how you expect him to use it. Do this several times, until you feel he understands what you are saying.

- *Encourage him to sit on the potty at least three times each day, particularly after mealtimes.* He can't gain bowel and bladder control until he is able to sit on it for a few minutes. This may be strange and uncomfortable for him at first, but, with your encouragement, he'll soon get used to it. You can reasonably expect him to have established a routine for sitting on the potty within three weeks of starting training.

- *Use any positive incentive to keep him on the potty.* Some children like to look at a book while sitting there, or to listen to music or to play games with mum and dad. Don't worry if he stays there for 20–30 minutes, thoroughly enjoying himself – potty-training should be fun, so if there is something in particular that makes your child feel comfortable and relaxed on the potty, use it!

- *Link potty-time to his body's natural cycle.* You will very soon learn your child's bowel and bladder rhythms, and potty-training will be more successful when it ties in with his body's natural level of activity. For some children this may mean sitting on the potty three times a day, while for others it may mean five times.

- *Give him lots of praise when he uses the potty appropriately.* He'll love being made a fuss of when he succeeds with the potty (and he will probably have his first success within seven days of starting training); a big cuddle from you, a beaming smile on your face, and words of praise will make him want to do the same again the next time.

- *Let your child run about the house without any nappies or pants on, two or three weeks after potty-training begins.* Of course, this strategy inevitably results in a wet or soiled carpet, especially in the early stages, and some parents would rather avoid such a mess at all costs. But it does make things easier for your child.

- *Once he appears to have some bowel and bladder control (probably within 14–28 days after training begins), give him trainer pants.* This signifies another stage in independence, and is another boost to his self-confidence. Remember that trainer pants only absorb some fluid, not all.

Be prepared to persist. Some children become trained very quickly (e.g., within two weeks), while others take months. This can be very frustrating for you, especially when you know other children of the same age who are already past this stage. Stick with it, though, until success is achieved. And remember that all children have toilet 'accidents' during potty-training – treat these in a matter-of-fact way, without losing your temper. As a rough guide, a child aged 30 months may have up to four 'accidents' each week, whereas the rate will have dropped to around two per fortnight by the time he is three years old.

When your child is using a potty regularly during the day, let him use the toilet. This can start at the age of two (though a young child may be frightened and insecure sitting on a full-sized toilet). Use a special child's toilet seat which fits into the one that's already there. Even then, however, he may want to take your hand, or to hold on to the sink. He may also need a small step so that he can climb on to the toilet seat. At this stage, you can also begin to teach him to wipe his own bottom (wiping from the front to the back). Some children are keen to do this because it helps them maintain independence and privacy, while others prefer someone else to do it for them. By three years, he may be able to clean himself adequately.

See also **Bed-Wetting**.

Pre-Natal Development   Life inside the womb is fascinating! The process of development from the moment of conception to the moment of delivery is divided into three phases:

- *the ovum*. This phase lasts about 10–14 days; it is the period from the moment when the nucleus of the sperm fuses with the nucleus of the ovum until the fertilised ovum becomes firmly implanted in the wall of the uterus. From then on, the ovum is dependent on the mother, and the next phase of pre-natal life begins.
- *the embryo*. Progress is rapid in subsequent weeks. The embryo becomes surrounded by membranes which form a sac, filled with a watery liquid. The embryo floats in this liquid, but is attached to the sac by the umbilical cord, which itself is attached to the placenta. The pla-

216

centa acts as a filter for the embryo (and foetus). During this period, which lasts until about eight weeks after conception, an embryo starts to develop many major organs, including eyes, ears, the mouth (which can open and close), limbs and the all-important spinal cord.

- *the foetus*. This third period of growth lasts from around two months until the birth itself, and sees further development of body systems already laid down during the embryo period. By 12 weeks, muscles are well developed, eyelids and lips are present, toes and fingers are observable, and foetal sex can be identified. Around the end of the 16th week, a mother may report that she feels her foetus beginning to move. It is now over four inches long, and the ears are formed. By 24 weeks, eyes are completely formed (but closed), and taste buds appear on the tongue. A foetus is capable of surviving if born at this point.

Knowledge of foetal capabilities from the 24th to the 40th week has been compiled from two sources. First, studies of premature babies born from the 24th week onwards have been able to plot changes in the senses of the foetus. By that week a baby's nervous, respiratory and other bodily systems have advanced to such an extent that it can survive outside the womb, with special help. As a result, we now know, for instance, that a foetus born at

- 28–33 weeks will make mild attempts to avoid bright lights and loud noises, may have a weak cry, and will have some movements;
- 33–36 weeks has stronger movements, a stronger response to bright lights and loud noises, and will give a good cry when hungry;
- 36–40 weeks will begin to track movements of objects with its eyes, will be active, and will have a very solid cry when distressed.

The sensory abilities of premature babies under 40 weeks are not developed to the same extent as those of full-term babies. For instance, their sense of touch is not so highly attuned and they are not very sensitive to pain. Yet they do respond to other types of sensory stimulation. Research has confirmed that babies born from 28 weeks onwards can

217

differentiate basic tastes such as sweet, sour, salt and bitter, and basic odours.

A second source of knowledge about the sensory skills of an unborn foetus comes from the widespread use of ultrasonography. Examinations carried out with this technique demonstrate that a foetus spends a great deal of time moving around the womb. And since these movements tend to be coordinated, this probably means it has a good sense of balance. Ultrasound techniques have shown that an unborn child will give a startled response to a loud noise. Eye movements have also been detected.

With this level of sensitivity, it is hardly surprising that a foetus can be affected by stimulation outside the womb. However, the fact that an unborn foetus at 28 weeks responds to noise does not mean that it hears these noises in the same way as an already born foetus of similar maturity. Remember that an unborn foetus is surrounded by fluid, which is not very good at transmitting sound. Think for a moment about your own experiences in your local swimming-baths. The pool area may be very noisy, with lots of people shouting to each other and splashing around. The sound echoes loudly from one wall to another. However, as soon as you put your head under water, sounds become muffled. Submerged in water, you have great difficulty picking out individual sounds and specific voices. Scientists believe that's what it is like for a baby surrounded by liquid in the womb.

As well as this, the outer ears of a foetus are covered by a creamy material known as vernix, which will act as a further barrier to clear hearing inside the womb. Studies have also shown that although an unborn baby may be startled at first by a loud noise (indicated by an increase in foetal heartbeat), the effect soon fades.

There is no direct connection between the mother's nervous system and that of her foetus. Yet, as early as the 1940s, scientists proved that there is an indirect connection between a mother's emotional condition and her foetus's physiology. This happens because emotional arousal – such as anger or fear – causes a physical reaction which releases chemicals into the bloodstream. Hormones are also secreted. These biochemical changes are transferred through the placenta, causing the foetus to become agitated. Foetal movements in the womb increase many times over when the mother experiences emotional stress. If the period of excitation lasts for weeks, the foetus may persist with this higher rate of movement for the remainder of the pregnancy.

See also **Memory; Ultrasound**.

Q

Quality Time Family life is hectic, no matter what age your children are. When they are babies, their physical care takes up so much time, what with the constant washing, changing and feeding; when they are toddlers, they demand a lot of attention because they want to be amused so much of the time; when they're pre-schoolers there's the fetching and carrying to playgroups and nurseries, and the endless rounds of parties; and when they reach school age they suddenly become involved in a whole new range of educational and social activities which occupy so much of their day. And you have your own busy lives to lead.

No wonder, then, that family communication can falter in the hubbub of everyday life. That's why it is so important to make 'quality time' – a time when outside pressures are laid aside, when every member of the family sits down and shares his feelings and ideas, while the others listen. Quality time is the opportunity for parents and children to keep in touch with each other about what's happening in their lives.

Quality time can be individual – for instance, between you and just one of your children. It can be achieved by setting aside a specific time each day to be with him, talking to him about his experiences that day, or perhaps playing a game with him. Some children are pleased just to have the chance to talk about their favourite television programme with their parents. Even if you can manage this for only a few minutes each day, your child will benefit from it.

Or quality time can be a whole-family event. Mealtime is often the best time, since this is perhaps the only moment of the day when all the members of your family sit down together. Unfortunately, the lure of television is often too great, and they may prefer to sit with their meals on their laps, eyes glued to the box, without a word passing between them. But do make a point of encouraging a family meal, and make sure that everyone round the table has a chance to share their experiences. A small amount of quality time gives a large amount of psychological satisfaction.

See also **Bonding; Emotional Deprivation; Working Mothers**.

Quarrels No parents can deal with all the stresses and strains of everyday life without occasional disagreements – but no child likes to witness mum and dad quarrelling.

Tension between you and your partner can show itself in many ways. Raised voices are not the only means of conveying the fact that there are ill-feelings in the household. Many parents hold the mistaken view that if they do not actually scream at each other in front of the children, the children will have no idea there is any problem. Unfortunately, the statement 'We may not get on well with each other but at least the children don't see that' is rarely borne out in reality.

The non-verbal communication that goes on between couples – the gestures, the unsaid comments, the looks on faces, the expressions in the eyes – is just as meaningful to a young child as the spoken word. Children are as sensitive to body language as they are to what is actually said.

Research has shown that young children are sensitive to particular marital tensions – tension over dissatisfaction in the sexual relationship, tension over one parent feeling the other is not as considerate as he or she should be, tension arising from emotions not being expressed openly, tension about matters not being discussed openly, and tension over one spouse feeling dominated by the other. If you and your partner do have conflict over any of these issues, or any others, treat them as high priorities and make an effort to resolve them as quickly as possible.

Regular quarrels between parents can have a bad effect on their child for a number of reasons. First, he needs a stable family in which to thrive, and if he feels this stability is threatened – by repeated disagreements between mum and dad – he'll become unsettled. Loss of family security disturbs a young child. Second, parents who fight frequently with each other are more likely to disagree about the way their child should be disciplined, and this confuses him. Third, a child models his behaviour on his parents, to a large extent. If they quarrel a lot, then he is likely to repeat this behaviour in his own relationship with others of his age. Lastly, a child is affected by parental arguments because he wants to remain loyal to both of them, irrespective of the

221

reasons underlying the arguments. Witnessing mum and dad fighting tears his loyalties in two.

Yet disagreements are a normal part of family life. And a child has to learn to cope with this. Negative emotions – such as anger, dislike and jealousy – are experienced by everybody at some time or another. This is perfectly normal. But some parents feel that they, and their children, should always repress these negative feelings, in the hope that they will go away. In fact, this tends to have the opposite effect. Repression of such feelings injects even more tension into a relationship. And a child brought up to think that only pleasant feelings are to be allowed free expression will eventually feel guilty every time he has an unpleasant thought. He has to learn that there are appropriate ways of expressing anger and ill-feeling, that the release of negative emotions need not necessarily be destructive.

This doesn't mean that you should have regular arguments in front of the children. Of course not. But a child who sees that his parents argue, yet still love each other, will eventually understand that arguments and love are not mutually exclusive. He will learn that it is possible to be angry with someone and love that person at the same time. An occasional parental disagreement in front of children need not be harmful, if handled properly.

In addition, if a child sees that arguments can have a beginning and an end, that they do not have to drag on for days and days, and that two people arguing can settle their differences, then something positive has been achieved. You can teach your child, by example, that disagreements can be resolved without any long-term damage to a relationship. This will help him handle conflict in his own relationships.

Should your child see you quarrelling, reassure him that the fight does not really mean anything. Tell him explicitly that although you are angry with each other, you still care for each other. Make sure he understands that it is not wrong to feel angry with someone, and encourage him to discuss his feelings rather than conceal them.

There are certain limits to this. Physical aggression, or even the threat of physical aggression, between you and your partner should never be witnessed by your child, under any circumstances. A child will always become terrified and insecure if he sees one parent struck a blow by the other. He may become afraid to leave the house in case something dreadful happens when he is out. Or he may become afraid that one day he himself will be hit.

See also **Aggression; Body Language; Fighting; Modelling; Separation and Divorce; Unhappiness**.

Questions Once your child starts talking, she will soon realise that asking questions is one way of finding out more about her world. And the wonderful thing about asking questions (as far as she is concerned) is that it involves social contact with you – it's a very pleasant way for her to learn. A young child's questions generally fall into one of these categories:

- *facts*. 'Why is grass green?' 'Who makes dogs have a tail?' 'When is my favourite TV programme on?' 'Why is rain wet?' This sort of question enables her to acquire information about specific aspects of her life that interest her. Some of these questions can be very complex, even though they appear straightforward.
- *permission*. 'Can I have another sweet?' 'Will you take me to the park?' 'Is it all right if me and my friend play outside?' 'Can I draw now?' This sort of question lets a child test out the limits of acceptable behaviour, and helps her establish the boundaries within her immediate environment.
- *ideas/feelings*. 'Do you think I should buy a present for dad?' 'Why are you crying?' 'What will happen if I don't go to nursery today?' 'What do ice-cream and chips taste like together?' This sort of question allows her to express her ideas and feelings, and to assess how other people react to them.

Much to your dismay – and irritation – you may find that your child asks you the same question again, even though you gave her a satisfactory reply a few minutes ago. She does this for a number of reasons. First, asking questions is a good way of getting your attention, because most parents are pleased when their child shows interest in something – and it doesn't take her long to realise this strategy is very effective. In some instances, two-year-olds and three-year-olds repeat questions solely to attract more attention. Second, your child may not understand the answer you gave, even though she seemed satisfied at the time. Asking the question again gives her another opportunity to think about the issue, and to confirm what you originally told her. It is highly unlikely that she repeats questions just to annoy you!

Always answer her questions at a level appropriate to her age. There is absolutely no point in explaining theories of nutrition to a four-year-old who asks why hamburgers are so tasty. Don't be tempted to give the sort of in-depth reply you would give to an adult who asked you the same question. Look closely at the expression on her face when you answer her – if she seems bored and disinterested then you have almost certainly pitched your reply too high.

You may find she is adept at asking questions that you don't always have the right answer for. For instance, do you know why the sky is blue? Probably not – and there's no harm in admitting it to your child when she asks. Tell her you don't know, and encourage her to find the information in a reference book. This can be a fun activity that you and she can share.

She may ask a question which you find embarrassing but which she, in her innocence, does not (e.g., 'Why do you always fight with each other?' or 'Where do babies come from?') – a young child is much less inhibited about these issues, and is quite happy to ask about them. This may make you feel uncomfortable, perhaps because the question is about sex, or because she asks it very loudly in a crowded supermarket. Irrespective of your own feelings, however, if she cares enough to ask a question about something personal then she deserves a reply – one that is honest, yet worded so that she understands what you say. Never tell her that she shouldn't ask such questions, since she may become afraid to express herself openly.

See also **Knowledge; Learning Skills**.

R

Reflexes Healthy new babies have a number of reflexes (actions that they perform automatically, without thinking), some of which are used by paediatricians to assess them immediately after birth.

You may have noticed that as soon as your baby was born, she was briefly examined by medical and nursing staff, who gave her an Apgar assessment. Devised in the 1950s by an American doctor, the Apgar system gives a rating of two, one or zero to the following physical characteristics: heart rate, breathing, muscle tone, reflexes and colour. The higher the score, the better. A healthy baby will probably score at least seven; a score of less than this indicates she may be at risk, and a score of four or under indicates she may be in a critical condition. The Apgar assessment is repeated five minutes later. Reflexes, then, are a crucial part of early development.

A newborn baby's reflexes include:

- *swallowing*. She knows how to swallow and breathe at the same time, without choking.
- *sucking*. When a finger or nipple is placed in her mouth, she automatically starts to suck.
- *rooting*. She will turn her head towards a finger or nipple that is gently stroking her cheek.
- *grasping*. When an object or finger presses down on the palm of her hand, she will grasp it firmly.
- *walking*. When held upright with her feet barely touching the floor, she will take a few small steps.
- *the Moro reflex*. If she is moved suddenly so that her head drops back, she will fling out her arms and legs, open her hands, arch her back, and then bring her arms together as if trying to catch hold of something.

Some of these reflexes persist throughout a baby's life and are necessary for basic survival (e.g., sucking, swallowing), while others fade during the first year (e.g., the Moro reflex, rooting). Some scientists believe that many of those reflexes which disappear soon after birth were useful at an earlier period in human evolution, but are no longer required – for instance, a grasping reflex would have been helpful when humans' ancestors lived in trees. Although reflexes are inborn and are essential for healthy development, a baby also begins to learn actively about the world around her right from birth.

See also **Knowledge; Learning through Play**.

Religion Many families regard religion as important, and a home life with religious commitment provides a structure that can be a source of comfort and security for young children.

The mind of a child is particularly receptive to a belief in God. He might not have the same concept of God as adults, but he will happily accept the existence of a deity – he won't challenge the view that there is a God who makes the world the way it is, because this notion makes sense to him. And if you respect religious values, then your child will almost certainly follow your example in the pre-school years. (Of course, when he grows older – especially when he reaches adolescence – he may begin to look at alternative systems of belief.)

Nursery or school is often the first place outside home to involve a child in religious activities. Come Easter time, nearly every nursery and infant class has brightly painted eggs proudly displayed, and the walls covered in paintings of yellow chickens. Then in December there are the Christmas celebrations, playlets about Mary and Joseph, and lots of parties and presents. Other major world religions also have festivals which engage children in a hive of activity.

Children usually take great delight in the practicalities of religion. Whatever the persuasion, going to a place of worship can prove a fascinating experience for the eager young mind, and rituals and prayers can be a source of wonder. When a child develops an interest in religion early on in life, it is often maintained for some time, perhaps even into adulthood.

The Americans have a saying: 'The family that pray together, stay together.' While this may be true of some families, it does not apply to everybody. There are many religious families that experience conflicts, stresses and emotional difficulties. But a strong religious tradition within a family can give a growing child a sense of respect for himself and others.

See also **Religious Differences**.

Religious Differences　Parents don't always share the same religious beliefs. There are many 'mixed' marriages – that is, marriages where the partners have different religious backgrounds. In such instances, a child may find religion confusing rather than comforting, especially if his parents have not reconciled their differences.

The time for a couple to sort out their religious differences is before children are born. In fact, the best time to do it is before marriage itself – this way, there is plenty of time to consider all the angles. Religion usually engenders strong feelings, and giving up one religion for another – even when it is in the best interests of the family – can be a very painful process. Discussions on the religious upbringing of children should never be left to the last minute.

Some couples in a mixed marriage take the view that their child should be brought up to experience both religions in the house, and that when he is old enough he should choose for himself. Although this may seem a commonsense solution to the predicament, giving a child an opportunity to choose his religion in fact places too great a responsibility on to young shoulders. Religious systems are complex; many adults cannot explain the ins and outs of their own religion, so it is unreasonable to expect a young child to make such a decision. Parents must make the choice for him. In later years, he may elect to challenge their religious views – that is part of growing up. But parents should provide firm guidance at the start.

Even where partners in a mixed marriage agree to opt for only one religion, problems can arise through pressure from friends and family. Wars start through religious belief – hardly surprising, then, that family skirmishes can erupt for the same reason.

A child who experiences religious tolerance within his own family is likely to adopt a similar attitude himself outside the home. However, both partners need to have their own views clear before they can hope to provide an adequate example for their child to follow. If religious differences between husband and wife are not resolved, and if they continue into married life, their children will come to regard religion as a source of conflict, not as a source of security.

See also **Religion**.

Road Safety The prime responsibility for teaching road safety rules to your child rests with you. You can't wait until she is at school, in the hope that her teacher will present road safety to her as part of the curriculum – by then, it might be too late. Pedestrian road accidents are the major cause of deaths amongst children: figures from the World Health Organisation show that they constitute between 35 and 50 per cent of all accidental deaths of children under 14. Child pedestrians as a whole are a vulnerable group of road users, but the section of the population most at risk is children between 5 and 9 years of age; and about twice as many boys as girls are hit by cars.

The best way to teach your child about road safety is to use a method that involves action, not just talking. Of course, you need to explain to her about the dangers of traffic (and, depending on her age, you might even need to explain what 'traffic' is), about the effect that a car has when it hits a pedestrian, about the need to look and listen for cars when trying to cross the road, and so on. This is a very important part of road safety. But it won't be sufficient on its own.

Having given your child a basic explanation, go out on the street with her, in order to give her a practical opportunity to carry out your instructions. Demonstrate that some parts of the road are better for crossing than others, specify why that is (e.g., because of better visibility, less traffic congestion), and emphasise that she should always use a controlled crossing when getting from one side of the road to the other. Give her first-hand experience of using an appropriate crossing point, talking her through it stage by stage.

While giving this practical demonstration, ask your child lots of questions. What might happen if she runs across the road without first looking for cars? When should she start to cross? What should she do if the 'green man' starts to flash when she's half-way across? How should she cross the road if there isn't a suitable crossing point? Questions like this will encourage your child to think about road safety, and to see the purpose of it. And this way, she is more likely to follow the rules.

Encourage her to notice aspects of traffic when she is out of doors with you. For instance, she should be able to differentiate busy roads from quiet roads, and lorries from cars. She should also know that she can be seen more easily by drivers if she is wearing light-coloured clothing. She should realise that it is safer to cross at a point where there are no parked cars than it is to cross between parked cars. This will help her see road safety from the driver's perspective, as well as from her own.

See also **Hazards**.

Routine Every child needs consistency and structure in her life. Knowing that some events in everyday life are predictable gives her a sense of security, a sense of well-being. And a regular routine, especially in early childhood, also gives parents a sense of well-being. Ask any mum and dad who are woken up regularly through the night by a baby who wants to be fed or to play – they'll soon tell you how much they want to establish a night-time routine with their infant!

Routines help an older child as well. Most three and four-year-olds like to know, for example, that they go to playgroup on Mondays and Wednesdays, that they go swimming on Fridays, and so on. This sort of structure enables a child to plan ahead. Later in life, she'll be much more able to organise herself if she's had experience of doing it in childhood.

But too much structure and routine can be counter-productive. Some parents fall into the trap of pre-planning their child's day to such an extent that she is propelled from one activity to another, without having any time to reflect on her enjoyment of them. Her days and weeks should always be flexible enough to allow for a change of plan; and she should always have some free time in which to plan her own amusements.

Try to involve your child in planning her own routines, even at a very basic level. Naturally her idea of, say, a suitable time for bed will be different from yours, but she is more likely to feel comfortable with a routine that takes her own views into account than one which she feels has been imposed unfairly upon her.

See also **Bedtime; Discipline; Hospital; Illness; Over-Organised**.

230

Scapegoat Some children get blamed even when they haven't done anything wrong. Psychologists use the term 'scapegoating' when one particular child always gets blamed for mishaps at home, whether or not he is actually responsible for what has happened. This type of scapegoating occurs when parents cope with stress by inadvertently redirecting their anxieties on to their child. Scapegoating happens to some extent in every family; few parents are able to resist the temptation to shout at their child from time to time when they themselves are upset. Isolated incidents like this, however, will not cause long-term psychological problems for your child – though he won't like it, and you may feel thoroughly guilty yourself after your temper has cooled.

But when parents regularly scapegoat their child, there can be more serious emotional effects. He may become locked into a vicious circle of ever-lowering self-esteem. Scapegoating makes a child lose his self-respect, which adversely affects his relationships with others, which in turn decreases his self-respect . . . And so it goes on.

To determine whether scapegoating is happening in your family, ask yourself these questions:

– *Is your child willing to take the blame for things that go wrong at home, even when he is almost certainly not responsible?* A child who is scapegoated becomes conditioned to admit to any mishap, and automatically stands first in line to receive punishment even though he is totally innocent.
– *Do you find you nag at your child constantly over trivial matters?* Of course, he may be going through a genuinely difficult phase, and your non-stop complaints may be justified. But it could be that he has become a convenient punchball for you to release your own frustrations on.
– *Does he accept every reprimand without challenge, even when he initially appears surprised at the accusations?* Most children become upset when they think they are

unfairly blamed. A child accustomed to being scapegoated soon stops defending himself because he knows
it's not worthwhile.

– *Do you feel under a lot of stress, and that your child
never gives you any time to be on your own?* Emotional
pressure diminishes our patience in dealing with the
minor hassles of everyday life. In this situation, your
child's normal demands can seem intolerable, and you
may be reprimanding him when he's really not misbehaving at all.

The following suggestions may help you reduce – or avoid
altogether – scapegoating in your family:

● *Talk openly with your partner about your worries.*
Honest communication between couples is the best way
of alleviating the sorts of personal stress that can lead
to your children being scapegoated.

● *Be prepared to accept that you are not perfect, that you
can make mistakes just like anyone else.* Parents who
have trouble accepting their fallibility will always try to
put the blame on someone else – probably their child.

● *Explain to your child why he's being punished.* Instead
of merely blaming him for his actions, give him reasons
for *your* action. He is less likely to feel scapegoated if
he is given an explanation for each reprimand. And you
may even discover, when you hear your own explanation, that it isn't a very valid reason for punishing
him.

● *Be willing to say 'sorry' to him if you have wrongly
accused him of something he didn't do.* You are not
being weak by apologising. Your child deserves honesty
from you, and your willingness to show regret sets a
good example.

A child may make himself the family scapegoat – even
though he isn't consciously aware he's doing so – as a means
of getting attention. If you think this describes your child,
then it is you who have to change your behaviour, not him.
Instead of attending to him only when he misbehaves, give
him attention when he is behaving properly. Tell him how
pleased you are that he's not breaking any rules, and find
a few minutes each day when you and he can spend time
doing something together. This will reduce his need to

attract blame in order to get your attention. And try ignoring some of his disruptive misbehaviour. The more he realises that making himself a scapegoat doesn't get extra attention, then the less likely he is to behave this way.

See also **Attention-Seeking Behaviour; Bullying; Guilt; Lying; Stealing; Swearing; Victim**.

School, Choice of In previous years, parents couldn't choose which school their child attended because local education authorities had specific catchment areas for each school, and these boundaries could not be crossed. However, the regulations governing school selection have changed, and now parents have a broader choice. You are unlikely to pick a school for your child which involves lots of travelling each day, but you will probably find that there are at least four or five local authority primary schools within reasonable distance of your house.

Many parents opt for their nearest school (their local primary school) because this is the one that most of their child's friends will attend. Starting school is a new stage in his life and it is easier for him if his friends start school with him, at the same time. Another reason for choosing your local school is that your older children may already attend it; having children at two or three different schools can cause practical problems.

Whether or not your child does in the end go to his local school, you should be satisfied that whichever you choose is the one most able to meet his needs, that it is the one you definitely want him to attend. And the only way you can find this out is by visiting the school yourself or when choosing between a number of schools, by visiting each one. This may be time-consuming, but it is time well spent – after all, your child will spend six years there!

Phone each school well in advance – in the term before your child's starting date – in order to make an appointment with the headteacher. The response you receive to your telephone call will give you an initial idea of the way the school reacts to visitors. Don't bring your child with you when you go there (unless the headteacher asks), or you will end up thinking more about the impression he's making on the school staff than about the impression they are making on you.

During this visit, you need to know what to look for. Some parents are concerned about the general atmosphere, some are concerned about the reading scheme used in the infant department, while others may be more interested in musical activities. The following list gives suggestions for the aspects you should probably consider, but there may be others that are of particular concern to you (if there are, make a list of them and take it with you):

- *class teacher*. Meet the teacher who will be responsible for your child's class. Talk to her about the work she does, the equipment she uses, and the range of non-academic activities she provides for pupils. During your discussion – and don't be afraid to ask lots of questions – assess her attitude towards children, and decide whether or not you feel comfortable with the ideas she presents to you. Would you like to have been taught by this teacher when you started school? The impression made on you by the headteacher is also something you should consider.
- *staffing*. Aside from your child's teacher, you will want to know the number of other teachers, and the total number of pupils. The school may have specialist teachers who have responsibility for such areas as additional support for pupils with learning difficulties, music, drama or science. You can also inquire whether the first infant class has additional help from an auxiliary.
- *building*. A clean, solid school building does not necessarily mean that teaching standards are satisfactory. But children learn better in a fresh, appealing classroom with adequate heating than they do in a cold, shabby building, with paint peeling off the walls and water coming in through the roof. And have a good look round your child's prospective classroom – it should have a stimulating appearance, with plenty of wall displays, separate work and play areas, and a good range of books and equipment.
- *educational standards*. The early stage of schooling is more to do with settling in, learning to cope with a routine, being part of a group and being able to follow class rules, than it is with learning in the academic sense.

But your children do make great educational strides in these first few years, so ask about the school's approach to the teaching of reading, writing and maths – it should be systematic and well planned.

- *breadth of curriculum*. There's more to the school curriculum than the three Rs, however. Many subjects traditionally associated with secondary schooling are now also taught in primary schools, such as science, environmental studies, history, geography and modern languages. The headteacher will tell you which of these are covered, and how frequently they appear in the curriculum. You may also want to inquire about other subjects, such as drama, art, music and PE.
- *computing technology*. Although you may not be familiar with computers, your child will need to be by the time he leaves school. Every primary school has computers available for its pupils, but not all of them use them in an effective, structured way. Ask the teachers about this, how they use computing technology as part of the curriculum, and the amount of time available for individual children to have hands-on experience.
- *parental liaison*. Parents have a right to be made welcome in their child's school, and to be kept up-to-date with his progress. This can be achieved through home-school diaries, parent afternoons, parent helpers in the classroom, and parents' nights. Many schools operate an 'open-doors' policy for parents.

Having covered all these points during your visit, you're now well placed to make an informed choice. But if you are still uncertain, think about the issues that are troubling you, and perhaps make a second visit before reaching a decision. This advice also applies to private schools – don't assume that all private schools are of a high standard simply because parents pay for their children to go there.

Boarding school is an option for some families, especially if parents are in employment involving frequent travel abroad or if there is a family tradition of boarding school. This form of education requires a child to have a greater degree of independence and self-sufficiency, because of the extended separation from home; and boarding schools are infamous for bullying, particularly of younger pupils. A combination of these factors, coupled with high fees, has resulted in more parents sending their children to boarding schools as day pupils.

See also **School Readiness**.

School Readiness Most children are psychologically and physically ready for school when the first day of the infant class finally arrives. But some children are not, and they may find school a daunting experience because they will be unable to meet some of the new demands placed upon them. You can help your child reach a state of readiness for school by ensuring that, by the time she is of school age, she is competent in the following key areas of development:

social (independence). She should be able to:

- go to the toilet on her own, and tidy herself afterwards;
- wash her hands and face;
- take her coat off and hang it on a peg;
- share and take turns;
- listen to an adult and follow basic instructions;
- tidy up toys and books when requested to do so;
- play happily with a small group of children of her own age;
- deal with difficulties without having a tantrum;
- cope with lunch, without help;
- separate from you without becoming unduly upset.

educational. She should be able to:

- listen attentively to a short story;
- identify colours and give their names;
- correctly name one or two basic shapes;
- know her name, address and (possibly) phone number;
- talk clearly in sentences;
- recite a few favourite nursery rhymes;
- concentrate on an activity for at least five minutes.

physical. She should be able to:

- undo buttons and zips;
- untie her shoe-laces (although she may not be able to tie them);
- catch a large ball thrown gently to her;
- walk steadily along a straight line;

- run quickly without falling over;
- jump off the ground, with both feet in the air at the same time;
- take off her shoes and then put them on again.

Having these skills doesn't mean your child will manage everything in school without difficulty, but it will help her settle in more easily. Similarly, if she isn't able to do all these things, it doesn't mean that school will be too demanding for her. But do practise them with her at home, in order to boost her competence and self-confidence.

See also **Concentration; Coordination; Hand-Eye Coordination; Independence; Knowledge; Learning Skills; School, Choice of; Social Development**.

Self-Confidence Children with low self-confidence are more likely to experience emotional and educational difficulties, have little faith in their ability to cope with everyday problems, be afraid to express their own ideas for fear of ridicule, and prefer to play a passive role in social relationships.

The foundations for a strong self-confidence are laid at home – the way you interact with your child plays a major part. For instance, the more positive the interest you take in her life, then the more likely she is to realise you value her, and the more likely she is to value herself. Spending a few minutes listening to your child's tales – no matter how boring and trivial they may seem in comparison to your own life events – will have a positive effect on her self-confidence.

And consider how often you make derogatory comments to her about her behaviour. If she is going through a particularly difficult phase, in which she is disobedient and demanding, try to avoid falling into the habit of reprimanding her all the time. Repeated negative remarks from parent to child, even in justifiable circumstances, will reduce her confidence. Sometimes it is better to ignore small incidents of naughtiness, or even to take action without actually saying anything (for instance, by simply removing the pen she is using to draw on the back of her hand).

Psychologists have shown that self-confidence is also

237

related to the way discipline is exercised at home; children with a strong self-confidence tend to have parents who have a clear set of rules for behaviour and who are prepared to enforce them consistently. A child thrives best in a family environment that has predictable and consistent standards. Of course, there are times when you knowingly let your child break the rules, perhaps because you are too tired to bother. This is perfectly normal, but if it becomes a regular pattern, and if discipline fluctuates from day to day, then you child's self-confidence will drop.

The use of rewards and punishments is important. Parents of children with high self-confidence tend to use rewards to encourage their child's good behaviour rather than use punishments to discourage her when she is naughty. While there is undoubtedly a place for punishment in discipline, repeated punishment also has the effect of focusing attention on a child's wrongdoings. It emphasises her negative characteristics and consequently weakens her self-confidence. A more effective strategy is to reward her when she behaves well, when she does what you expect of her. This technique makes a child more aware of her positive characteristics.

You can increase your child's self-confidence by letting her make elementary decisions about her day-to-day care. True, family life is hectic, and it is often a lot easier for you to make all the decisions. Yet your child needs to have some control over her world. Allow her the opportunity to make some choices, whether about the breakfast cereal she eats or the colour of her new shoes. A child who has all these decisions made for her will tend to have low self-confidence.

There is no greater boost to self-confidence than achieving a task that was previously too challenging. You know what it's like when you are trying to learn a new skill, such as how to strike a golf ball so that it travels a long distance. At first you think you'll never do it because every time you swing the club you manage to miss the ball completely. Then (after extensive practice) comes that sweet moment of success, that moment when you feel club and ball connecting in the way they should. It's a great feeling, isn't it! A child feels the same way when she achieves success.

Whatever skill your child wants to master, a useful approach is to break the task into very small steps, each one a slight progression ahead of the previous one. For instance, the first stage in learning to ride a bicycle could be for her to sit on the bike, hands on the handlebars, while you hold it steady. The next step could be for her to sit on the bike while you push it along the road; and so on until the last step, when she can propel it herself without any support. Each stage should be just that little bit harder than the previous one, and yet not so difficult that your child feels it is beyond her reach. At every stage that she's successful, shower her with praise.

See also **Attractiveness; Discipline; Emotional Deprivation; Learning Skills; Routine**.

Separation and Divorce Every married couple argues from time to time – that's part of normal married life. But with some couples, the endless arguments are a symptom of much deeper relationship difficulties. And for these partners the outcome is separation or divorce. Over a third of all children born in this decade will spend some time living in the home of a single parent.

There are a number of reasons for this increasingly common breakdown of family life:

– *female independence*. Women as a social group are at their highest-ever level of independence. Many women are able to take on the role of 'provider', following separation or divorce, because they have a career.
– *female identity*. Many women realise that they have skills and talents of their own, that they are not simply adjuncts to their husbands. This increase in self-confidence and self-awareness means that a woman will not necessarily be prepared to sacrifice herself to years of unhappy marriage.
– *male ego*. Some men feel threatened by the change in a woman's position within the family and within society, and are unable to accept what they regard as an imbalance in their relationship; this eventually leads to the collapse of their marriage.
– *social tolerance*. Being a single parent has less social stigma attached to it. There are also welfare benefits – admittedly, less than sufficient – that can alleviate the financial plight of a single parent.

Members of older generations often yearn for the days

239

when 'marriages were for life'. While this philosophy should not be dismissed out of hand, it fails to acknowledge that many marriages which were superficially happy in the 'good old days' were actually miserable. Staying together in such circumstances may have looked good to outsiders, but those inside the marriage – including the children – suffered emotionally.

There is no psychological justification for the advice that a couple should continue with their unhappy marriage solely for the sake of their children. Some parents claim that, although they have no love for each other, their children are unaware of the true feelings existing between them. They believe that since they have not openly flaunted their disagreements at home, their animosity is concealed. But long silences at mealtimes, an absence of loving response between them, and a subdued family atmosphere all tell a child that something is wrong between his parents.

However, a couple who desperately love their children, and who don't want to separate because of this, may find this gives them enough motivation to change their marital relationship so that their partnership can continue in a revitalised way. This is totally different from staying together in a stagnant relationship for the sake of the children, because it involves positive change. It is a forward step.

Social attitudes towards divorce fluctuate from decade to decade. But children will always be at risk psychologically when their parents split up for these reasons:

- *A child needs stable family relationships.* Failure to form at least one firm emotional connection with an adult by the age of three of four can have long-term detrimental effects on personality development. Parents have difficulty giving their children that essential love and attention when they themselves are struggling to cope with life.
- *A child models his behaviour on his parents.* In a family beset with hostilities between the mother and father, a child is presented with a disturbed model of behaviour which he is likely to imitate.
- *Parents who fight constantly are likely to use their children as a way of retaliating against their partner.* One parent may deliberately exercise different levels of control than

the other one, for the sake of aggravating him or her. But using a child in this way will only upset him even further.
- *Every child wants to have both parents, and will do his best to remain loyal to both.* The end of a marriage does not mean the end of a child's love for either of his parents. He does not want to have to choose one over the other, or to form an adverse opinion about either parent.

Evidence from psychological research underlines the positive value of maintaining contact with both parents, following separation or divorce. One study of divorced families found that five years after the divorce about a third of the children were coping well and had no emotional difficulties, about a third were coping reasonably well, and the remainder were showing signs of emotional difficulties. The main difference between the 'copers' and the other two groups of children were that they saw both parents regularly. The children with emotional difficulties tended to be those who seldom, if ever, saw one of their parents.

The high incidence of divorce in recent years has allowed psychologists to look closely at the long-term psychological effects. And, encouragingly, evidence from research confirms that children from disrupted families are no more likely to be delinquents than other children. Nor are they more likely to present educational problems in school, or to have social difficulties.

Most of the bad psychological effects of divorce seem to lessen after a couple of years, once the family rebuilds itself and adjusts to the new circumstances. But the responsibility for carrying the family through the crisis rests with parents, not with the children. Any emotional damage resulting from parental separation will not be permanent if the adults act in a sensitive and reasonable way.

See also **Fathers; Modelling; Mothers; Quarrels; Single-Parent Family; Step-Parents; Working Mothers.**

Sex Education Do not avoid sex education in childhood. Even if you don't tackle the subject directly, your child will form an opinion about sex – based on what he hears others saying about it, on what he sees on television and on your reaction when he asks you questions about it. And a child who isn't given sex education by his parents may evolve his own theories, ones which may be totally ridiculous and possibly frightening. Proper sexual understanding will help your child cope better with personal relationships in adulthood.

In order to be ready for his questions, you need to clarify your own ideas and feelings. For instance, if you feel embarrassed talking about sex, then he will sense it. You could talk it over with a friend first, or with your partner; or maybe practice out loud using sex-related words, until you feel comfortable saying them. Preparation like this will help reduce your own tension.

Every family has its own ideas on nudity, but very often, in families where the parents sleep naked, or where the young children are allowed into the bathroom when mum or dad is having a bath, the children are able to talk about body parts in a casual way, without feeling embarrassed or guilty.

'Where did I come from?' is usually the first question that an inquiring four- or five-year-old asks about sex. And a satisfactory answer is to say that he came out of mum's tummy. Most children of this age will accept an answer like this and will ask no further questions, because their thought processes are not as mature as adults'.

Always pitch your answers at your child's level. Don't go into unnecessary detail unless he specifically wants it. Telling a child under the age of five about the ins and outs of the male and female reproductive systems, about eggs and sperm, will only serve to confuse him. Keep your replies simple and direct – treat sexual inquiries like any other aspect of his curiosity.

Never tell your child he is too young to know about these things. After all, if he is sensible enough to ask the questions in the first place, then he deserves a sensible answer. And don't tell 'white lies' in order to resolve the situation quickly; there is no justification for telling a young child that he was bought from a shop, or that the stork brought him. He might just believe it, and then you will have a hard time convincing him of the real version later.

He may ask the same questions over and over again, and require the same explanation to be repeated many times.

Be patient – this is a natural part of any learning process. Simply because you tell him once that a baby comes from mum's tummy, doesn't mean that he will remember it, or even that he will believe it! Your child should feel able to approach you about sex.

A child aged five and upwards may want to know how he got into mum's tummy in the first place. At this point, your explanations should start to involve the fact that sex occurs within a caring relationship. (Of course, you know that sexual intercourse frequently occurs in a casual non-loving relationship, but leave that aside until your child is much older.) Sex discussions should always be set in the context of a loving partnership. Explain that dad and mum loved each other so much that they wanted to have a baby, so dad put his seed into mum. For every question, give just enough information to answer it. Your child may quickly become bored with anything more complex – you may even find that half-way through your detailed explanation, his eyes have strayed back to the television set.

Books specially written for children can provide a useful starting point for sex education. Most of them provide very basic information on conception and birth, within a family setting. The advantage of using this sort of book is that it will give you the chance to prepare your ideas in advance. Your local library will probably have a reasonable range; make sure the book you choose portrays sex in a way that you are comfortable with. For example, some show the adults walking around the house naked, and this may not reflect your own family values; some may use sexual terms that you don't use, and this could cause confusion. Read the book carefully from cover to cover before selecting it for your child.

Sex education is a lifelong process which continues with, or without, parental guidance. If you use opportunities to discuss sex with your child, as they arise out of everyday life, then he'll have a basic understanding by the time he is seven or eight. But if you discourage sex discussions in the earlier years, you leave him vulnerable to the influence of the misguided tittle-tattle that perpetually circulates in the school playground.

See also **Masturbation; Questions; Sexual Abuse; Sexual Curiosity**.

Sexism   You probably don't regard yourself as 'sexist', and you are probably confident that you give your children equal opportunities irrespective of their sex. But think about your own attitudes for a moment.

Have you ever bought a friend's baby boy a pink outfit, or a baby girl a blue outfit? Probably not – the chances are that you automatically associate pink with girls and blue with boys. Have you ever described a boy as 'pretty' or a girl as 'handsome'? Probably not – we have certain words that we use only to describe boys and others that we use only to describe girls.

Virtually all of us are 'sexist' to some extent (i.e., we have a stereotyped view of the behaviour and emotions that we expect from boys and girls) even though we may not be consciously aware of having such an outlook. And children are affected by this. The sex-role stereotypes that you hold will influence your children's gender identity (their sense of 'boyness' and 'girlness').

Psychological studies have revealed that women behave differently towards boys than they do towards girls – without realising it – especially when the children are under five years old. For instance, it has been found that mothers tend to keep a baby girl closer to them and spend more time in direct contact with her than they do with a baby boy. They tend to encourage boys to be more adventurous than girls, and they also tend to praise and criticise girls more than boys.

Another investigation focused on the emotions that mothers assume their young children have. Detailed interviews with a number of mothers of children aged between two and three revealed that they are reluctant to admit that girls have negative feelings such as bad temper and aggressiveness. Yet they have no difficulty attributing these emotions to boys. In other words, mothers expect boys to be angry, hostile and anti-social at times, but not girls.

Your attitude towards gender will be reflected in your child's attitudes. If you have a lifestyle which is traditionally associated with your gender then your child is likely to regard this as the normal pattern. And if you have the attitude that boys are better than girls at sporting activities such as football and cricket, then your child will begin to think the same way. Children are more likely to be broad-minded when their parents are less sexist in outlook.

244

Sexism is often seen in literature. It is true that most contemporary writers of children's books present a more balanced perspective, but this change is relatively recent. Many children continue to read traditional books (e.g., Enid Blyton's *Famous Five* series) in which the boys are portrayed as intelligent, inventive and able to cope with challenge, while girls are portrayed as unimaginative, dependent and sedate.

No wonder, then, that children as young as two have very clear ideas about sex roles. At this age both boys and girls tend to think that girls like to play with dolls, like to help their mother, like to cook dinner, like to clean the house, talk a lot, never hit, and frequently ask for help; and both boys and girls think that boys like to play with cars, like to help their father, like to build things, and like to tell others 'I can hit you.'

By school age, these ideas have become even more firmly fixed. Most children at this age consider that:

– males have more physical strength than females;
– boys fight more than girls;
– girls get hurt more easily than boys;
– boys and girls wear different clothes;
– boys are not expected to show feelings as openly as girls;
– girls are expected to be more helpless when under stress;
– girls respond more to polite requests than boys do.

If you want to encourage your child to have a less conventional, less stereotyped view of sex roles, then:

- *Be aware of your own views*. You need to have a clear and honest understanding of your own thoughts about sex roles – only then will you be ready to change (if necessary) the way you interact with your child.
- *Provide your child with a wide range of toys*. Make sure you have a range of so-called 'boy' and 'girl' toys, and at times encourage him or her to play with toys traditionally associated with the opposite gender.
- *Be discriminating in your choice of children's books*. Read any books before you give them to your child; this way you can avoid any material that is stereotyped in the way sex roles are presented.
- *Offer examples of unconventional sex roles*. Make your child aware that there are many people who occupy jobs

245

that are usually associated with the opposite sex. Top cooks, for instance, are usually men, and there are more women engineers than ever before.

See also **Gender Play**.

Sexual Abuse   Physical contact between parent and child is a normal part of healthy family relationships. Therefore any definition of sexual abuse has to go beyond simply describing it as something that happens when an adult touches a child. In addition, some sexual abuse – such as self-exposure, or introducing a child to pornographic materials – does not involve any direct physical contact with the child.

The Royal College of Psychiatrists defines child sexual abuse as '*the occurrence of a sexually inappropriate act(s) involving a child, which is committed by a person who is five or more years older, or who, in initiating the sexual act, exploits the child in question*'. It adds three explanatory points to this definition:

- 'Inappropriate acts' include acts of exposure, genital fondling (whether the child's or the other person's), penetration (oral, vaginal or anal), and rape.
- 'Exploitation' refers to the balance of power between the child and the abuser, at the time the sexual activity first took place. In other words, exploitation happened if the action was unwanted when it first started, and if the abuser misused the status of his age, authority or gender.
- The five-year age gap between the victim and the sexual abuser is an important factor; but if a child under five years old is involved, then the above actions constitute sexual abuse irrespective of the age of the abuser.

Here are some questions that parents frequently ask about sexual abuse involving children:

Q. *Does child sexual abuse occur spontaneously, and is it due to the abuser's sudden and uncontrollable sexual urges?*
A.   Some acts of child sexual abuse are spontaneous, but most abusers are quite calculating in their actions. They often manipulate their child victims into obedience and

silence by using threats of further abuse ('If you tell, I'll do it to you again and nobody will be able to make me stop'); by introducing the notion of shame ('Your mother will be so ashamed of you if she finds out what you've been doing'); or even loyalty ('You shouldn't tell on me because we've known each other for years'). The idea that child sexual abusers have no control over their actions implies they have no responsibility for what they do.

Q. *Does sexual abuse occur only in families who are living in poverty and environmental deprivation?*
A. There is no basis to the belief that child sexual abuse is confined to one particular social class, or to one specific type of area. Although it has been reported more in low-income families, it has also been shown to exist at all levels of society and in many different countries.

Q. *Is child sexual abuse really such a big problem, or is it simply a case of the media blowing up a few isolated incidents out of proportion?*
A. Facts and figures are hard to find because children – and adults who were abused as children – are reluctant to make accusations. Even so, studies suggest that child sexual abuse is widespread. A 1985 British survey of over 2000 men and women over the age of 15 revealed that 10 per cent claimed to have been sexually abused during childhood; this led the researchers to conclude that over 100,000 children will be sexually abused before the age of 15.

Q. *Are child sexual abusers old men in dirty raincoats?*
A. The majority of child sexual abusers are not old men but are aged somewhere between teenage and the early thirties. One study found that abusers of girls have an average age of 31, while abusers of boys have an average age of 27. Be wary of any adult who wants to be on his own with a child, or to be in situations where the child is undressing or bathing or going to bed. A significant proportion of offences is committed, for example, by babysitters. Sexual abuse often takes place in the perpetrator's own home.

Q. *Don't children who become sexually abused bring it on themselves by being promiscuous and by encouraging adults to touch them?*

A. Blaming the victim turns attention away from the perpetrator of the abuse and towards the child – and that's wrong. Children are open and trusting; love and affection are an essential part of the childhood years and so a child often willingly seeks physical contact with an adult. This is innocent child behaviour that sexual abusers take advantage of in order to meet their own needs. Promiscuous behaviour in childhood and adolescence is more likely to result from, not cause, child sexual abuse.

Q. *Is it true that girls most at risk of sexual abuse are those who have reached puberty, and who therefore have developed secondary sexual characteristics?*
A. Studies have revealed that pre-pubertal girls are most at risk of sexual abuse, especially during the primary-school years. (Girls also tend to be sexually abused at a younger age than boys.)

If a child of any age tells you that she has been sexually abused, take the comment seriously. Don't react in a way that makes her feel embarrassed or guilty. Reassure her that she has done nothing wrong by telling you what has happened to her. After that, either report the situation directly to the Social Work Department in your area (telephone or visit personally) or contact the child's health visitor or GP who will pass on your concerns to the Social Work Department.

See also **Sexual Curiosity; Violence**.

Sexual Curiosity Children are fascinated by breasts, bottoms, penises and vaginas. Most giggle uncontrollably at the very mention of these body parts – or even at the suggestion that they might be mentioned. It's not surprising, though, that children react this way, because these are the organs that adults get so anxious about and make considerable effort to conceal. With this almost taboo atmosphere surrounding nudity and sexuality, no wonder young children can't wait to find out more about it all.

If they were left to their own devices, without parental interference and restriction, they would probably demonstrate a significant amount of sexual interest anyway. As early as 1927, a researcher investigated the behaviour of a primitive tribe who neither encouraged nor discouraged their children from sexual explorations, and found that a large part of the children's spontaneous pre-school play was sexually orientated.

Sigmund Freud maintained that childhood sexuality is more complicated than simple idle curiosity. He believed that childhood is the period in which the foundations for later adult sexuality are laid down. According to his psychoanalytic theory, different body parts become the focus of a child's sexual feelings as she grows through the pre-school years.

Freud proposed that psychosexual development consists of three phases in early childhood. First, there is the oral phase – in the first year of life – during which a baby derives strong erotic satisfaction from stimulation of her mouth during feeding and sucking. This is followed in the second year by the anal phase, in which the focus of erotic pleasure is redirected on to the anus. Toilet-training, says Freud, encourages this in infants. And third, there is the phallic phase – ranging from ages three and four upwards – in which the genitals become the main source of erotic satisfaction. However, many contemporary psychologists reject this extreme view of childhood sexuality.

Some parents attempt to control their child's sexual behaviour – whether it is active inquisitiveness involving another child or simply passive curiosity – by punishing her immediately (e.g., with a swift smack, a stern warning about the consequences of a future repetition, or deprivation of sweets); or by rebuking her with old wives' tales which misinform about the dangers of sex; or by suggesting another activity that could be more enjoyable, and thereby distracting her away from the sexual activity she is engaged in.

But none of these are suitable long-term strategies because either they encourage a child to associate her genitals with guilt (she may think anything to do with sex is naughty, and if this feeling persists in subsequent years her adult sexuality may be adversely affected), or they simply sidestep the central issue of her sexual curiosity.

If you do want to manage your child's sexual curiosity satisfactorily, then:

- *Avoid showing embarrassment about sex.* You can't expect her to develop a mature sexual attitude if you start to giggle and redden every time the subject is raised. She'll sense your discomfort.

- *Pitch your explanations at the level of her understanding.* Telling her 'Your friend won't want to play with you if you keep pulling her pants down' will make more sense to her than the more general comment, 'It's not nice to put your hands up someone's shorts.' Your advice should be very specific.

- *Keep calm.* If you over-react to your child's sexual behaviour, she'll soon realise that what she is doing is one way of gaining your attention. This realisation can make her feel very powerful, and may, in fact, encourage her to persist. Far better to stay relaxed and level-headed than to let her see you become angry.

- *Explain about the importance of privacy.* Remind your child that everybody – no matter what age they are – has a right to decide who touches them and who does not, and that just as she has times when she doesn't like being kissed and cuddled, so do other people. Explain to her in very basic terms about respecting the personal rights of others. And if it is masturbation that is worrying you, tell her that other people don't like to see her do that.

- *Be prepared to physically discourage her from persevering with her behaviour.* There is no harm at all in your taking direct action to stop her behaving overtly sexually – as long as that action isn't punishment, and as long as you explain the underlying reasons to her. If, for example, she always strips off whenever she is alone with a particular friend, stop her playing with that friend for a while. Tell her why you are unhappy about her behaviour, but let her know that she can resume playing with her friend once she is able to play more appropriately.

See also **Comforters; Masturbation; Sex Education; Sexual Abuse; Unhappiness**.

Shyness Is your child shy? If he is, don't worry – every child is shy sometimes. Even the most vivacious, talkative child can 'dry up' when he suddenly finds himself in a new situation or in the company of other children and adults that he doesn't know very well.

Shyness depends to a large extent on age. Although every child matures at a different rate, the following guidelines apply to most children:

1 week A newborn baby cannot differentiate one person from another, and therefore does not show any signs of shyness. It is true that some will take a feed only from one person in particular, and not from anyone else. But apart from this, most babies will happily interact with anyone who shows them kindness and interest.

6 months By this age, an infant has begun to differentiate familiar faces from unfamiliar faces, and he can recognise the people closest to him – namely, his parents, and his brothers and sisters. He will probably be shy and tearful when he sees a stranger.

1 year He now has greater awareness of who is familiar and who is not. He remains shy and clingy in new situations, however, and may even cover his eyes with his hands or arms when a stranger approaches. At mother-and-toddler group, he often sits 'glued' to his mother, keen to join in the fun and games yet not secure enough to go off on his own into the playroom.

2 years A child of this age has a greater degree of self-confidence, yet may still hesitate to talk to people he doesn't know. A stranger is more likely to be greeted with silence than with tears. Because a two-year-old is able to walk, he can now remove himself physically from any situation he doesn't like – so when he feels shy he simply runs out of the room.

3 years Many children of this age are confident enough to accept attention from children and adults that they do not know well. A typical three-year-old is more able to cope with meeting new children and adults; playgroup and nursery are well suited to his social needs.

5 years Most of the earlier signs of shyness have gone, partly as a result of the increased confidence that comes with growing up, and partly as a result of the experience of meeting others in earlier years. Even so, a child aged five and upwards may still show shyness in a totally new situation – e.g., the first day at primary school.

Although shyness is a passing phase for most children, there are some who retain their shyness longer than others. And some people remain shy all their lives. An investigation in the USA studied people who had been described as shy when they were children and then interviewed them 30 years later. How had shyness affected their lives? Shy people (compared to those who weren't shy) were found to have

- married later;
- become parents later;
- entered a stable career later;
- a stereotyped gender role within the family;
- achieved less in their job;
- a higher rate of divorce;
- a very conventional lifestyle.

These findings don't mean that a shy person is inadequate or unhappy. However, if you want your shy child to become more outgoing, then:

- *Build up his self-confidence.* His shyness stems from a lack of self-confidence in his own abilities. So encourage him to feel competent and capable by discussing his strong points with him (e.g., he's good at singing, he's kind). Emphasise these positive attributes; tell him they will make other children like him.
- *Give him lots of opportunities to mix with others.* You can't expect a shy child to become outgoing unless he meets other children. If he's not at nursery or school, make sure he has the chance to play with children of his own age.
- *Don't let him avoid people.* He would much rather be on his own – but that's the easy way out. The more you let him avoid meeting other children, then the more his shyness will increase.
- *Encourage him to think of the other person.* When a shy child meets someone, he usually spends the first few moments thinking about himself (e.g., about his appearance, about whether the other child likes him or not).

Suggest that, instead, he imagines what the other child is thinking and feeling; this will distract his attention away from himself.

- *Teach him 'opening strategies'.* Show him specific approaches to use when he meets new people (e.g., inviting the other child to play a game, or asking him about his favourite television programmes). A definite plan of action will help him cope with these first awkward moments.

Shyness can have benefits – for instance, it can protect a child from danger. A shy child who will not go off in a car with a total stranger is behaving much more sensibly than a talkative one who is prepared to go with anyone who is friendly towards him. (It's ironic that a four- or five-year-old has to be warned about strangers just when his confidence is strong enough to cope with unfamiliar adults. But it needs to be done.)

Explain to your child why he shouldn't talk to strangers. Tell him that not all adults are kind to children, and that he can't tell who is a kind person and who is a nasty person just by looking at them. Lay down very clear guidelines and keep them simple – e.g., 'Don't talk to any stranger, no matter what he says to you' or 'Never take sweets from people you don't know.'

Now that you have established these rules, however, he may sensibly ask what he should do if he gets lost. Tell him to ask for help from any person in a uniform, or from a woman. Of course, this is no guarantee he will be safe, but it does increase his chances of coming into the temporary safekeeping of a harmless adult.

See also **Friendships; Playgroup/Nursery, Starting; Self-Confidence; Sociable Play; Social Development.**

Sibling Rivalry 'He always gets more than me', or 'He's allowed to stay up later than me and that's not fair' are familiar cries in most families. This jealousy between the children – 'sibling rivalry' – is a normal state of affairs, and arises because they have to share their parents' attention, time, interests and financial resources.

Most parents will readily admit that family arguments are

frequently caused by jealousy between their children. Sibling rivalry can affect every child – although the oldest is most prone to jealousy, the youngest too will have moments when he is convinced everyone else in the family gets more than he does.

Don't dismiss your child's cries of 'That's not fair!' out of hand. If he feels strongly enough to voice his opinion of unfair treatment, then he deserves to be listened to. Ask him why he feels this way. His accusation will probably be completely irrational (and probably won't take any age difference into account) – but he should nonetheless be given a reasonable reply.

Sensible explanations (e.g., 'Your brother stays up later at night because he's older and doesn't need as much sleep as you do' or 'Your sister doesn't have to wash the dishes after meals because she's too young to handle the crockery without breaking it') are far more convincing than an irritable retort (e.g., 'You'll go to bed when I decide, whether your brother's in bed or not').

Parents can unwittingly cause sibling rivalry. It is very tempting to encourage one child in the family to behave better or to try harder at school, by comparing him with one of his brothers or sisters. But this technique is unlikely to have the desired effect. In fact, it is virtually guaranteed to intensify feelings of jealousy between them. Judging a child's achievements against those of his older brother or sister will only make him feel inadequate. And the older child may not like such a comparison, either. A more effective strategy is to use a sibling's superior achievements as a 'carrot', rather than as a 'stick'. For instance, a younger child who is struggling to learn to read will benefit more from his older sister's help with his reading homework than he will from an unfavourable comparison.

Encourage your children to play together, and to share their toys. The more they understand and accept each other, the less likely there are to be jealous scenes. And make sure it's not always the oldest one who gets the new sweatshirt – let the younger child have a turn too.

Some parents do prefer one of their youngsters over all the others. This happens for many different reasons: perhaps because he is good fun to be with, or perhaps because he's very quiet and well behaved. Whatever the circumstances, jealousy will emerge when love is distributed unfairly in a family. If you do have a favourite, don't let it show, either by your words or by your actions.

A child has to learn to cope with feelings of jealousy towards his brothers and sisters, and he needs to develop a way of keeping these natural – but unpleasant – emotions under control so that his enjoyment of life is not impaired. You can help your child cope with sibling rivalry in the following ways:

- *Don't confuse differential treatment with preferential treatment.* One of your children may need lots of cuddles before going out to school in the morning, while another may prefer just to have a smile from you. Each has different emotional needs, and you should try to meet these needs even though this may result in the children being treated differently. This is unlikely to lead to sibling rivalry; differential treatment and preferential treatment are not the same.

- *Give each of your children individual attention.* Simple logistics dictate that the more children you have, the busier you become. But whatever time you have available, spend some of it with each child on his own, whether it is reading a story at bedtime, or taking him for a walk in the park.

See also **Age Gap; Birth Order; Equality; First-Born Jealousy; Jealousy**.

Single-Parent Family This term covers several kinds of families, each with quite different backgrounds. For instance, it can apply to a family that has experienced the death of one of the adults, or to a family headed by a mother who was never married, and who has always raised her child alone. However, by far the largest number of single-parent families are those arising from a dissolved marriage.

The period following separation or divorce is usually one of chaos and turmoil. Every child – especially boys under the age of five – is affected by the impact of changing to a single-parent family, and may become anxious when leaving the remaining parent, or behave badly at home and at school. Fortunately, these short-term effects pass. The long-

255

term psychological effects of becoming a single-parent family are not entirely predictable; some children continue to yearn for their absent parent while others do not.

Living in a single-parent family poses particular difficulties:

- *physical demands*. A single-parent usually has to work in order to pay the bills, and as a result has little energy left to deal with home life at the end of the day. And if she doesn't work, there may be the strain of new-found poverty. This takes place against a background of having meals to prepare and shopping to do, and managing children who are themselves emotionally weakened by the marital split. Then there are dealings with her former marriage partner, in-laws, and so on. The sheer volume of these demands dictates that a single parent cannot do justice to them all.

- *emotional demands*. The head of a single-parent family has no one to support her everyday decisions, and this can undermine her self-confidence. Whereas in a two-parent family a woman has her partner to reassure her that what she thinks and says is valid (and, of course, vice versa), a single parent doesn't. She has no feedback to tell her that she's right or wrong, apart from her children – and they'll probably be challenging her authority anyway. This means a single parent is likely to be less effective and less powerful in leading the family.

- *age gap problem*. Parents in a two-parent family may use the fact that they are adults to encourage their children to behave properly; in other words, they can use the age gap between themselves and the children to establish their authority as parents. But a single parent often confides in her children because she does not have a partner to share her concerns with, and this means that she may have difficulty acting authoritatively towards them.

- *dependence*. In a single-parent family, parent and children depend on each other more than they normally do in a two-parent family. This happens simply because there are now fewer people in the house. While this can be very positive and can enhance a parent-child bond, it also means there is less freedom to release feelings. When a single parent gets angry with her child, there is no one else to take over from her – and, also, her

child doesn't have another parent at home to turn to. Consequently, single parents often have to check their emotions.
- *lack of money*. Another difficulty usually facing a single-parent family is the abrupt economic change, a factor that has indirect psychological effects. Now that her former partner's income has to maintain two homes (and possibly two families, if he has left to live with another woman), there is less cash available to be spent on food and clothes, and luxuries become a thing of the past. This too adds stress.
- *poor housing*. Single-parent families often have accommodation difficulties. If a marital separation is sudden and unplanned, the mother may be forced to leave the family home very quickly, taking her children with her. Urgently needing somewhere to live, they may have to turn to their local council for emergency housing – and anything available under this type of allocation is usually basic. Such an environmental change is yet another pressure on a single-parent family.

All of this sounds a bit 'doom and gloom'. But many single parents are quick to point out that life in a two-parent family also has stress points, especially if the parents have relationship difficulties.

Psychologists have found that children in a single-parent family (compared with children in a two-parent family) tend to be less capable socially and intellectually when starting school, and to achieve less educationally throughout life. On the positive side, though, they tend to have satisfactory sex-role identities, a keen desire to get on in life, good parent-child relationships, and satisfactory psychological development.

A child from a single-parent family, therefore, experiences a combination of positive and negative influences. The happiest single-parent families have the following features:

- *good parent-child communication*. This is positively related to the family's mental and physical health; the more openly parents and children can express their feelings and ideas, their anxieties and their happiness, then the better for all of them.
- *stable home routine*. A clear structure in family life helps

a child adjust to having a single parent, and gives her a feeling of security.

- *frequent access to the non-custodial parent*. In most instances it is in a child's best interest to maintain regular contact with her estranged parent.
- *no arguments between the parents*. No child likes to see her parents quarrelling, whether or not they are separated. She is more likely to adapt to living in a single-parent family if she doesn't see her parents fighting in front of her.

See also **Fathers; Mothers; Parents; Quarrels; Separation and Divorce; Step-Parents; Working Mothers**.

Sleep Isn't sleep wonderful! Your child may be exhausted at the end of the day, with aching muscles and drooping eyelids, but you know she will wake up fully refreshed after she's had a good night's sleep. Sleep is a way of replacing lost energy, a way of recharging her batteries. Yet nobody knows exactly why children (or adults) need sleep.

Scientists have proved, though, that:

- *physical changes take place during sleep*. For instance, a child's pupils become very small; the rate at which saliva, digestive juices and urine are secreted drops sharply; the volume of air breathed diminishes; heart rate slows; electrical brain waves change their character; and consciousness is lost.
- *sleep is essential for physical and mental health*. A child who does not get regular sleep at night will become irritable and depressed, difficult to manage, and will not be able to concentrate in school. She may also lose her appetite, start to lose weight, and eventually become ill.
- *nobody can go without sleep indefinitely*. In 1986, an American established a new world record when he managed to go without any sleep for 453 hours 40 minutes, while sitting in a rocking chair.

A new baby

- sleeps up to 80 per cent of the day;
- takes seven or eight naps every 24 hours;
- dreams 50 per cent of sleep time;

- sleeps anywhere and at any time;
- drifts imperceptibly in and out of sleep.

As your child grows older she will develop a more predictable sleeping routine, although not every child has settled sleep during the night. In fact, night waking – defined as waking up one or more times during the night, at least four nights a week – is the most common problem reported by parents when their infant is between the ages of 12 and 18 months.

Over 20 per cent of one-year-olds wake up four or more nights each week; at 18 months, 17 per cent wake that frequently. Encouragingly, the rate of night waking then begins to decline, although at four years there are still 10 per cent of children reported by their parents as waking regularly each night. In addition, at each age, around 10 per cent of children wake two or three nights a week.

You can help your child have untroubled sleep, by using strategies involving:

- *comfort*. An uncomfortable child will not sleep, even though she's tired. Make sure yours isn't hungry, thirsty, feeling unwell, in pain, cold, or too hot.
- *contentment*. She won't fall asleep unless she feels loved and secure. Soothing cuddles before bedtime relax her; reading a short story to her will also have a settling effect.
- *routine*. Your child is more likely to sleep well when she follows a predictable routine each evening – e.g., undressing, followed by bath-time, followed by story-time, followed by lights out.
- *security*. She may be unable to get to sleep in the dark. A night-light can be useful – once she has fallen asleep, it can be turned off.

And try to avoid:

- *naps*. Cut out unnecessary naps during the day. Children older than three or four should play quietly when tired in the afternoon, rather than have a daytime nap.
- *background noises*. Your child may be disturbed by outside noises, such as heavy traffic, barking dogs, noisy neighbours. Eliminate these sounds where possible, and reassure her they aren't harmful.
- *unhappiness*. A troubled child won't get to sleep easily.

Worries that keep children awake include arguments with friends, fighting between parents, and anxiety about starting playgroup or school. Ask her what she is worried about.

See also **Bedtime; Crying Baby; Dreams; Nightmares; Routine; Unhappiness**.

Smacking Children have a knack of pushing parents to the absolute limit . . . and beyond. If you can put hand on heart and swear truthfully that you've never raised a hand to your child, then you're in a small minority – surveys have shown that most parents smack their child at some point during the pre-school years. The constant nagging of a demanding toddler can use up the patience of even the most placid of parents, as can the antics of a five-year-old who thinks it's good fun to draw all over the sitting-room walls with his felt-tip pens. Like most of us, some time or other you've probably been at that low point where you felt such over-whelming frustration and fury at your child's behaviour that you forgot all your good intentions and smacked him.

But there are good reasons why you shouldn't use smacking as part of your discipline at home:

– *It doesn't work*. Studies have found that being smacked at the age of seven doesn't prevent children from being troublesome when they are 16. In fact, the opposite occurs – children are more likely to cause their parents problems at 16 if they were smacked frequently when they were seven. And toddlers who are smacked are the ones least likely to obey instructions not to touch breakable objects. So you might smack your child in the hope that it will work, but the reality is that it doesn't have any positive long-term effect.
– *It sets a bad example*. From your child's point of view, if smacking is good enough for you to use when you're angry, then it's good enough for him to use when *he's* angry. Aggression breeds aggression, and sets a bad example which your child will probably follow.
– *It's dangerous*. There's a very fine dividing line between a carefully measured smack on the legs or bottom and an over-zealous assault that injures a child. Of course,

few parents deliberately set out to seriously hurt their child with a smack; in most instances it's intended as a 'short, sharp shock', a reminder of who's boss at home. Yet smacking is usually done in temper – and that's a time when people don't have full control over their actions. So you might hit your child too hard; or he might move at the wrong moment, causing the smack to land across his face instead of a part of his body protected by clothes.

– *It makes you feel bad*. If you have ever smacked your child, the chances are you felt terrible afterwards. No parent likes to see their child looking at them with fear in his eyes. We all want our children to value us, not to be afraid of us; feeling like a school bully is not pleasant. And these very normal 'post-smacking blues' outweigh any momentary satisfaction you felt when you delivered the smack.

There are effective ways of exercising discipline without smacking your child. You will find the following list helpful:

- *Tell him why rules matter*. Use explanations he can understand – e.g., that throwing his toys in temper will break them. He is more likely to follow your rules if he thinks they are sensible.
- *Emphasise that he'll benefit from rules just as much as anyone else*. For instance, the rule that children shouldn't punch each other means he doesn't need to worry about being hit by another child.
- *Keep rules consistently*. This is so important – if you have set limits, in most cases, make sure your child sticks to them.
- *Take action if he regularly breaks your rules*. If you've warned him that he will be punished, then stick to what you have said. Empty threats only teach him that you don't mean what you say.
- *Use rewards and praise to encourage good behaviour*. Praising a child when he is behaving well is very effective – so is the tactic of giving him a special treat for having a particularly good day.
- *Time rewards and punishments properly*. They will be most effective when given immediately – rather than, say, waiting two hours to punish him for behaving badly,

or waiting a week before rewarding him for behaving well.

- *Don't try to bully him into good behaviour.* You're bigger than he is and you can intimidate him. But the impact lasts only for a few moments – he'll misbehave again as soon as you turn your back.
- *Use threats of punishments that are realistic.* Only make threats that you know you can carry out. Short punishments (e.g., reducing television viewing time by 10 minutes) are very effective.
- *Be prepared to reach a compromise.* There should always be room for reaching a compromise with your child. Most rules can be bent sometimes.
- *Walk away when you feel tempted to smack him.* This isn't a sign of weakness – it's a realistic acceptance that you have taken as much as you can at this moment.

See also **Aggression; Attention-Seeking Behaviour; Crying Baby; Discipline; Modelling**.

Snacks No matter how much effort you put into food preparation, no matter how meticulously you plan your child's daily menus, there will be times when he is hungry between meals. This doesn't mean he should have eaten more at lunch (although there's no harm in reminding him that he wouldn't be so hungry if he had). A small snack between meals can take the sharp edge off a child's hunger, putting him in better spirits when the next meal arrives. It can also turn a bad mood into a good mood.

So don't take the high moral ground when your child complains that he is hungry, even though the next meal is due within the hour. Nutritious food is good for him, whether he eats three large portions each day or six small ones. Of course, you don't want the day to deteriorate into a never-ending series of small snacks, because that will reduce his interest in family meals – and will also have you permanently stuck in the kitchen. An occasional snack between meals, however, is acceptable.

A child likes snack-type foods because they are:

- small and easy to consume;
- less structured than family meals;

- different from usual main courses;
- chosen by him (he asked for them).

These positive reasons mean that you can be sure he will eat whatever snack you serve him. And this opportunity can be used to reinforce good eating habits: give him nutritious snack foods. Be careful, though, that the snack doesn't make him so full that he can't eat the next meal.

Healthy snacks include sliced fresh fruit or vegetables (e.g., apple, pear, orange, seedless grapes, carrot sticks, green pepper strips), finger-food (e.g., meat/cheese sandwiches with wholemeal bread, pizza strips, cheese on toast), and dairy products (e.g., cheese cubes, yoghurt, low-fat cheese spread, cottage cheese). Low-fat crisps can be given occasionally. Never give a peanut to a child under the age of five, because he could accidentally inhale it and choke.

There is a difference between 'snacks' and 'sweets', although your child may not agree! Sweets, cakes, biscuits and fizzy flavoured drinks should be avoided when possible. Aside from giving him an excess of carbohydrates which may turn into fat, sweets cause tooth decay. And don't be fooled by supposedly healthy cereal and muesli bars: read the contents label carefully, since many of them contain a lot of sugar.

But be realistic. Every parent starts off determined not to let their child eat 'rubbish', yet soon realises this isn't always possible. At times, you are bound to give him the packet of sweets he's been screaming for, simply to get some peace and quiet. He'll survive that nutritional lapse! Likewise, there's no need to feel bad because he has binged on sweets, crisps and fizzy drinks at a party. Just as long as he doesn't do it too often.

Opinions vary about 'junk' foods. In many instances, junk food has nutritional value (e.g., carry-out hamburgers, pre-filled pancakes, fish and chips), as long as it is eaten as one small component of a well balanced diet. (The danger is that these foods might become an integral part of a child's weekly food consumption.) So don't feel guilty letting him have a carry-out hamburger, or small pieces of breaded chicken – it can be a fun way to end a day out.

See also **Additives; Eating; Eating Out; Fussy Eaters; Healthy Eating; Overweight.**

Sociable Play   Sociable behaviour has three main features, all of which can be encouraged through play:

- *sharing*. There are two forms of sharing. First, a child might share in order to benefit personally – for example, she shares her sweets with others in the hope that this will make them want to play with her. Second, a child might share even when there is no obvious personal benefit – for example, she shares her new toy with her friends simply because she likes them. This, perhaps, is a more genuine type of sharing because it involves a child doing something for nothing.
- *cooperation*. This happens when a child works with a number of others so that every single one of them benefits – for example, when a group of children work together to build a 'den' for them to play in. This is quite different from competition which happens when each child works alone, trying to get the reward for herself – e.g., when children race against each other on sports day.
- *empathy*. The ability to share and experience the emotional state of another person. An empathic child (unlike an anti-social one) is able to understand and appreciate the emotions of somebody else.

Many parents have an intuitive feeling that specific toys can have an adverse influence on their child's behaviour; consequently, they may not allow her to have toy guns, knives and swords because of the worry that this might encourage her to behave aggressively towards others. Research findings suggest there is some foundation to this concern.

In one study, investigators examined the extent to which the characteristics of a toy determine the way a child plays with it. Over 60 boys, aged between three and six, were involved, and they played in pairs, in a series of 12-minute sessions. During these play periods the children were given toys, three of which were designed to present aggressive cues (an inflatable doll in the form of a well known space villain; mechanical boxing robots; small *Star Wars* characters with a spaceship), and three of which were designed to present sociable cues (a basketball, with a hoop which had to be held by one player while the other threw the ball into it; a peg-board which lit up when one child pressed a switch

264

while another inserted pegs; a toy ambulance with small paramedic figures). Results confirmed that sociably cued toys encourage children to take turns and cooperate with each other, while aggressively cued toys encourage them to be verbally and physically hostile towards each other.

So make a list of all the toys your child plays with, and then categorise them as either 'sociable' or 'anti-social'. You may be surprised to discover the range of toys that present anti-social, aggressive cues.

Psychologists have also found that when children play at games requiring sociable behaviour, they become more sociable and caring towards others. Such games can be very simple. For instance, lay a piece of newspaper on the floor, and tell your child and some of her friends that they all have to place at least one foot and one hand on the paper. The smaller the piece of newspaper and the larger the group, the more interesting the game becomes. This activity has the two key characteristics that make a game sociable – first, the children have to cooperate with each other in order for everyone in the group to make contact with the paper, and second, they have to share the space on the paper with each other. As well as this, it's great fun – children take great delight in twisting and tangling themselves.

See also **Gender Play; Kindness; Learning through Play; Play; Playing with Your Child; Zero-Sum Games**.

Social Development   When you hear your new baby screaming day and night because she's hungry, or because she needs her nappy changed, or simply because she's in a bad mood, it's hard to imagine that within a couple of years this same individual will be able to mix with other children of her own age, will probably be able to share her toys without complaint, and may even be popular. But she will.

Getting on with others is so important. A sociable child has many advantages compared with one who does not mix well – e.g., she has greater self-confidence, she enjoys a more stimulating way of life. There are, of course, children who deliberately choose to be solitary, and they appear to be very contented, but in most instances an isolated child is an unhappy child.

Despite having inherent tendencies towards social

involvement, your child still needs to learn 'social' skills, such as the ability to communicate her feelings accurately. A child who learns to say, 'It's me next' will be more socially acceptable than a child who simply grabs a toy without any explanation. Even a two-year-old can be encouraged to do this. Another important social skill is knowing what to say in the first few moments when meeting someone for the first time – teach her what to say and do in these situations (e.g., she could offer the other child a toy to play with).

Encourage her to think about the way she behaves towards other children and about the gestures she uses. Some gestures are aggressive (shouting, scowling, clenching fists and swearing), while others are pacifying (smiling, showing approval, holding out a hand). Children who mix well are usually those who use more pacifying gestures than aggressive ones.

The three most important social skills that will help your child get on with others of her own age are the abilities to share, to take turns, and to follow rules. A child who does not have these skills will have social difficulties. Explain to your child why they are important (e.g., because others will like her), and give her plenty of opportunities to practise them at home (e.g., sharing sweets with her friend, waiting her turn to have a glass of lemonade, playing games with rules).

A good level of hygiene is also necessary. Life is unfair, and although it is not your child's fault if she has dirty clothes or is unwashed (this is your responsibility), this gives her an uphill struggle when it comes to mixing with others. Encourage her to take an interest in her appearance, in her clothes, and in her personal cleanliness. Good eating habits also help.

Your child's social development in the early years occurs in stages:

3 months She will have already shown her first smile (usually around six weeks), and she clearly enjoys the company of familiar people. She will probably watch you closely as you move around the room.

6 months When she's happy playing with you, she will smile consistently or even laugh. However, the first signs of shyness may appear when she sees people she doesn't know.

9 months She is now ready to take the social initiative when she is with other children and adults (e.g., she may approach another child). She can readily identify a familiar face from that of a stranger.

12 months A typical one-year-old loves action rhymes which involve her parents tickling her or moving her about (e.g., pat-a-cake, 'Round and round the garden'). And she will like sitting on your lap, being cuddled by you.

18 months The first signs of genuine cooperation show through when your child begins to help with dressing and undressing. She may try to pull her vest off herself, or perhaps to put her slippers on.

2 years Unfortunately, social development takes a temporary downward turn at this age. Instead of increasing her social skills further, she becomes more concerned with herself – tantrums predominate when others don't do what she wants.

2½ years Your child likes being with other children, although she won't actually play with them yet. She is still cautious about sharing her toys, and isn't ready yet for cooperative play.

3 years She will love playing fantasy games with other children, each absorbed in their own make-believe role. She is more aware now that games can't take place unless everyone plays according to the same rules.

4 years Your child should be able to mix cooperatively with other children of her own age. She may not be thrilled at having to wait her turn, share, or follow the rules of someone else's game, but she can cope with this if she wants.

5 years She will have developed social competence and will be able to join the company of others of her own age, without much problem. Of course, she may be shy and withdrawn, but she can cope without adult supervision.

See also **Fighting; Friendships; Hygiene; Kindness; Manners; Politeness; Shyness; Sociable Play**.

Special Needs All children need to be loved, need to be physically cared for, need to feel secure, need to have self-confidence, need to have structure and consistency in life and need to mix with other children. But there are some children who have special needs in addition to those described above, needs that arise because their development is atypical.

Until the 1980s, these children were called 'handicapped' or 'subnormal', but this form of labelling is no longer used. Now, children with developmental problems are described as having 'special needs'. The problems with the terms 'handicapped' and 'subnormal' are that they focus on a child's weaknesses instead of on his strengths, they are too general, they don't indicate that certain supportive measures may be taken to help him cope with his difficulty; and they also encourage people to consider his condition rather than the child himself. This shift from 'handicap' to 'special needs' allows him to be treated as an individual.

Parental reaction to the realisation that their child has special needs varies from shock to denial, from grief to acceptance, from fear to despair. Although there are parents who don't experience such negative emotions, feelings of confusion and distress usually follow the diagnosis that a child has a serious developmental problem. Being honest with yourself will help you get through this early stage. It's not pleasant to know you feel guilty or afraid, but these are common reactions that you shouldn't try to hide. There is no shame in feeling anxious or embarrassed about having a child with special needs.

Find out as much as you can about your child's problem and the impact it may have on his development. Ask the professionals who are involved with him, and keep asking until you receive adequate answers. You may find it helpful to contact other parents who have a child with similar difficulties; sharing your worries with someone else is often beneficial. This can usually be arranged through organisations specifically formed to help parents.

Right from birth, play is vital to every child's development because it is through play that he explores the world around him – he learns through play. But a child with special needs may require extra encouragement to play because he may not show that active sense of curiosity that most children have. Be prepared to get involved with him – if he doesn't reach out for toys, take them to him and put them in his hands; if he doesn't squeeze a squeaky doll, then put his fingers round it and gently squeeze them yourself. This will provide him with a suitable model of behaviour that he can copy, and that will also stimulate his interest.

The chances are that you have other children as well (the majority of children with special needs have at least one brother or sister), and their development is just as important. Common complaints from siblings include that they are asked to do too much around the house (because their parents' time is entirely taken up by the child with special needs), that they feel neglected (because the child with special needs is the centre of attention), and that they are pressurised to be high achievers in school (because their parents expect too much of them).

Bear in mind that all your children have their lives to lead, not just your child with special needs. They all need to develop their full potential. In the same way that you shouldn't cover up your child's special needs, neither should you make them a permanent and all-encompassing focus. Tensions often arise in a family with a child who has special needs when the other children don't fully understand the nature of those difficulties. So give them as much information about the problem as you can, and encourage them to ask you questions.

Many parents become over-protective of the child with special needs, and are more lenient with him than they are with their other children. They probably do this because they feel he is more vulnerable than the others. But your child with special needs will benefit from a consistent family discipline, so avoid the temptation to spoil him because of the difficulties he is experiencing.

See also **Cerebral Palsy; Down's Syndrome; Integration, Educational; Language Difficulties; Learning through Play; Milestones; Over-Protectiveness; Play; Playing with Your Child; Sibling Rivalry; Spina Bifida.**

Spina Bifida Caused by a spinal column defect in which one or more of the bones forming the backbone (the vertebrae) fail to join properly, leaving a gap or a split; one of the most common congenital abnormalities in children. Every year in the UK approximately 3000 children are born with this condition, and learning difficulties occur in around 50 per cent of them. More boys than girls are affected.

The condition varies in severity. At one end of the scale *spina bifida occulta* is very mild, and usually goes unnoticed. The visible sign may be a dimple in the back, but most people with this are unaware they have an abnormality because they don't experience any symptoms at all. At the other end of the scale, *spina bifida cystica* is more serious. The visible sign is a cyst (or sac), almost like a large blister, on the back. It is covered with a thin layer of skin.

There are two types of spina bifida cystica:

– *meningocele*. Occurs when the cyst contains some of the meninges (membranes which cover the spinal cord) and the spinal fluid which surrounds the brain and spinal cord. In most instances, damage to the nerves is limited, and so a child with meningocele is only mildly affected.
– *myelomeningocele*. This occurs when the cyst contains the meninges and spinal fluid, and also part of the spinal cord, which is therefore damaged. Myelomeningocele is a more serious form of spina bifida. It always involves some degree of paralysis. Most children with this condition have difficulty with bladder and bowel control, and may never be entirely continent.

In addition, a baby born with spina bifida usually has *hydrocephalus* (i.e., brain fluid cannot drain into his bloodstream). The effects of hydrocephalus vary, but often include visual and learning difficulties, fits, and coordination problems.

The precise cause of spina bifida is not known. The nervous system is one of the first parts of the body to develop, and the neural tube – from which the brain and spinal cord develop – is formed within the first 25 days of pregnancy. Spina bifida arises when the neural tube grows abnormally.

Evidence does suggest, though, that spina bifida is partly inherited. A woman who has already had one child with spina bifida has an increased chance of having another with the same problem. The chance of an adult with spina bifida having a child with spina bifida is one in 20. Genetic counselling is available, and there are also tests which can determine whether the foetus is affected.

A large-scale survey found that in over one third of families with a child who had myelomeningocele, the mother admitted that she had been influenced against having any more children, and around 25 per cent stated that having a child with spina bifida had made them very anxious about possibility of subsequent pregnancies. However, nearly 20 per cent of the mothers felt that having a child with spina bifida had not influenced the size of their family; they either intended to have more children, or had decided before the birth of the affected child that they would not have any more. A small number of mothers reported that having a child with spina bifida made them decide to have a larger family than they had originally planned – perhaps to prove to themselves that they could have a non-affected child.

Most children with spina bifida are able to attend their local school. Segregated special schooling is recommended only when a child's learning difficulties are so severely impaired, or when his physical difficulties are so extreme, that his needs cannot be met within an ordinary classroom.

See also **Hydrocephalus; Integration, Educational; Special Needs**.

Spoiling Spoilt children are rarely liked by others. Yet it's unfair to reject a spoilt child, because it's certainly not her fault that she behaves this way – no child is born spoilt, nor does she make herself spoilt. Spoiling is caused by parents (and often grandparents), and they do it for many different reasons, including:

- *a desire to give their child everything possible*. Parents who had a very deprived upbringing are often determined to make sure their own child doesn't have that experience. Spoiling is one outcome of this approach.
- *compensation for a difficult childhood*. Everyone feels sorry for a child who, say, has long periods of ill-health, so it's natural for parents to shower their sick child with toys, games, and as much attention as possible. But if they take it to extremes, this form of compensation will turn into spoiling.

271

- *it is easier to say 'yes' to a child than to say 'no'.* A demanding toddler wants her own way, and her parents have to be quite determined in order not to always give in to her demands. Yet life is easier in the short term if she is given what she wants, because this avoids confrontation; in the long term, however, it will make her grow into a spoilt child.

- *they were spoilt by their parents when they were children.* We all react to the way we were brought up, sometimes by mirroring it with our own children and sometimes by turning against it completely. Parents who have fond memories of being over-indulged in childhood will consider it to be a suitable way of raising their own children.

- *there is only one child in the family.* Holding the centre position in the family – without ever having to share it with any other children – means a child may become spoiled as her parents smother her with clothes, toys, gifts, love and attention.

A spoilt child usually becomes unpopular because she thinks only of herself, because she's unable to share and take turns and because she's insensitive to other people's feelings. If these personality traits continue into adulthood, rejection and unpopularity will also continue. That's why it is best to tackle spoiling right at the outset.

People differ in their attitudes to over-indulging babies. Some think that babies can't possibly be spoilt because they don't know what's going on around them. Others think that spoiling can start at birth, and that an over-indulged baby will develop into an over-indulged child.

It is true that even a young baby can soon learn that crying is an effective way of getting attention from mum and dad, but failure to react to a crying baby can have the serious effect of teaching her that she is not very important. It communicates the message that, although she is unhappy, her parents are not going to do anything to make her feel better. Repeated experiences like this can reduce a baby's feelings of security, and she may even cry more frequently as a result. The best approach is one which achieves a balance between rushing to her every time she whimpers and ignoring her completely when she cries between meals.

But spoiling is not just a matter of giving a child too many toys, or too much attention – it's more about the way these things are given to her, why they're given to her, and how she understands the situation. And there should be occasions when she's not given what she wants. Naturally, she'll react badly when this happens, but it will teach her how to adapt when things don't go her way. This is not being cruel or letting her down; rather, it's a sensible strategy to stop her from becoming spoilt.

There are other ways to avoid spoiling your child, including the technique of asking her to justify why she wants something. It's tempting to accede to her perpetual nagging demands, simply for the sake of a quiet life. But then she may not value what she gets – instead, the act of acquisition may become more important to her than the actual enjoyment of the object. Asking her to explain why she wants something forces her to think about her request. (And show her by example that it's better to ask nicely for something than to stomp about angrily.) Try to encourage her to accept a compromise between what she wants and what you want, and once a deal is struck, don't go back on it later when she starts nagging at you all over again.

A young child who is spoilt sees the world around her only from her own point of view. She thinks only about herself, and her desires; therefore, she needs to be encouraged to appreciate other people's feelings – e.g., you could point out how terrible her friend felt when she snatched her toy away from her. She may be completely uninterested at first in what you have to say, but she'll get the message eventually.

See also **Crying Baby; Discipline; Grandparents; Only Child**.

Stealing A child under the age of three does not usually have a full understanding of the significance of personal possessions. True, a young child can get very agitated when his friend takes one of his favourite toys without asking, but he cannot generalise this concept to other people's possessions. So he doesn't 'steal' in the adult sense of the word; there is no malicious intent underlying his action.

However, he does need to learn the basic meaning of ownership. That's why minor incidents of theft by a child under the age of four should be dealt with firmly, but reasonably. Tell him that it is wrong, that others won't like him if

273

they think he takes things without asking, but don't make a big issue out of it. And if he does tend to take things without permission, there's no harm in giving him a fresh reminder before you visit someone else's house with him.

By the age of four or five, your child will know right from wrong and will know that stealing is not allowed. But he may be tempted to 'try it out' at some time or another, even though he knows he shouldn't do it, because stealing,

- *gives him what he wants, without having to wait.* A child who wants sweets but has no money can solve this problem by stealing money from his classmate's desk or from home; and a child who wants a computer game but hasn't got one can change the situation by stealing from someone else.
- *can appear exciting and adventurous.* The thrill associated with stealing (e.g., fear of discovery, excitement at disobeying adult rules) can be very attractive to a child – at least, until he is caught, at which point he wishes he had never thought of the idea in the first place.
- *may maintain his status amongst his friends.* Your child may be tempted into theft because his friends steal and he doesn't want to be left out of the crowd. It's not easy for a child to resist pressures like this.
- *is something that he has seen you do.* You would probably be outraged at the suggestion that you might be a thief. But have you ever brought some paper or sellotape home from the office without paying for it? Have you ever been undercharged in the supermarket, yet not declared it? Double standards of morality confuse children.

If you do discover your child has stolen something, nip it in the bud there and then. Treat the matter seriously (even if the item he has taken is insignificant), explain the consequences of his behaviour, ensure that he is involved in compensating the victim, and punish him reasonably. As long as he knows that you strongly disapprove of his behaviour then he is unlikely to repeat it again. But don't make a meal of it; the fact that he has pinched a sweet from a shop without paying hardly puts him in the same league as a bank-robber. A one-off incident does not mean a regular pattern will be established.

Persistent theft by a school-age child is a genuine cause for concern, however, because it may be a sign of a deeper emotional problem. A child who fails to get love and attention from his parents may decide – perhaps unconsciously – that at least he is going to get something from them – and so he steals money from his mother's purse even when he does not want to spend it, or biscuits from the food cupboard even when he is not hungry. Many psychologists claim that this unconscious motivation frequently underlies incidents of repeated theft.

Of course, a child who steals for these reasons still needs to have moral rules explained to him and still needs to be treated firmly. But stealing is only the symptom of his underlying difficulty – it is not the real problem. And the best way to tackle that more serious issue is for his parents to think long and hard about their child's development. They need to examine his life closely, and their relationship with him.

See also **Emotional Deprivation; Guilt; Lying; Scapegoat; Swearing.**

Step-Parents Just as marriage has increased in popularity this decade, so too has remarriage – the remarriage rate is now over 50 per cent higher than it was thirty years ago, which means that almost 3 children out of 10 are living with one natural parent and one step-parent. Yet the chances of a second marriage succeeding are even less than the chances of a first marriage succeeding. Of those couples who reconcile their differences and remarry the same partner, over 50 per cent separate within two years. Of those who marry a new partner, 50 per cent separate within three years.

Couples in a second marriage experience different problems from those in a first marriage. Surveys have shown that difficulties in a first marriage usually stem from emotional immaturity, sexual dissatisfaction, and worry over money – problems with children come bottom of the list. But couples in a second marriage report the greatest area of conflict is the management of their children.

Parents shouldn't expect their child to welcome a remarriage with open arms; previous experience has taught him that mums and dads don't stay together for ever. No wonder he is apprehensive about the possibility of living through

275

another period with lots of arguments and ill-feeling. He has to learn to trust the stability of his new family, and this takes time.

A child's adjustment to a remarriage depends on factors relating to:

- *acceptance of the previous loss*. He may unconsciously deny that his parents have separated – this is a natural defence; but the remarriage won't work until he accepts that the previous marriage is over.
- *gap between marriages*. A short gap leaves a child too little time to get over the trauma of divorce before facing the impact of the new family. But a long gap between marriages is not the best solution either, because he may become used to having mum all to himself and may be reluctant to share her with a step-parent.
- *divided loyalties*. Where a family break-up arises from divorce, a child really has three parents – his two natural parents and his step-parent – and he may feel his loyalties are stretched. Yet, in many happy remarried families, a child still sees both his natural parents.
- *parental jealousy*. Ex-spouses may be jealous when their former partner remarries, and this may influence a child's perception of his new step-parent. However, every child is capable of having a good relationship with a step-parent and a natural parent at the same time. Each relationship contributes to his development in its own way.
- *child's age*. Younger children are better at adjusting to a new step-parent than are school-age children. Adolescents frequently have problems adapting to a new family structure.
- *parental responsibilities*. The step-father often assumes full responsibilities too soon, before his step-child is ready to accept him. It is usually best for a step-parent to take parental responsibilities gradually.

Many second marriages involve an amalgamation of two sets of children from two previous marriages, and there may be jealousy between them. This is most marked when the children are of the same age – each child feels threatened by the others, afraid his parent's love for him will diminish. However, most parents are able to form good relationships

276

with their step-children when they have their natural children living with them as well.

When a second marriage produces a new baby, any existing children in the family may feel insecure. They need reassurance. Some couples in a remarriage decide not to have a baby of their own because of the detrimental effect this could have on the other children. This is a personal decision, but it does seem a rather drastic measure to take in order to avoid a potential pitfall. Every child adds a new and unique dimension to a family. In fact, one study has demonstrated that relationships between parents and children in step-families, and between the children themselves, are better when the couple have children of their own. A natural child in a step-family seems to act as a binding force.

Although the stereotype of a step-parent is someone who is wicked, uncaring and selfish, there is little basis in reality for this pessimistic view. Studies on the effects of remarriage on children (involving thousands of step-families with at least one step-child) have found that:

- 6 out of 10 families think family relationships are excellent, 2 out of 10 think family relationships are good, and only 2 out of 10 think they are poor.
- the age of the step-mother at the time of remarriage is important. More step-mothers over the age of 40 report excellent relationships with their step-children than younger step-mothers. The age of the step-father does not appear to matter so much.
- nearly twice as many children under the age of 13 have excellent relationships with their step-mothers than older children, although the age of the children has no effect on their relationships with their step-fathers.
- step-fathers are more likely to form close connections with their step-children than are step-mothers, particularly if the step-child is a boy; they also tend to be more competent than fathers in intact families.
- the self-image of a child in a remarriage is no different from that of a child in an original family. Being in a step-family does not adversely affect the way a child sees himself, or his feelings of personal worth.

See also **Separation and Divorce; Single-Parent Family**.

Supervision Children need their parents' supervision – there's nobody who would argue with that. What is debatable, however, is the type and level of supervision that parents should exercise over their child at different ages. Should you let your three-year-old play in the sitting room while you lie upstairs in bed having a short nap? Is it acceptable for your four-year-old to play in an enclosed garden while you prepare a meal in the kitchen? Is it reasonable to allow your five-year-old to play in a park with her friends while you sit some distance away reading a magazine?

There are no easy answers to these questions – and what suits one parent may not suit another. Yet part of growing up is being allowed an increased degree of independence without mum or dad in close attendance. No matter the age of your child, consider the following factors when determining the level of supervision required:

- *your child's ability*. There is no point in leaving her unsupervised during an activity that she doesn't have the ability to cope with on her own. For example, a three-year-old will be unlikely to complete a complex jigsaw puzzle without her parent's help, and so requires supervision in that situation.
- *the nature of the activity*. There are some activities that are unlikely to cause your child harm – e.g., playing with building bricks, drawing with crayons. Here, supervision can be minimal. But there are other activities that are potentially dangerous and consequently need closer supervision – e.g., playing close to a pond, cutting with scissors.
- *your child's maturity*. Some children take longer to develop a sense of danger, and are unaware of everyday hazards. Closer supervision is necessary for immature children, in case they unknowingly place themselves at risk.
- *past experience*. If you have found previously that your five-year-old becomes wild and irresponsible the moment she is out of your sight, then clearly she is not ready to be left unsupervised. However, if she has coped with a reduced level of supervision on previous occasions, then you can afford to lessen it even further the next time.

Supervision should be decreased in slow, gradual steps, as your child progresses through childhood. If you do it too quickly, she won't be able to cope. Although she may moan because she wants to be independent as soon as possible, your supervision keeps her safe.

But you can't wrap your child in cotton wool. She has to be given regular opportunities to stand on her own two feet, without you watching over her, or she will never attain a satisfactory level of independence. Too much supervision will reduce her self-confidence and her ability to look after herself when she is away from you. In situations where she doesn't have you to tell her what to do, where she has to make a decision on her own, she will struggle.

As a rough guide, a child under two should rarely, if ever, be left unsupervised for more than a few moments (unless she is at home, playing quietly and safely). From the age of three upwards, start to allow her times when you and she are not together – playgroup provides ample opportunities for this – and gradually increase these times over the next couple of years. By the time your child reaches school age, she will probably be sensible enough to manage many tasks within her daily routine without close parental supervision. At that age, explain to her why you want to keep an eye on her for some activities, while you are prepared to give her more freedom for others. She may not like what you say, but she will understand it.

See also **Hazards; Independence; Over-Protectiveness; Road Safety**.

Swearing Watching your child develop language is one of the rewards of parenthood, as you witness her progressing from mere babbling towards more mature sounds, and then on to actual words and sentences. But this joy soon turns to shock when you suddenly hear her cursing and swearing.

Since a young child does not have a well developed moral understanding, the blame for most instances of children under the age of three or four using foul language can be laid at the door of adults or older children. A pre-school child who, entering an untidy room, puts her hands on her hips, furrows her brow and admonishes the occupants with 'What a bloody mess this is!' is almost certainly mimicking adult behaviour that she has seen. She is unlikely to have any idea of what the words actually mean – just that it's the sort of thing grown-ups say when they get angry.

If you hear your young child swear, you will probably react in one of the following ways:

- *with uncontrollable laughter.* The incongruity of her using very adult language can seem comical, even though you disapprove of the language itself, and you may burst out laughing. Unfortunately, she may interpret this as your approval of swearing.
- *by giving her a severe telling-off.* You may be so annoyed that you reprimand your child strongly, with the aim of ensuring she doesn't use these words again. But this strategy may backfire. If you draw undue attention to swearing, she will immediately realise that a swear-word is a special word with a special effect – and that it is a good way to get your attention. This awareness may make her want to continue swearing.
- *by ignoring her.* This is probably the best way to deal with an incident of swearing at this age. The chances are that she has only used the word casually and that it will quickly pass out of her vocabulary.

A child of school age is often attracted to swear-words precisely because she knows they are used by adults, and she thinks that by adopting grown-up mannerisms she will become more grown-up herself. But she also knows the distinction between a 'good' word and a 'naughty' word. So explain to your child that swearing is something neither children nor adults should indulge in, and that other children may not want to play with her if she swears. (Never tell her that swearing is something only adults are allowed to do.) You can't prevent her from hearing others swear when she is outside the house. But setting a good example yourself will provide her with an alternative model to imitate.

See also **Discipline; Guilt; Lying; Modelling; Politeness; Scapegoat; Stealing.**

T

Tantrums   Young children are prone to temper tantrums, particularly around the age of two – which is why this stage is often referred to as the 'terrible twos'. At this age, a child begins to assert himself and tries to exert his authority over his parents. In time, he will learn that family life involves give and take and that there are occasions when he does not get his own way. But at two, he still thinks he can rule the roost. When his wishes are blocked, his feelings of anger and frustration may be so strong that they explode into an uncontrollable tantrum.

You may be tempted to give in to your toddler when he loses his temper, if only to calm him down. But you won't be doing him any favours by behaving in this way. Such a response simply teaches him that when you say 'no' you really mean 'Yes, but you must have a tantrum first.' And it will encourage him to have even more tantrums.

Stick to your guns. If you have said 'no', then make sure you mean 'no'. Although there are times when household rules should be flexible, in most cases where parental rules have been set, your toddler should be expected to follow them, whether he is happy with them or not.

Once in a temper tantrum, however, he may need your help to get out of it (but this does not include your screaming at him to be quiet). Some children calm down quickly when they are put out of the room for a few minutes, because they hate losing their parents' attention, and this forces them to gain control. Some calm down quickly when they find that mum and dad ignore their outbursts. And some need their parents beside them, to provide calming reassurance. There isn't a 'right' way of dealing with tantrums – a lot depends on the child, his parents, and the setting in which the tantrum occurs.

Prevention is better than cure. It is better to try to prevent your child having a tantrum than it is to scold him after the event. And because tantrums are often predictable, you may be able to take avoiding action. If you know that he is in a situation that usually agitates him (for instance, trying to do jigsaws that are too difficult), either give him something else to play with or share the activity with him, all the time keeping him calm. Also, tantrums tend to be more frequent when a child is tired – so try to avoid confrontations just before bedtime. Of course, there are times when attempts at prevention simply do not work, and your child goes on to have a full-blown tantrum. Try to be calm at this point. The chances are that he has little control over his outburst, and so there is no point in your screaming at him.

Most children have fewer tantrums as they grow older. By the age of five, a child is more able to talk about his anger and frustration, rather than having to rely on actions to release these pent-up emotions. Some, however, continue to have tantrums even when they reach school age – though the size and strength of an older child means that his tantrums are far more harrowing and destructive than those of a younger child. On the positive side, a school-age child has greater insight into his own reactions during a temper tantrum. He will be more aware of what happens as his temper builds up, and he will probably regret his outbursts afterwards. You may be able to use this awareness to help him gain control of his anger (e.g., by encouraging him to walk away when he feels his temper building up).

Relaxation techniques have become increasingly popular for helping older children control their frustration and rage. This involves learning how to induce a feeling of calmness through muscle exercises and breathing exercises. Although these methods have been widely utilised for many years by adults as a way of managing stress and anxiety without the use of drugs – in circumstances ranging from ante-natal classes to treatment for phobias – it is only in recent years that their potential for helping children has been recognised.

A child around the age of five or older is more likely to respond to strategies which put him in charge of controlling his temper, than to methods that his parents may use to control him. That's why teaching him preventative methods of temper control – such as avoiding potential frustrations or using relaxation techniques – is the best course of action.

See also **Aggression; Discipline**.

Teeth Every tooth consists of an outer coat of hard, dead enamel and an inner core of softer, living dentine. We start to feel toothache when decay is so severe that it bores its way through the enamel into the inner living core. Dental care, therefore, is very important for your children.

Sometimes a baby is born with a tooth already in his mouth, but most babies don't have their first tooth until around six months (although with some it's not until at least a year). This first set of teeth (known as *milk teeth*) is found in girls earlier than in boys, but boys tend to lose their milk teeth earlier. All twenty milk teeth are already formed at birth – you may be able to feel them as bumps in your baby's gums before they have actually broken through.

The teething stage (when your baby's teeth are beginning to erupt through his gums) can cause him extreme discomfort. You may notice he salivates a lot, or chews hard on his rattles. In many instances, a teething baby has red cheeks, diarrhoea, and even a rash on his bottom. (But be careful not to attribute every ailment at this stage to teething, since there may be another cause for your baby's distress.) You may be able to ease his discomfort by gently massaging the gum area with your clean finger. Teething gels, which act as mild anaesthetics, are available from chemists', but these don't seem to be very effective. Some parents recommend something hard and cold for the baby to chew on, such as a cooled teething ring.

Milk teeth are particularly vulnerable to decay, which is why you should avoid giving your infant sweet drinks and foods. His first teeth should be treated with care, as they lay the foundation for subsequent healthy jaw and gum growth. They also guide the second teeth through.

From the age of five, your child's milk teeth will begin to loosen and fall out, usually in the front lower jaw first. You may be able to see the second tooth as soon as the milk tooth has come out. And by the time he is seven, a good many of his first teeth will have fallen out – ask a group of children this age to smile, and you'll have great difficulty counting all the gaps between their teeth! The legend of the generous tooth fairy comes to the fore at this point; although your child may have a hunch that in reality you are the tooth fairy, he'll be quite willing to push these doubts to the back of his mind, as he savours the prospect of finding a coin in place of the tooth he left under his pillow the night before.

Since dental care is so important, introduce him to tooth-brushing very early on. At first, simply let him chew on a small, soft toothbrush, and let him watch you brush your teeth in the morning. This sets a good example. He will probably prefer children's toothpaste, which is milder. Ask your dentist's advice on the proper technique for brushing teeth (regular dental appointments should be made when your child is three or four years old). It's not a case of scrubbing them as hard as you can – rather, you should be gentle but thorough. When he reaches the toddler stage, make toothbrushing a regular routine after mealtimes and before bedtime. Never let him have sugary products in his mouth once he has brushed his teeth at night.

Despite your best intentions about not letting him develop a 'sweet tooth', the chances are that he will want to eat more sweets than you would like. Try to reach a balance on this. If you forbid him to have any sweets, he will probably get some from his friends. A better strategy is to give him some, say, after a meal and before he brushes his teeth. His teeth are most at risk from decay when he eats a small number of sweets throughout the day than when he eats a large number all at once.

Dentists point out that up to 30 per cent of the population over 16 have no teeth of their own at all. That's a frightening thought; so encourage your child to have good dental care habits, right from the start.

See also **Eating; Healthy Eating; Snacks**.

Twins Over 8000 sets of twins are born every year in the UK – averaging 1 in 90 pregnancies – and this number is increasing steadily year by year. (Multiple births are also on the increase; in England and Wales in 1982 there were 70 sets of triplets and 6 sets of quadruplets, whereas in 1988 these figures were 157 and 12 respectively. And the Walton children, born in 1984, were the first all-girl sextuplets to survive.)

This growth in the rate of twins is due to the wider avail-ability of infertility treatment. However, parents rarely undergo this treatment with the hope of having twins or multiple births; their aim is usually to have one healthy baby – more than one at the same time is a bonus.

Research confirms that:

- twins tend to run in families, and so a woman who is herself a twin or has a twin relative is more likely to give birth to twins than a woman who has no twins in her family;
- women who conceive after the age of 40 are four times more likely to produce twins than are women who conceive at the age of 20;
- it is quite usual for the birth of twins to follow the birth of a single child;
- doctors are often able to diagnose twins as early as the 16th weeks of pregnancy;
- most twins are born prematurely (the average gestation period is 37 weeks) and are underweight;
- there is a higher incidence of cot deaths in twins;
- twins tend to be slower to acquire speech, and are more likely than other children to have speech problems that require specialist help.

Twins are either identical or non-identical. When identical twins are conceived, a single egg that is already fertilised separates into two identical parts. Each part develops into a baby. Since each child comes from the one egg, these twins (monozygotic) are always of the same sex and possess the same inherited characteristics. When non-identical twins are conceived, two entirely separate eggs are fertilised by separate sperm at the same time. Since each child comes from different eggs, these twins (dizygotic) are no more alike than any other brother and sister.

Yet studies show that even identical twins are not exactly the same in every way. While it is true that they have a greater similarity of heartbeat and pulse rate than non-identical twins, clear differences often emerge in other areas. For instance, parents frequently find that one identical twin is right-handed while the other is left-handed. The left-handed child is likely to be the smaller twin. Twins often have different handwriting styles, and there are likely to be personality differences. It is normal for twins to pass developmental milestones at slightly different times.

The birth order of the twins (i.e., which one actually emerged first) has no effect on their psychological development. But people are often fascinated by the question of which child is a few moments older than the other, especially with identical twins, because it provides a way of distinguishing between the two look-alikes. The inherent danger in such a labelling, particularly if it originates from their parents, is that it can cause unnecessary rivalry between the children. The so-called older twin may feel pressure to be dominant even though she would prefer not to be. Or she may feel inadequate if the so-called younger twin develops at a faster rate.

There is a widely held view that twins have a special psychic relationship which allows them to be constantly aware of the other's thoughts. Although there is no scientific evidence to support this idea, there have been many instances where twins have fabricated a secret language between themselves. They tend to give up this form of communication before they reach school age. But the existence of a special language between children is not unique to multiple births – parents of non-twins often find their young children are able to communicate using terms adults can't understand.

Twins present certain practical difficulties in the early years, difficulties to do with their basic management – e.g., who to give attention to first, who to feed first, who to pick up first when they are both crying. Indeed, the main complaint of parents, during the first twelve months after their twins' birth, is the physical strain of managing two feeding and sleeping schedules simultaneously.

Fortunately, this very exhausting phase of the babies' lives does pass quickly, although it might not seem that way at the time! And their parents often look back on those early months as a period when they themselves became very close. They have no choice but to share childcare, and this sharing process often enhances their relationship.

Once a basic routine has been established, parents then have to cope with life outside the home. Have you ever tried going shopping with two young children of the same age? Double buggies are available, but they are difficult to get on and off public transport – and even harder when carrying the week's shopping. The toddler stage carries hazards of a different sort because the children's increased mobility means that their parents may have two infants darting off in opposite directions at the same time. This is probably why twins are usually kept in their buggies for longer periods than single children.

As twins grow older, their parents have to choose whether to place both in the same class in nursery or school, or whether to separate them. Separation can make starting at nursery difficult, since each child will have to cope without the support of his twin; but this may be offset by the advantage that each can establish his own identity. At some point, twins do have to develop separate lives, and the later parents leave it, the harder it becomes for the children. Parents often report that each child positively thrives when given the chance to be in a class of her own, away from her twin, because each is treated individually.

See also **Birth Order; Independence; Language Development; Zygote**.

U

Ultrasound Scientists have learned a great deal about foetal growth inside the womb, largely through the development of the technique known as ultrasonography. An ultrasound examination of a pregnant woman involves a probe, pressed against her abdomen, which sends acoustic impulses into her body. These impulses are then deflected at different angles by foetal bones and tissues of varying density. All of this information is fed back to a television screen, on which the strong signals (from areas of high density) are seen as white while the weak signals (from areas of low density) are seen as black.

These techniques have shown, for example, that the foetus

- spends a lot of time moving around the womb, and probably has a good sense of balance;
- gives a startled reaction to a loud noise occurring outside the womb;
- has slow eye movements as early as the 16th week after conception;
- begins to have rapid eye movement (REM) sleep around the 23rd week, and this continues until around the 36th week, when long periods of quiet sleep take over;
- appears to have identifiable facial expressions, such as disgust, unhappiness, joy and fear.

Psychologists have also used ultrasonography to reduce maternal anxiety during pregnancy. One study monitored the psychological effects of letting mothers see a video of their ultrasound assessment in order to reassure them of the foetus's well-being. The researchers found that infants of these mothers (compared with infants of mothers who didn't receive this information) were less active in the womb, had higher birthweights, and were less irritable in the early weeks of life.

See also **Pre-Natal Development**.

Unconscious Sigmund Freud (1856–1939) identified three levels of a child's (and adult's) mind. First, the conscious level: this consists of everything a child is aware of at any given time. Second, the pre-conscious level: everything a child is unaware of at any given time but which she can easily remember if asked. Third, the unconscious level: aggressive instincts, nasty thoughts and selfish feelings, which are concealed in the deepest part of a child's mind (she is totally unaware of these emotions) and yet have a profound influence on her behaviour and personality.

Freud claimed that the unconscious is like the large part of the iceberg that lies below the water line – it is completely hidden yet is extremely powerful. He argued that every bit of behaviour in childhood and adulthood is caused by unconscious thoughts. For instance, a child who spills her juice over a drawing of her father unconsciously wants to hurt him – the action of spilling her juice allows her to release her unconscious feeling harmlessly. And a child whose behaviour suddenly deteriorates may be troubled by a fear that lies deep in her unconscious – e.g., the fear of being rejected by her parents. Even such simple acts as a slip of the tongue, or forgetting an appointment, are caused by unconscious thoughts.

While Freud developed psychoanalysis (the 'talking cure') for use with disturbed adults, his daughter, Anna, developed play therapy for use with troubled children. Play therapy rests on the assumptions that play, not language, is a child's main means of communication and that through play she will be able to release unconscious feelings that disturb her. Despite the widespread use of play therapy and psychoanalysis, however, there is little scientific evidence that these methods work, and they have been heavily criticised as a result.

See also **Personality; Play**.

Unhappiness No children are happy all of the time – like adults, they have ups and downs. But there is a difference between a child who is momentarily sad in reaction to a particular occurrence (for instance, because someone has broken his favourite toy), and a child who is regularly unhappy (for instance, because he is unable to make friends,

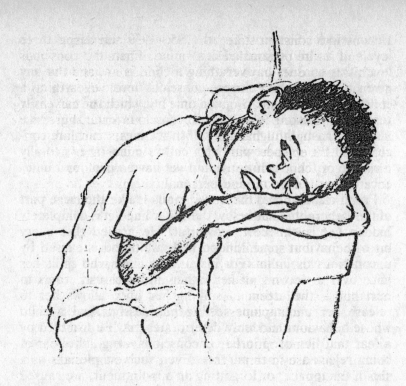

no matter how hard he tries). This latter child is so affected by his sadness that his self-image, and his relationships with other children and adults, suffer. This severe degree of dissatisfaction is quite different from the brief tearful moments that are a part of every child's life.

Young children demonstrate their unhappiness in many different ways. One may show it by being passive and withdrawn, while another may express his distress in the opposite way, by turning his inner turmoil into outer turmoil. At first glance it may not be obvious that he has underlying worries, but the picture becomes clearer when the troubled behaviour persists.

The most important aspect of your child's early life – which is necessary for later happiness, though by itself will not guarantee it – is the affectionate relationship he has with you. The quality of this bond determines many of his emotional characteristics, including his feeling of inner happiness. A child who has not forged secure emotional relationships with at least one adult before the age of four may be in a constant state of unhappiness and despair, and will find future personal relationships difficult.

Childhood does have its moments of stress, and the way you help your child through these periods will affect his level of contentment. For instance, a first-born may have problems adjusting to a newborn brother or sister, but sensitive and thoughtful handling by his parents can help him through this episode without a residual feeling of unease. Similarly, a child whose parents separate wants to remain loyal to both, even though the adults themselves do not get on together. Handled badly, parental antagonism causes the child deep-rooted sadness; but if it is handled well, he can learn to accept his new family circumstances. And another stress point that some children have to face is the bereavement of a close relative – if his grief is ignored or if it is relegated to second place after the adult's grief, then his unhappiness will deepen.

Temporary unhappiness is an inevitable part of growing up. But if your child is allowed to express his distress as it arises, and is not ignored or made to feel guilty about it, then it will ease in time. The onus is on you to make sure this happens.

See also **Bonding; Emotional Deprivation; First-Born Jealousy; Grief; Separation and Divorce**.

V

Victim Some children seem to fall foul of bullies, time after time, no matter what situation they are in. These children appear to attract bullying wherever they go. And it's not simply a matter of being small, or of being bookish, or even of being slightly built and underweight. There are many children who have these characteristics and yet never become the focus of bullying.

A child who is consistently bullied may be behaving in a way that actually encourages others to be hostile to him. He may do this because of his need for:

- *attention*. Being bullied is an effective way of getting his parents' attention, or maybe attention from other children. A victim of bullying nearly always attracts sympathy, and for some children that is the only type of attention they are able to get – an attention-seeking child is willing to put up with an attack because of this. However, a child like this will be attention-seeking in other areas of his life as well, and so is readily identifiable.
- *punishment*. A child who has a strong feeling of guilt – for some real or imaginary wrongdoing – may unconsciously seek punishment as a way of expiating that guilt. One way for him to be punished is to have another child physically attack him; through this, he obtains emotional satisfaction.

These explanations may sound like a case of blaming the victim. But the fact is that some children do unconsciously encourage others to bully them, and you should exclude this factor first before trying to resolve your child's complaints of being bullied in school. Another pointer to the 'willing victim' is the number of children bullying him. The greater the number of assailants, then the greater the likelihood that the child is unwittingly inciting the attacks.

If your child regularly comes home complaining that he is being bullied by a particular child, spend some time considering whether he is behaving in a way that is contributing to the problem. Ask yourself the following questions:

- *Does he get bullied by more than one child?*
- *Is he attention-seeking in other ways?*
- *Do you constantly have to reprimand him at home?*
- *Is he willing to take the blame for something that he hasn't done?*
- *Does he seem to deliberately provoke you into punishing him?*

If you answer 'yes' to most of these questions, it is likely that your child is making himself a victim of bullying, in order to meet his psychological needs. Talk to him about it, and try to find out why he feels this way. If you answer 'no' to most of these questions, then it is highly unlikely that he is in any way responsible for being bullied.

See also **Attention-Seeking Behaviour; Bullying; Scapegoat**.

Videos Parents who are concerned about the influence of television on their child have been safe in the knowledge that films shown before 9pm are suitable for younger viewers. This time provides a neat cut-off point for sensible parents wishing to exercise a degree of control over their child's viewing habits. However, the advent of the home video means that young children can now access films previously denied to them on scheduled television.

Few parents, of course, intend their five-year-old to watch a film rated '18' (or even '15' or '12'). But there are three main factors that make this sort of viewing a possibility. First, there is the 'morning after the night before' scenario: parents have watched a video the night before, and next morning their children – who are up and out of bed while the parents are still asleep – have ample opportunity to watch it themselves. Second, although cinemas adhere to age guidelines when admitting audiences, many video stores are less rigorous. This makes it easier for children to obtain films which they couldn't see in the cinema. And third, a child may be able to watch an inappropriate video at her friend's house.

There is little doubt that an '18' horror film can have a disturbing influence on an impressionable young mind. This

is precisely why you need to provide some degree of supervision over your child's home-video diet, especially when
she is young.

See also **Aggression; Nightmares.**

Violence Hardly a day goes by without some of our
national newspapers carrying a story about a child who has
been physically abused. But this doesn't mean that violence
towards children is a phenomenon of the 90s, or even the
80s – one of the earliest-recorded court cases of a child
being repeatedly beaten and cut with a sharp implement
happened in New York in 1874.

The whole issue of violence towards children is controversial because of people's varying attitudes. Some argue
that any physical assault on a child should be regarded as
an unacceptable act of violence and treated as such, while
others maintain that parents have a right – and a duty – to
smack their child when she misbehaves. The problem is that
there is no clear dividing line between a justifiable smack
(is there such a thing?) and a violent assault. There have
been many cases of parents who over-enthusiastically
smacked their child, only to be shocked subsequently by the
level of injury they had inflicted upon her.

It's a myth that all parents who are regularly violent
towards their children are seriously psychologically disturbed; less than 10 per cent come into this category. There
is no single explanation to account for the reasons why
some parents beat their children. However, analysis of over
20,000 cases of child physical abuse in the USA revealed a
strong association between violence against children and
environmental deprivation (unemployment, poor living conditions, inadequate housing and large families). All the
same, this cannot account for all instances of violence
towards children, since there are many families living in
these circumstances who do not assault their children.

See also **Sexual Abuse; Smacking.**

Vision Sight is only one of five senses – yet it is possibly
the most important, since a great deal of learning takes

294

place through vision. A baby uses his eyes to explore the environment; an infant uses vision to judge the expression on his mother's face; a toddler uses sight as he wanders about the room, avoiding the hazards as he goes; a pre-school child uses vision to fit blocks into his shape-sorter; a school-age child uses sight to learn to read. Vision, therefore, is central to a child's development, and a child with impaired vision may be slower to learn basic skills than a sighted child.

William James, one of the first psychologists, believed that a baby is born with very little visual ability. He described a new baby's visual experiences as a 'buzzing, blooming confusion'. But we now know that James was wrong – research has shown that a baby arrives in the world already pre-programmed to attend to specific features in the environment. At birth, he

- *is sensitive to light*. If a very bright light shines into his eyes, he will shut them tightly and keep them that way until the light source is removed.
- *can track large moving objects*. A baby is able to notice movements of large shapes, and may watch his mother as she crosses from one side of the room to the other.
- *detects contours*. If he is shown a solid black shape against a contrasting white background, he will spend most time looking at the points where black and white meet.
- *prefers patterns to colours*. A new baby will look longer at a patterned picture than he will at a solid-colour picture.
- *focuses on objects between 8 and 10 inches away from his face*. This means he can look closely at his mother's face during feeding.

A major change in the way an infant uses vision occurs at around the age of two months. Until then, he uses his 'secondary visual system' – i.e., he is concerned only with the whereabouts of an object; he will watch an object as it moves around, will focus on something that comes near to him, and will look at edges of things. After this, a baby's 'primary visual system' takes over: he now becomes more interested in what an object actually is. He starts to attend more to details, such as whether an object is straight or curved, light or dark, and so on; and instead of peering at only one specific feature of a picture (as does the very young baby), an infant of two months and older begins to scan the whole picture.

These early visual skills enable a new baby to begin to make sense of the world around him, to distil meaning from all that is happening in his immediate environment. Lack of such visual skills hampers this process.

See also **Bonding; Eye; Learning through Play; Visual Difficulties.**

Visual Difficulties   Although total blindness in childhood is rare, many children are partially sighted – i.e., they have sufficiently bad eyesight to require some form of visual aid over and above the normal range of glasses obtainable on prescription from an optician.

There are many causes of partial sight in childhood, including:

– *cataract*. An opaqueness in all or part of the lens (the bit of the eye that lets the light shine through, allowing it to activate nerve ends in the retina). Corrective surgical work is possible, but this is rare for a baby unless there is a genuine risk of blindness in both eyes.
– *glaucoma*. Occurs when the eye's natural fluid can't drain away. The build-up causes an unnatural pressure, resulting in blurred vision. Treatment can remedy the potential loss of sight.
– *squint*. With this condition, a child's eyes appear to look in opposite directions. In a baby under six months, a squint is normal. However, if a severe squint continues and remains untreated until the child is two or three years of age, blindness in one eye may occur. Treatment for squints varies from temporarily covering up the good eye to surgery.
– *toxocariasis*. A rare disease passed to a child through contact with dog or cat excrement, usually when he is playing in a public park or a garden used by animals.

There are many children with much less serious visual defects, but there is little cause for concern in these instances because wearing prescription glasses remedies the difficulty. Common remediable defects include short-sightedness (a child sees objects that are near, but an object far away appears blurred) and long-sightedness (he sees objects far away clearly, whereas a nearby object appears blurred). Routine medical screening is a worthwhile and efficient means of detecting these minor visual defects.

Sight is only one of five senses, but it is possibly the most important, since a great deal of learning takes place through vision. A child with impaired vision may be slower to learn basic skills than a sighted child. However, your baby has to learn to use whatever vision he has, no matter how slight it may be.

Unlike a baby with normal vision who can sit unaided and use his eyes to observe his environment, a partially sighted baby needs the environment to come to him. Objects have to be brought close to him, and people have to be nearer than normal when talking to him. A baby with partial sight needs a lot more touching and other physical communication with his parents. He will rely on sounds and smells to gain understanding of what is going on around him. Talk to him while playing with him. Just like a sighted baby, he needs to be placed in different positions in order to encourage his physical development. A partially sighted baby should have a normal range of opportunities to be in his pram, walker, buggy and 'relaxer'. He should also be allowed to experience rolling about on the floor.

Don't become over-protective of your partially sighted child when he reaches the toddler stage. He needs to be allowed to move around his environment. As long as sensible safety precautions are taken (i.e., a cooker guard, a rail across the top of the stairs, covers for the electric sockets), then the few bumps and bruises that he acquires will be more than offset by the benefit he gains from exploring.

Toys are as important to a partially sighted child's development as they are to a sighted child's, although buying a toy for a child with limited vision requires a bit more thought. There are toys designed specifically for a partially sighted child, but these are not readily sold in most toy shops. When choosing toys, consider the following features:

- *stimulating*. Your child will prefer toys that are interesting to touch, which rattle or make any sort of noise when played with, and which even have an interesting smell.

297

- *colourfulness*. A partially sighted child may have some vision, however slight. Toys in vivid yellow, blue, red or green are easier to see than dull colours.
- *play potential*. Some toys, such as jigsaws, are only usable in specific ways, whereas other toys, such as building bricks, modelling clay and paper and paints, can be used in a variety of ways. This latter group – with a greater play potential – is the kind of toys most suited to the needs of a child with partial sight.
- *purposefulness*. Toys aimed at developing specific skills – for instance, form-boards, finger-puppets, pedal-cars, and shape-sorters – are as appropriate for a partially sighted child as they are for any other child.
- *safety*. A partially sighted child is more vulnerable to everyday hazards, and the choice of toys has to reflect this. Avoid play objects that have sharp edges, that are easily breakable, or that are small enough to be swallowed.
- *cleanability*. All children go through a phase of exploring objects by putting them in their mouths. A child with a visual difficulty is likely to continue with this habit for longer than a sighted child, and so toys should be able to be cleaned without suffering damage.

See also **Bonding; Eye; Hazards; Over-Protectiveness; Vision**.

Weaning Babies have to be weaned off milk (whether breast-milk or bottle-milk) on to solid foods because after a certain age milk alone doesn't give them enough nourishment. However, you should not start your baby on solids earlier than is recommended – they won't make her grow better.

Current medical opinion holds that early introduction of solids could be harmful. In 1980, the American Academy of Paediatrics stated that no nutritional advantages result from the introduction of solids before a child is between four and six months. In 1981 a British medical report took a slightly more lenient view, but still cautioned against solids before an infant is three months old.

Despite this advice, in 1986 a survey of mothers found that 8 per cent gave their babies solids before they were two weeks old, 40 per cent before they were six weeks old, and 74 per cent before they were 12 weeks old. These data prove that many mothers do ignore official advice, often because they find that solid food doesn't appear to do their baby any immediate harm, or because they believe that it is nutritionally superior to a liquid diet. Some parents find that the early introduction of solids is an effective way of soothing a hungry, fractious baby. Yet there is no scientific evidence to suggest that early weaning does lead to a good night's sleep, and indeed some studies have said that it has no effect.

Your baby's behaviour is the best way of deciding when to start her on solids (assuming, of course, that you don't break the three-month limit). If you find, for instance, that your four-month-old is still hungry after a feed, even though you have increased the amount of milk, then it is probably time to try solids. But don't rush into it.

Approach weaning gradually, giving your baby one new food at a time. This will enable you to monitor whether or not she likes it, and whether or not it agrees with her. Give her a drink of milk first, then mash or liquidise a small amount of food and give her that. You may find that she spits it out at first, but don't worry – she'll probably take time to get used to the new taste and texture. Remember that a baby still gets her main source of nourishment from milk until she is 12 months old.

Some parents let their infant taste the food by putting some on their finger (freshly washed), which they then place in her mouth. Some offer her solids from the tip of a small spoon. Other parents sit her on her high-chair, place a few small pieces of food on her tray, and then leave her to explore. Every baby is different. Once you have got yours interested in solids, and she is older than six months, then gradually make the food less smooth. She should be encouraged to get used to foods of different textures, but never force-feed her.

Commercially prepared foods, in tins or packets, are very convenient and may suit your lifestyle. Be careful, though, that they don't have added sugar (that could damage her milk teeth) or any kind of additives. The fresh food that you eat will be suitable for your baby, but avoid adding salt to it. Once your infant is well established on solids, make sure she continues to take a satisfactory amount of liquid throughout the day.

See also **Additives; Eating; Fussy Eaters; Healthy Eating; Teeth.**

Working Mothers The number of working mothers of young children returning to full-time employment will probably continue to increase in future. In many instances, a mother goes back to work because she needs the money; in some instances, she does so because she doesn't want to risk losing a promising career. Whatever the reason, there is no evidence that returning to work – even during the pre-school years – inevitably has an adverse effect on her child's psychological development.

But this lifestyle is not without its problems. From a woman's perspective, being a working mother may mean having to cope with double the normal amount of tasks. Very few working mothers would say that their partner actually agrees to split the domestic chores evenly down the middle – the man generally assumes that the prime

responsibility for running the house continues to rest with the woman. The woman's job is frequently given a lower priority. (Of course, there are couples who exercise a much more even balance, but this is hard to achieve, and requires consistent determination from both partners – something that often fades after a few years.) The net effect of the usual imbalance in task allocation is that a working mother's role has expanded, rather than changed: she now does more. In such a situation, the physical and emotional strain of being a working mother is high.

Critics of this less rigid role for mothers express concern that a child will lose out psychologically by not having his mother close by him at all times during the pre-school years. However, while it is true that the pre-school years see the formation of the child's fundamental characteristics, the fact is that there is nothing to suggest that the quantity of time a woman spends with her baby is what matters. On the contrary, research findings indicate that what matters is the quality of the mother's time with her baby. Five minutes with a loving, relaxed mother are worth more to a baby's psychological development than are fifty minutes with a rejecting, tense one. If going out to work improves a woman's self-confidence, and consequently helps her relate more positively to her child, then he will benefit psychologically as a result.

Yet there are two unwelcome side-effects of this new opportunity for women to combine a career with parenthood. Some women who *want* to give up their job to be a full-time mother are aware of social pressures against such a move. They feel embarrassed admitting to their friends that they do not want to go back to work after the birth of their baby.

Second, some women who opt to combine parenthood with full-time employment are not completely comfortable with their choice. They will have chosen this course of action only after weighing up the pros and cons, but that doesn't mean they are entirely happy about leaving their baby in the care of someone else during the working week. Women in these circumstances often experience guilt feelings, which may persist throughout their child's life.

When selecting a childminder to care for your child while you are at work, it is absolutely essential that you choose one who is registered with your local authority – the law requires that all childminders have to register in this way. Visit a couple of childminders from the list you are given, and ask how many children each looks after, what age the children are, and so on. And watch how she interacts with the children she cares for. If you are not happy with her attitude and capabilities, then don't employ her.

The same applies to nannies and au pairs (although there isn't the same legal requirement of registration). Many nannies are fully qualified nursery nurses, who have undergone a nationally recognised training course. Whether an applicant is sent from an agency or whether she makes direct contact with you, get in touch with her previous employer and ask for references. When interviewing her, satisfy yourself that she is the sort of person with whom you would like your child to spend each day. An enthusiastic and capable nanny can add a new, dynamic dimension to a child's life.

See also **Fathers; Mothers; Quality Time; Single-Parent Family**.

X

Xmas This is such a happy time for children, a time for having fun and for giving and receiving presents. However, Xmas can also be a time of confrontation between you and your child.

One source of this potential family conflict stems from the way parents can misuse their child's desire for a gift as a means of controlling his behaviour. They sometimes try either to use the promise of a present on Xmas Day as a 'carrot' for encouraging his good behaviour, or to wield the threat of no present on Xmas Day as a 'stick' to discourage his naughtiness. But it usually takes more than the prospect of a gift to motivate a child to improve. So a strategy that tries to combine pleasure on Xmas Day with good behaviour is one that is doomed to failure – the most common outcome of this method of discipline is tears.

Another source of conflict is the often unrealistic expectations that parents have of their child on Xmas Day. Most assume he will be delighted with his presents (which he probably will be), that he'll play happily all day (which he probably won't, because the boredom factor soon sets in), and that he'll be settled all day (which he probably won't be, because by the afternoon he'll be drained after all the excitement). When he doesn't fulfil these expectations, tempers become frayed.

The best way of helping your child get the most enjoyment out of Xmas is to make his gifts unconditional and to have realistic expectations of his behaviour on the day itself.

See also **Discipline**.

X-Ray The most common medical procedure carried out in childhood, largely because of the high number of children under the age of seven admitted to hospital as a result of broken bones. Unfortunately, many children are upset and uncooperative during this procedure – even though having an X-ray isn't painful – and this makes the radiographer's job extremely difficult.

A child's agitation is probably due to a combination of factors: the clinical surroundings, the protective robes that the medical staff have to wear, and the fact that his parents may not be allowed to accompany him while the X-ray is being taken (especially if he attends a general hospital rather than a paediatric one). Whatever the cause of his distress, his reaction may mean that proper medical treatment is delayed.

Psychologists have found that the most suitable strategy for helping a child through this situation is patience and calmness – not easy when you know your child is injured and needs immediate treatment. However, when accompanying him in hospital, reassure him that he's only having a picture taken of his arm (or whatever), that it won't hurt him at all, and that he'll be perfectly safe. Try to be with him in the X-ray room, because your presence will help to calm him.

The use of 'negative discipline' (physical restraint or punishment in the X-ray room in order to coerce a child into cooperating with the radiographer) rarely works. In most instances this tactic simply upsets him even more, further delaying important treatment. So don't use threats to cajole him into cooperating with medical staff.

See also **Hospital; Illness**.

Y

Young Parents   The age of first-time parenthood continues to rise steadily, as more and more couples prefer to acquire financial security and broader life experience before starting their family. Even so, statistics suggest that up to 10 per cent of new parents are under 20 years old.

Young parents are no different psychologically from older parents. They tend to share the same values, and have the same hopes for themselves and their children. But they are particularly likely to be isolated from important family and social networks, for these reasons:

- Their families may disapprove of the partnership and therefore reject them.
- Their friends are probably single, or married but with no children, and so have a more flexible lifestyle.
- Their neighbours may not approve of them and may regard them as irresponsible.

Unemployment is an additional stress which young parents often have to face. Untrained under–20s rarely find jobs easily, and many young parents have trouble making ends meet because of dual unemployment. Sociologists call this the 'spiral of disadvantage' – the young parents' inability to find work plus their inability to move around the country easily in order to do so result in a low income, which in turn results in poor housing. The circle of poverty is hard to break.

These psychological and environmental influences can combine to place young parents in a vulnerable situation, although many do cope well with parenthood. Childcare professionals should be prepared to give young parents and their child extra attention and advice whenever necessary.

See also **Fathers; Mothers; Older Parents; Parents; Single-Parent Family; Working Mothers.**

Z

Zero-Sum Games Most games that your child plays, beyond the age of three or four, are competitive (e.g., football, running races, board games) and have winners and losers. Psychologists term these *zero-sum games* because they offer a mixture of positive outcomes (when your child wins) and negative outcomes (when she loses). Activities of this sort have an important place in childhood, and can encourage a child to develop very positive characteristics such as determination to succeed, an ability to withstand pressure, and tolerance of failure. But zero-sum games can also encourage her to develop negative qualities, such as aggressiveness, selfishness and the desire to achieve without thought for others.

Positive-sum games provide an alternative: here children work together cooperatively, rather than against each other competitively, and the outcomes for each child are always positive. The following positive-sum game involves minimal preparation. Get an empty plastic lemonade bottle, and four chunky pencils whose diameter is slightly less than the neck of the bottle (one pencil for each child who plays the game). Tie one end of a piece of string round one of the pencils and lower it into the bottle, leaving the other end of the string trailing down the side. Repeat this with the other three pencils.

When your child is at home with two or three of her friends, tell them that you want them to play a new game. Using the equipment you've prepared, ask each of them to hold one of the pieces of string. Explain that when you say 'Go' they have to pull the strings to get the pencils out of the bottle as quickly as possible, and that the game is won by the whole group when the last pencil is removed. (The relative widths of the pencils and bottle-neck mean that only one pencil can be pulled out at a time – so the children have to cooperate in order to complete the game quickly.)

You may find that they start to bicker with each other at first, because they are competing rather than working together. But after a few attempts they will begin to work more effectively as a team. You can time their performances, and keep a score chart for them. Positive-sum games of this sort – unlike zero-sum games – encourage desirable characteristics such as sharing, cooperation, and sensitivity to the strengths and weaknesses of others.

See also **Friendships; Kindness; Sociable Play; Social Development**.

Zygote   Conception occurs when a sperm from a male pierces the wall of the egg (ovum) from a female. This is only possible during a specific physiological phase: once every 28 days an ovum in one of the two ovaries ripens and begins its journey (which usually takes between three and seven days) down the fallopian tube, towards the uterus, pushed along by small hair-like cells which line the tube. If the ovum isn't fertilised by a sperm during this time, it disintegrates in the uterus after a few days and its remains are dispersed.

However, if a male sperm is present in the fallopian tube when the ovum is there, the two may join together, and conception may then take place. At this point the fertilised ovum – known as a zygote – is only about 1/175 of an inch in diameter, but it begins to grow immediately. In the next 10–14 days the zygote continues travelling through the fallopian tube until it reaches the uterus, where it becomes implanted; by then, it is approximately the size of a pinhead.

The zygote also determines whether twins will result. With identical twins, a single zygote splits into two identical parts, each of which will develop into a baby. Since each child comes from the one egg, these twins are always of the same sex and have the same inherited genetic characteristics. With non-identical twins, two separate eggs are fertilised by separate sperm at the same time. Since each child develops from different eggs, they are no more alike than any other siblings.

See also **Pre-Natal Development; Twins**.

ADDRESSES

Association for Post-Natal Illness, 25 Jerdan Place, London SW6 1BE (071–386 0868)

Association for Spina Bifida and Hydrocephalus (ASBAH), ASBAH House, 42 Park Road, Peterborough PE1 2EQ (0733 555988)

British Epilepsy Association, Anstey House, 40 Hanover Square, Leeds LS3 1BE (0532 439393; Epilepsy Helpline 0345 089599)

College of Speech and Language Therapy, 7 Bath Place, Rivington Street, London EC2A 3DR (071–613 3855)

Cry-sis (Association for Parents of Sleepless Children), BM Cry-sis, 27a Old Gloucester Street, London WC1N 3XX (071–404 5011)

Cystic Fibrosis Research Trust, Alexandra House, 5 Blyth Road, Bromley, Kent BR1 3RS (081–464 7211)

Down's Syndrome Association, 153–5 Mitcham Road, London SW17 9PG (081–682 4001)

Dyslexia Institute, 133 Gresham Road, Staines, Middlesex TW18 2AJ (0784 463851)

Education Otherwise, 36 Kinross Road, Leamington Spa, Warwicks CV32 7EF (0926 886828)

End Physical Punishment of Children (EPOCH), 77 Holloway Road, London N7 8JZ (071–700 0627)

Enuresis Resource and Information Centre (ERIC), 65 St Michael's Hill, Bristol BS2 8DZ (0272 264920)

Family Planning Association, 27–35 Mortimer Street, London W1N 7RJ (071–636 7866)

Gingerbread Association for One-Parent Families, 35 Wellington Street, London WC2E 7BN (071–240–0953)

Hyperactive Children's Support Group, 71 Whyke Lane, Chichester, Sussex PO19 2LI (0903 725182)

National Association for Gifted Children, Nene College, Park Campus, Broughton Green Road, Northampton NN2 7AL (0604 792300)

National Association for the Welfare of Children in Hospital (NAWCH), Argyle House, 29–31 Euston Road, London NW1 2SD (071–833 2041)

National Autistic Society, 276 Willesden Lane, London NW2 5RB (081–451 1114)

National Childbirth Trust (NCT), Alexandra House, Oldham Terrace, London W3 6NH (081–992 8637)

National Deaf Children's Society, 45 Hereford Road, London W2 5AH (071–229 9272)

National Toy Libraries Association (Play Matters), 68 Churchway, London NW1 1LT (071–387 9592)

Pre-School Playgroups Association, 61–3 King's Cross Road, London WC1X 9LL (071–833 0991)

Royal National Institute for the Blind, 224 Great Portland Street, London W1A 4XX (071–388 1266)

Spastics Society, 12 Park Crescent, London W1N 4EQ (071–636 5020)

Twins and Multiple Births Association (TAMBA), P.O. Box 30, Little Sutton, South Wirral, L66 1TH

Working Mothers' Association, 77 Holloway Road, London N7 8JZ (071–700 5771)

INDEX

(main entries are in **bold** type)